GREEK SCULPTURE

TEXT AND NOTES BY REINHARD LULLIES

PHOTOGRAPHS BY MAX HIRMER

HARRY N. ABRAMS, INC., NEW YORK

TRANSLATED FROM THE GERMAN BY
MICHAEL BULLOCK

LIBRARY OF CONGRESS CATALOG CARD NUMBER: 60-10887

FIRST PUBLISHED 1957
REVISED AND ENLARGED EDITION 1960

FOREWORD

Nearly all the plates are reproductions from photographs specially taken for this book in the Museums of Greece, as well as those of London, Paris, Rome, Vatican City, Venice and Munich, by the undersigned in collaboration with Miss Julia Asen.

My sincere thanks are due to the Directors and Departmental Heads of the Museums for permitting me to photograph the sculptures and for the support and assistance they so willingly gave me. They are: in Greece, Prof. Christos Karusos, National Museum, Athens; Dr. Jannis Miliadis, Acropolis Museum and Ceramicus Museum, Athens; Dr. Joannes Papadimitriu, Piraeus Museum; Dr. Joanna Konstantinu, of the Museums in Delphi and Chaleis; Dr. Nikolaos Saphiropulos, of the Museum in Olympia; Dr. J. P. Kondis, Rhodes; Dr. M. N. Nikolaidis, of the Museum in Cos. Also Prof. Bernard Ashmole, formerly of the British Museum, London; Dr. Jean Charbonneaux, Musée Nationale du Louvre, Paris; Prof. Renato Bartoccini, Museo delle Terme (Museo Nazionale Romano), Rome; General Director Prof. Filippo Magi, Vatican Collections, Vatican City; Dr. Bruna Forlati Tamaro, Museo Archeologico, Venice; Prof. H. Diepolder, Staatliche Antikensammlungen, Munich. I wish to extend my particular thanks to Prof. Marinatos of the Ministry of Public Worship and Education in Athens, and to the Director of the German Archaeological Institute in Athens, Prof. E. Kunze, for their ready cooperation. I am indebted to the Heads of the Museum of Fine Arts in Boston, and of the Metropolitan Museum of Art in New York for the loan of important Museum photographs; likewise to Prof. Carl Blümel, Director of the Department of Antiquities of the State Museums in Berlin.

My grateful thanks are also due to Dr. Reinhard Lullies, who wrote the text for this book, for his useful advice in the choice of works of art to photograph. Finally, I take this opportunity to thank Miss Julia Asen for her enthusiastic collaboration. To her I owe the success of what often proved to be tricky photographic undertakings; she is also largely responsible for the preparation and processing of the picture material.

Max Hirmer

FOREWORD TO THE REVISED AND ENLARGED EDITION

The favourable reception which this book has had from experts and art-lovers alike has merited the publication of a second edition, not only in Germany but also in the United Kingdom and the U.S.A. This second, revised, edition contains a number of new plates, with appropriate supplementary text matter, in particular of works from the important collection of antiquarian objects in the Archaeological Museum in Istanbul.

The undersigned would like, in this connection to extend his thanks to the Directors of the Archaeological Museum in Istanbul, Mr. Rüstem Duyuran, and his colleagues Dr. Nazih Firat and Dr. Zeikye Basak, as well as to Dr. Jole Bovio-Marconi, Soprintendente alle Antichità, Palermo, and Dr. P. C. Sestieri, Soprintendente alle Antichità, Salerno; and lastly to the Director of the Glyptotek Ny Carlsberg in Copenhagen, Dr. V. H. Poulsen, and to Dr. M. Gjödesen.

Max Hirmer

Our link with Classical Greece is so close that whatever we write on the subject tends to assume the form of a personal declaration of faith. Our response to Greek art – and, in particular, to Greek sculpture – is, if anything, even greater than our response to the epics of Homer, the Attic tragedies or the philosophy of Plato. For Greek sculpture is the visible and, one might say, the living testimony to the greatness of Greece. It would, however, remain a closed book without scholarly historical research, like everything belonging to the past. Yet the meaning of Greek sculpture far transcends its importance as an historical document. The truth of this – which the Renaissance later adopted as its guiding star – was first recognized during late antiquity. The art which the ancient Romans admired and which had a vital formative influence on the artists of Europe from the 15th century onwards, was to become the sole subject worthy of study for Winckelmann and his contemporaries and, in more recent times, to inspire poets of the stature of Rilke. This powerful influence is due above all to the profound humanity of the Greeks, which is nowhere more manifest than in the dominant place held in Greek sculpture by the human figure. Outlasting two thousand years, these works of art have remained a life-giving source for Western art, and beyond that, a generally accepted measure of human values. Whoever approaches Greek sculpture, be he a layman or a scholar, be he in search of enjoyment or of historical facts, will become aware of its decisive influence, but he must consider at the same time the far-reaching importance of the image of man it has created.

The foundation of the Greek style of sculpture was probably laid by the peoples who came in the Dorian migration, about 1200 B.C., from the North to the Greek peninsula and to the coast of Asia Minor, mixing there with the earlier settlers and initiating Greek culture in the true sense of the word. Before this, the art of monumental sculpture had been highly developed in Egypt as well as in the Near East. While we today admire the statues and reliefs by the artists belonging to these early civilizations, we realize that with Greek sculpture a new chapter in the history of world art began. There is an essential contrast between the sculpture of Egypt and the Near East on the one hand and that of Greece on the other. To reduce this to a simple formula: the Egyptians made symbols of reality, but the Greeks created living beings out of stone. In depicting abstractions meant to last into eternity, the Egyptians evolved an immutable artistic language. They reduced the human figure to geometrical shapes meant to be viewed from the front or in profile only and did not suggest a relation of any kind between their statues and the surrounding world. The Greek approach was essentially different, in that the artist sought to create a perfect and living organism, to infuse his statue down to the finger-tips with the breath of life and to endow it with a natural relationship to space. Any work of Greek art, be it a temple or a drinking cup, a statue or a relief, has been realized by the artist as an organism, alive and coherent down to its smallest part. The athletic bodies of young men were the perfect natural model for the Greek artist. Therefore the male nude remained throughout history the starting point for the Greek sculptor and the foremost subject of his art.

Greek sculpture has its roots in the needs of the religious and communal life of the city-states. Votive offerings, either presented to the gods on the sacred precincts or in the public square, and pious dedications to the deceased – these are the two purposes from which stems the meaning of all Greek works of art, be they statues big or little, votive or funerary reliefs, or the sculptural decorations of temples, treasuries and implements. We may assume that these pious ends were combined at least to a certain degree with an ornamental purpose, but it must be stressed that, until well into the Hellenistic period, Greek sculpture was not made for the pleasure of an aesthetically-minded public.

The Greeks regarded their gods as real persons. In the Homeric epics some gods fight on the side of the Trojans while others assist the Greeks – in the tragedies of the 5th century B.C. they take part in the action alongside the mythical heroes, – and in the same way they appear in marble on the frieze which surrounded the cella of the Parthenon, graciously receiving the Athenians who are celebrating the Panathenaea, the great quadrennial feast of Athene. We see them approaching her sanctuary in solemn procession. The gods, descending from Mount Olympus where they reside in a state of perennial youth, or emerging from the depths of the earth or the sea, appear every now and then to take an active part in the lives of men. There is nothing vague, nothing obscure and nothing mystical about them. The radiant sunlight shining over Greece that illuminates the landscape, making its features stand out in almost crystalline clarity, has given Greek religion its character and helped to shape the individualities of the gods. This tangible reality of the gods is reflected in every way in the works of the Greek sculptors. These works have no hidden or obscure meanings, they are never mere symbols of invisible powers, but always clear, single-minded factual representations of their subject.

Whether they were public commissions or donated by citizens, the works of the Greek sculptors invariably had some more or less direct relationship to the state, the source and centre of all religious and political activities. This close relationship to communal and religious life, by which the form and content of the artist's work was determined, explains not only the inner logic of the general development of Greek sculpture but also its purposeful unity of form. Not until the Hellenistic period, when the old religious beliefs were fading and the Greek city-states had ceased to exist, did Greek sculpture begin to be determined no longer primarily by the limitations arising from the artist's commission, but increasingly by his own individuality as well as by his public which began to take a hitherto unprecedented interest in works of art. The growing interest in the theory of art which becomes noticeable from the 3rd century B.C. onwards is a characteristic symptom of this development. The collating of information relative to artists' biographies indicates the nascent interest in historical research, among the earliest exponents of which were Xenokrates of Athens and Antigonos of Karystos, two scholarly writers of the

8

I/II Sculptures from the pediment of the Old Temple of Athena on the Athenian Acropolis. Limestone. Acropolis Museum, Athens Top: Right half of the pediment with the three-bodied monster Bottom: Forepart of the three-bodied monster

highest rank. The collection of a number of famous old statues from the Greek mainland which was formed by Attalos I of Pergamon (241–197 B.C.) and displayed in his residence is a pointer in the same direction. Later on, when the realms of the Diadochi had been absorbed by the rising Roman Empire, the heroic artistic concepts gradually faded and with them the inspiration that had sustained the Greek sculptors through so many centuries. This is the reason why, from about the middle of the 2nd century B.C. onwards, Greek sculpture imitating earlier Classical styles began to be produced beside original works of art. This is the source and first instance of those Classical revivals which were to play so prominent a part in the history of European art. Under the Roman Emperors this novel form of artistic activity flourished intermittently. Copies and free versions of Classical masterpieces began to be made about the same time. A constantly mounting demand for reproductions of works by famous Greek masters called forth growing numbers of copyists, who were most active during the first two centuries of the Roman Empire.

It was, of course, impossible for a copyist to reproduce the qualities that gave his Classical original its uniqueness and charm: the freshness of its conception and its artistic unity. Although most of the copyists bore not only Greek names but were also trained in the Greek tradition, they lived and worked centuries after the time when their model was created and in a different spiritual climate. They were therefore at best only capable of an externally faithful imitation of their models.

Nearly all the sculptures illustrated in the present volume are Greek originals; therefore much had to be omitted that would be indispensable for a complete survey of the historical development of Greek art. However, to reward us for this self-imposed limitation, we are allowed to feel across the intervening centuries the direct impact of the Greek sculptor's artistic personality. We are able to observe the mark of the artist's own chisel on the stone and to feel the undiluted power of his creative genius.

Yet there is one important element which is left to the power of our imagination, even when looking at Greek originals, and that is their colour. Bronze is an alloy of tin and copper. Greek bronzes originally had a surface bright and shining like gold. During the passage of centuries the varying shades of patina we see today on ancient bronzes were created by the impact of the elements. The colours may be grey or black, dark or light green, reddish brown or even blue, according to the chemical agents, among which the composition of the atmosphere and the degree of moisture it contains are the most decisive. We are used to regard Greek stone sculptures as works of art in monochrome, mainly in plain white marble, but also in the grey or yellowish tones of limestone and occasionally in those colours which are caused by prolonged contact with the soil. Originally all Classical statues and reliefs were painted with colours which have disappeared almost completely from the smooth surface of marble; they are slightly better preserved on porous limestone and best on terra-cotta, as the latter material was burnt a second time after the colouring had been applied. As terra-cotta was mainly used to make figures destined for funerary offerings, these were generally consigned to the comparatively safe keeping of the soil soon after they had been completed, but large-scale marbles usually remained exposed to the weather for centuries. Their original colouring has therefore only been preserved in a few exceptional cases, thanks to certain unusually propitious circumstances, and even then only in infinitesimal vestiges; these help us, however, to visualize what they originally looked like.

It must not be supposed that colour was a mere superficial adornment of Greek sculptures, which could have been omitted without making much difference. On the contrary, in Greek sculpture colour played a part as vital as form, indeed the two were regarded as indivisible elements by the artists. Changes in sculptural style therefore caused corresponding alterations in the colour scheme. Thus early Greek works were painted in strong colours, mainly in red, blue, green, black and yellow. These colours were applied with a definite predilection for contrasting effects obtained by setting complementaries next to each other. Another characteristic feature is an occasional neglect of realism, for which the blue in the beards and the hair of the three-headed monster from the Acropolis is a good example. Deep and luminous hues are characteristic of the 5th century B.C.; lighter and more gentle colours, like pink, sky-blue or violet, harmonizing with the softer more picturesque character of the sculptural style, began to be used from the middle of the 4th century onwards.

26, I, II

Today we rarely have a chance of seeing Classical sculpture in its original setting under the open sky and in bright Mediterranean sunlight. What we see are mainly fragments dispersed over all the countries of the Western world; regarded as the most valuable treasures of public and private collections, they are exhibited indoors. Of the many reasons for the destruction and the complete loss of so many important Greek sculptures we shall mention only the principal ones. Acts of war naturally take first place, with the lack of artistic sense of later generations next in importance, for statues as well as reliefs were frequently used as ordinary building materials with a complete disregard for their carved surfaces. For the same sad reason, sculptured marbles were frequently relegated to the kilns, from which they emerged as distemper, a custom first introduced in late antiquity but persisting into very recent times. Bronzes were melted down for the sake of their metal value. From the 3rd century B.C. onwards, the Romans carried off countless Classical statues among the booty acquired in their conquest of southern Italy, Sicily, Greece and Asia Minor. They bore away what they liked from the conquered cities as well as from sanctuaries and cemeteries. At first they treasured the sculptures they had brought home according to their true value and erected them in temples, public squares, private gardens and villas, but in the early centuries of our era most of these works perished. Many were destroyed by the early Christians and during the migration period. In Greece, havoc among monumental sculptures was wrought by earthquakes, the worst of which occurred in the 5th century A.D., when the temple of Zeus at Olympia collapsed with all its statues and reliefs.

The most usual similes for designating single periods of history are those derived from the ages of man. Thus it has become customary to describe the development of Greek sculpture by referring to its birth, its childhood, youth, maturity and, lastly, its old age. The same subdivisions might be described equally well by botanical expressions for growth and decay, like germination and growth, flowering, fruition, deterioration and final decay. When using these categories it must, of course, be realized that there are limits to the extent to which they can

12

III   Girl (kore) by a master from Chios. From the Athenian Acropolis.
Marble from Chios. Acropolis Museum, Athens

serve to describe the constant and variegated flow of history. Their legitimate usefulness is limited to the purpose of rendering the comparative survey of different periods less confusing.

Epoch, a Greek word, designates the point where one part of a movement ends and a new phase begins. Today we use the word epoch in a sense that is in contrast to this original meaning, for we term an 'epoch' a period in time which is marked at its beginning and end by important events and vital changes and which has, moreover, a recognizable evolution and individual characteristics of its own.

The history of Greek art is generally divided into five main epochs – the Geometric, the Archaic, the Classical, the Hellenistic and the Roman. Each of these has been subdivided into a number of secondary periods based upon historical events or stylistic changes. It is scarcely necessary to mention that the transitions from one epoch to another are fluid, that the end of one epoch runs over into the beginning of the next, according to the age and talents of the individual artists and the position and temperament of the various provinces of art.

The Geometric epoch takes its name from the prevalence of geometric patterns in the pottery decoration of that period. In broad terms, it comprises the four centuries from the end of the Dorian migration to the disappearance of geometric forms during the second half of the 8th century B.C. 'Archaic' comes from the Greek *archaios*. Herodotus and Thucydides used this word in the 5th century B.C. to describe the ancient world that lay far back in the past before their own period. In current parlance the Archaic centuries of Greek art are the 6th and 7th centuries B.C., that is to say, the span of time between the Geometric and Classical periods, of which the latter covers the 5th and 4th centuries B.C. Since the Greek Classical epoch properly so-called was not fully realized in plastic art until the Parthenon sculptures (448–432 B.C.), the transition from the Archaic epoch to the Parthenon era is distinguished as a period on its own known as the 'Severe Style'. The term 'Hellenism' as a description of the three centuries from the death of Alexander the Great (323 B.C.) to the accession to the throne of the Emperor Augustus (31 B.C.) was introduced into historical writing more than a hundred years ago by the historian Johann Gustav Droysen. The term was then applied by archaeologists to the art history of this epoch.

During the period of the Roman Empire the living stream that had fed Greek sculpture for a full millennium began more and more to run dry. The splendid Greek sculpture became an imperial art in Roman dress. Apart from portrait busts and historical reliefs such as we see on the Ara Pacis, the triumphal arches, and the columns of Trajan and Marcus Aurelius, it consisted essentially of copies and adaptations of older Greek statues or classicizing productions. Most scholars therefore regard the history of Greek sculpture as basically terminating with the end of Hellenism. True, even during the period of the Roman Empire the plastic artists were predominantly Greeks. But the Greek sense of form had been increasingly modified by a new mingling of peoples and the influence of the Roman mentality. The last phase of Greek art, often known as the 'period of the copyists' for short, does not come under consideration in this book.

People have always been conscious of the differing nature of the various periods of Greek sculpture and their opinion of these has been expressed by predilection and acknowledgement, rejection and silent neglect. In this connexion it is interesting to observe how the attitude of later generations to the works of art of a bygone age reveals what they bring to it themselves, what they lack and therefore seek in the past as a supplement to their own being. The value attached to the individual epochs has also played a part in the transmission of Greek sculpture, in so far as only an antiquarian and historical interest was felt for Archaic works during the Hellenistic and Roman periods, and Archaic sculpture was rarely copied. The oldest Greek sculptures of which Roman copies have come down to us date from about 480 B. C. During the period of the copyists all Greek sculpture older than this was obviously considered still imperfect and unfree, still too firmly attached to the ancient forms, for it to arouse the same enthusiasm as the works of Classical art. The verdict on Hellenistic art pronounced by Pliny the Elder in the 1st century A. D. is typical of the attitude of the early Imperial period to the older Hellenistic art. In his *Naturalis Historia* (34, 52) he appends to a discussion of Lysippus and his school the sentence, *Cessavit deinde ars ac cursus olympiade CLVI revixit*, which means in English, 'Then art ceased and awoke to fresh life in the 156th Olympiad' – the years 156–152 B.C. Pliny therefore regarded art as being virtually non-existent during the hundred and fifty years between the turn of the 4th to the 3rd century and the middle of the 2nd century B.C. – in other words, during the whole of the period from the end of true Classicism to the rise of pseudo-classical imitation. In accordance with the view of their own time held by the classicizers, he erased a whole period from the history of Greek sculpture, although works from this period, of whose art Pliny wished to take no account – such as the statue of Demosthenes from the market-place at Athens and the great votive offering for the victory of the Pergamenes over the Gauls – were esteemed and copied even during the Imperial epoch.

The fluctuation of opinion regarding individual periods of Greek sculpture during recent and very recent times is again particularly evident from the attitude to Archaic and Hellenistic sculpture. Until the immediate past, the new approach to art in Germany was still influenced by the views of Lessing, Winckelmann and the German classical authors. The old view held by Lessing and derived from Aristotle that art is the imitation of nature, and Winckelmann's oft-quoted comment on the 'noble simplicity and tranquil grandeur' of Greek statuary, determined people's approach to Greek sculpture until well into the 19th century. The section of the public interested in art did not warm to the statues of early Greece until relatively late. Goethe, for example, who had such an admiration for Classical art and who described and appraised its works in phrases that have become famous, seems to have found no proper access to Archaic art throughout the whole of his life. His adverse comments on the pediment sculptures at Aegina, whose beauty and significance had been recognized by less prejudiced contemporaries, can only be understood as due to a fixed ideal notion of the plastic art of the Greeks and the classicizing taste of his age. These marble sculptures dating from the late 6th and early 5th centuries B. C. *72–77; 82–87* were discovered on Aegina in 1811, and soon came to Goethe's notice through descriptions and drawings. He considered their stylized, unnaturalistic forms primitive. They must have appeared to him positively ugly. At all events, they cannot have appealed to him much when he wrote in 1818, 'there is little pleasure to be had from the Aeginetan sculptures'. They were 'carelessly

16

IV   Charioteer, votive offering of Polyzalos of Gela for Delphi. Head. Delphi. cf. Plates 102–104

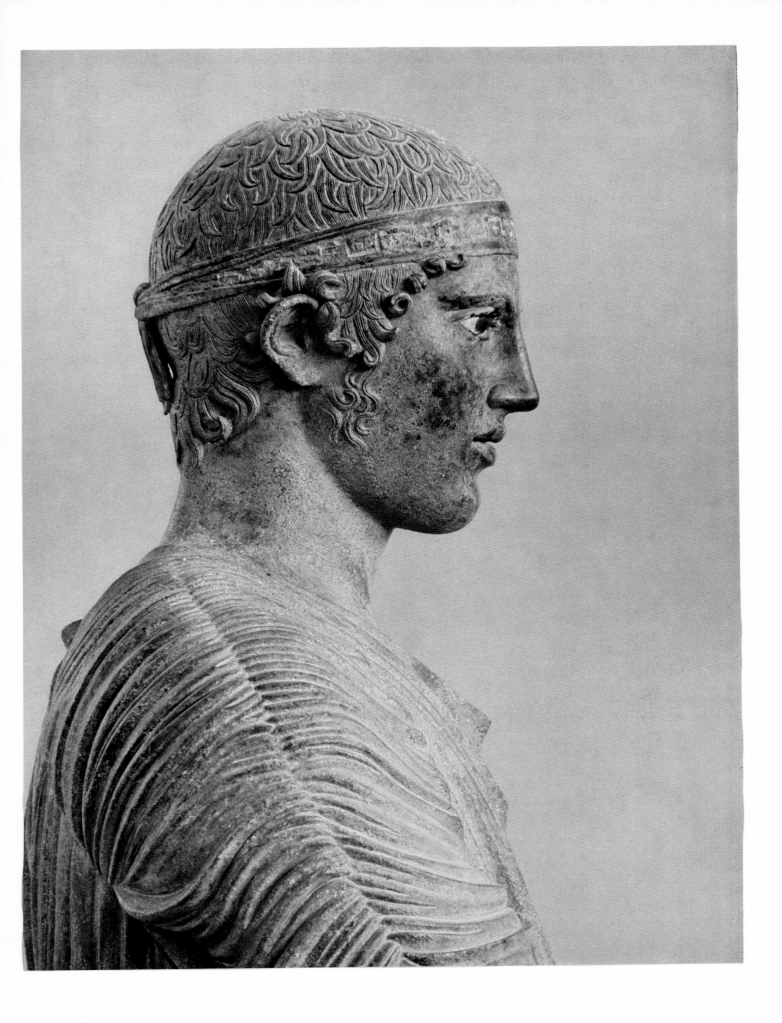

knocked-up temple images of completely disparate artistic value (the reclining figures perhaps added later), which must always remain problematical. Let us not believe that the ancients cut all their coats out of the same cloth'.

The attitude to Archaic art did not change in wider circles until excavations in Greece and Asia Minor during the second half of the 19th century had brought to light abundant finds of early Greek sculpture in Olympia and Delphi, on the Acropolis of Athens and the Greek islands, and these had been submitted to scientific investigation. Hand in hand with the historical understanding of early Greek sculpture went its growing aesthetic appreciation, a process that was furthered by the Viennese art historian Alois Riegl with his concept of 'artistic volition' (*Kunstwollen*). The discovery of Archaic art as the pure expression of the early Greek spirit, and its high artistic evaluation as an ideal of unbroken vigour and youthful vitality, was reserved for the beginning of our century. This discovery is inseparable from the whole spiritual situation of the age, the new advances in science and the aims of plastic art, which, in its conscious repudiation both of naturalism and of all Classicism, felt itself akin to the principles of early Greek art. The sonnets to Apollo in R. M. Rilke's *Neue Gedichte*, written in 1903/08, may be taken as typical declarations of the attitude to Archaic sculpture prevailing at the time.

Unlike the Archaic works, certain sculptures from a later period have gone down in contemporary estimation in comparison with the importance attached to them in past centuries. The Laocoön group, for example, was regarded by Lessing and the art theory of the 18th and well *278, 279* into the 19th century as the supreme embodiment of agonized suffering captured at the 'fruitful moment' with the highest means of the sculptor's art. There was no limit to the admiration felt for the way in which the artists had fused idea and reality in this group. Now that – thanks to a far more comprehensive body of monuments – we have a better knowledge of the development of Hellenistic art than earlier generations, and are thus able to assign also to the Laocoön group its place in the art history of the 1st century B.C., we are mainly struck – despite all the grandeur that is a feature of the group – by an impression of extreme virtuosity and exaggeration in the forms, coupled with classicizing tendencies, which are especially manifest in the composition.

The beginnings of Greek sculpture go back to the end of the 2nd millennium B.C., when the Greeks, after the Dorian migration, were founding new cult places and altars, some of them on top of ancient Creto-Mycenaean shrines. The earliest Greek sculptures, corresponding in time to the proto-Geometric and early Geometric vases, are votive offerings for these sanctuaries, grave goods and decorations on vessels and implements – small, unassuming figures of baked clay, copper or bronze. They represent animals, especially cattle and horses, and, in the early stages more rarely, human figures. The terra-cottas are made by hand, that is to say, without a mould. In a few cases they have been turned on the potter's wheel. The Greeks picked up the technique from the older peoples. Whereas in pottery fine, mature results were achieved during these early centuries, sculpture remained at a simpler stage of development. It did not aspire to anything much superior to the statuette. Its evolution was relatively slow until its culmination in the 8th century B.C., during the second half of which the Geometric style gradually lost its vitality and began to disappear. As yet few differences are discernible as between one province and another. The new and typical element in the Geometric figures, as compared with the earlier Creto-Mycenaean sculpture, is a sense of power and compactness that springs from the logical coherence of the parts. In the Geometric period men certainly did not live far from nature. Rather than a withdrawal from nature, the apparently abstract figures represent a compression of the natural model, which the artists of this early age reproduced according to its essential components and characteristics in the most concise shape and with clearly defined outlines.

With the 8th century B.C. the species of animals, the types of human figures and the poses become more numerous. In addition to isolated figures we find groups, created by placing single figures either side by side or facing one another. The first mythical themes now appear in sculpture in the round or in relief. The introduction of metal implements from the East and the adoption of oriental motifs becomes of great importance.

1 The bronze statuette of a horse shown in our first plate – one of the greatest and most beautiful works of art of its kind – already belongs to the second half of the 8th century. With its long legs, its short, thin body, broad, flat neck and upswept mane it already shows an exaggeration of the strict Geometric forms. But the most promising development that took place in the Geometric style was not increasing consolidation of its abstract tendencies, but their dissolution and transformation into more organic and living shapes. In the warrior from the Acro-
2 polis at Athens, which was produced at the turn from the 8th to the 7th century B. C., the parts of the body fuse together with a more unified flow than in the older, Geometric figures. They are rounded and more powerfully animated from within, the outline has lost its simple firmness and has become comparatively softer and more differentiated. Taken as a whole, the figure creates a more labile impression and loses its isolation in relationship to surrounding space.

In addition to small-scale sculpture in terra-cotta, bronze, wood and precious materials such as ivory, there must also have been large-scale wooden sculpture in Greece contemporary with the statues of warriors on the Acropolis. There are frequent references in Classical literature to *xoana*, very ancient carved images of the gods – some of them dating from the Geometric period – of which a few were considerably larger than statuettes. These may be regarded as forerunners or early stages of monumental sculpture. The decisive step towards a monumental sculpture in stone was taken by the Greeks shortly before the middle of the 7th century B.C. At this period a tendency to inner and outer monumentality imbued all works of plastic art. It is as manifest in the pottery and bronze-ware of this age as in the first life-size and over-life-size statues and in the monumental temple architecture. Temple and sculpture were intimately connected. The great religious image demanded an architecture in keeping with it: the monumental temple called for appropriate sculpture on its pediments and over its entablature. According to ancient tradition, Greek monumental sculpture was born in Dorian Crete and linked with the artist Daedalus, whose eloquent name means something like 'skilled craftsman' or 'maker of beautiful and magnificent things'. Various imaginary and historical conceptions meet in his person. He was regarded by later antiquity as a mythological figure, as the first artist of all, credited with making various new discoveries at a very ancient but historically verifiable period, and as a

20

V Zeus and Ganymede, from Olympia. Terra-cotta. Olympia

very early sculptor, mainly in wood, who was the head of a school of sculptors whose names have been handed down by tradition. Apart from Crete and the Peloponnesus, the Ionian Cyclades also played a leading part in the development of monumental sculpture during the 7th century – above all, the islands of Naxos and Paros, whose glorious white marble was famed and favoured throughout the whole of the ancient world.

The first half-century of the monumental style in Greece is still called the Daedalic period of Archaic art, after Daedalus. The huge bronze griffin's head from a kettle *protome* found at Olympia and the slightly later statuette of a standing clothed woman in the Louvre, a typical example of early Cretan stone-carving, date from the beginning and middle of this period. By contrast with the labile posture and fluid outline of the Acropolis warrior, the sculptures of the mid-7th century B.C. have attained a new statuesque firmness. The figure in the Louvre is built up of large sections placed one on top of the other. The lower part of the trunk disappears under the thick material of the dress and remains enclosed in the block. Nevertheless, the powerful, ample forms of the body are everywhere perceptible beneath the taut surface. The life of the spirit is accumulated in the triangular face with the mobile lips and the firm, clear and steadfastly forward-looking gaze. In the female head from the metope at Mycenae, dating from the end of the Daedalic period, the features are already one degree more mobile and communicative. A new sensuous vitality begins to break through in the face, as though heralding the so-called 'Archaic smile'. It would be wrong to interpret this 'smile' – which invades Greek sculpture around the turn from the 7th to the 6th century B.C. and is retained throughout the whole of the 6th century – as the expression of a momentary feeling of joy; it is not confined to figures who have reason to smile by virtue of their situation or the nature of the composition in which they appear; for even the wounded warrior on the western pediment of the 'Temple of Aphaia' on Aegina wore the 'Archaic smile'. The practice of invariably carving the features in such a manner as to make them appear gay must be regarded as part of the general tendency of Archaic art to concentrate on the universal and typical. At the same time, this smile mirrors the unbroken energy and freshness of a young epoch that found its fulfilment in this world and whose interest was focused upon earthly beauty and joy.

The first monumental statues of nude youths – probably the most important creations of Daedalic sculpture – were doubtless also produced around the mid-7th century B.C. They are the point of departure and the prerequisite for the unique development of the nude male figure that reached its goal and fulfilment in the Classical statue of the 5th and 4th centuries B.C. The Greeks had adopted the outward appearance of the erect male figure from the Egyptians. But in their free pose that dispenses with any outside support, the vigorous tension of the limbs and the coherence of all the parts within the framework of a closed whole, the early Greek youths are essentially different from any Egyptian work. They are purely Greek, the earliest no less than the later. Once it had evolved the type of figure with one foot to the front, the eyes looking straight ahead, the arms hanging at the sides or drawn slightly in towards the body, and the hands closed into a fist and resting on the thighs, Greek sculpture kept to it throughout the whole of the Archaic period.

23

When, after the first half of the last century, early Greek youths were unearthed in ever-growing numbers, they were at first thought to represent the god Apollo, and many of them are known to this day as statues of Apollo. In fact, only a few of them are entitled to this name – those which are marked as Apollo by the possession of such attributes as a bow and arrow. Their significance was much wider and more comprehensive. They might portray a god or a hero, but they could also represent the donor of the statue or the dead man over whose grave they stood as a monument. They give no indication of age, profession, origin or rank: they were images of the man as such in the glory of his naked, athletically fashioned body and in the prime of life.

Like all Greek sculpture, the stone statues of youths belonging to the Archaic period were no mere copies or imitations of the physical and mental aspect of a man. They possessed an unsurpassable reality, they were simultaneously stone and living beings. According to the belief of the time, a life-force entered into the work of the Archaic sculptor that might express itself in various ways. The statues could speak like living men through the inscriptions that were incised or chiselled on the figures themselves or on their pedestals. Thus a statue of Apollo, now
3 in the Boston Museum, addresses the spectator and tells him through the distich on its thighs: 'Mantiklos dedicated me to the god with the silver bow who strikes from afar.' Marble youths extol their own beauty and say they are splendid and wonderful works of sculpture. The statue
32, 33 of Hera from Samos, in the Louvre, proclaims through the inscription on its veil that Cheramyes gave it as an offering to Hera. The women in a large Samian marble group dating from the mid-6th century B.C. announce through the inscription on their base: 'Geneleos made us.' The same life-force that was contained in the human figures also inhabited the Archaic animals and hybrid creatures – the lions and panthers, the sphinxes and sirens – which stood in the sanctuaries and cemeteries. These were great emblems of fierce, daemonic strength. One such
17, 18 emblem was the winged Gorgon, whose grotesque face grinned down from the height of the temple, as may be seen in the Corfu pediment. The gods and heroes of legend that were placed on the pediments, friezes and metopes of Archaic buildings and on all kinds of implements, or depicted on tablets and vessels by the hand of the painter, possessed the same actuality. The spheres of artistic, mythological and real existence had not yet been separated in Archaic times.

In all, six statues of Archaic youths are shown among our illustrations. Each of them is characteristic of its period and the province from which it originated. Apart from the brothers Cleobis and Biton in Delphi, they are all probably funerary statues. The Youth in New York and the memorial from the tomb of Kroisos at Anavyssos are representative of the early period and of a late high-water mark reached by this type of figure in Attica.
11-13 Almost a century lies between them. In the early statue in New York, dating from the end of the 7th century B.C., the dominant features are the unrelenting severity of the pose, the systematic lucidity of the construction, the consistent integration of the parts into the whole, and the abstract treatment of the skeletal framework, joints, muscles and sinews. By contrast,
57-61 the Anavyssos monument is livelier, one might even say more naturalistic, more a creature of flesh and blood, so to speak. Whereas the sculptural construction of the older work is seen to

24

VI   Poseidon, head in frontal view. National Museum, Athens. cf. Plate 131

be the issue of a preponderantly mental process, in the later it grows out of a feeling for the life that flows through the whole body. In its totality, the figure is more corporeal, the forms are round and swelling. Looking at the Anavyssos Youth we receive the impression that the time cannot be far off when its fullness of life will burst the old conventional mould asunder. It is important to recognize that the years during which this statue was carved saw the rise of the early red figure vases in Attica. This new form of ceramic decoration, which replaced the older black silhouetted figures that lay flat on the surface, consisted of lighter figures that stood out from the dark wall of the vessel with growing corporeality and independence.

The statue of Cleobis, by virtue of its massive corporeality, its almost architectonic structure and *14, 15* its monumental appearance, is an outstanding example of early 6th-century Argive sculpture. Furthermore, the pair of Delphic brothers is well adapted to illustrate the additive method of grouping adopted at that time. The Youths from Melos and Tenea illustrate the differing potentialities of two provinces of art at the same period of time. They both date from the mid-6th century B.C. The Melian statue with its excessively tall, delicate and unathletic forms testifies, in *34, 35* the plant-like growth of the figure, to the sensuous vegetal style of Ionian art; the Tenean sculpture *36–38* exemplifies the powerful, resilient vitality and spiritual alertness achieved by the Corinthian master.

The individual style of each province appears more and more clearly in Greek sculpture after the end of the Geometric epoch and with the rise of monumental statuary. The stylistic differences that exist even between neighbouring districts are doubtless connected in the main with the inherited characteristics of the various Greek tribes, with the geographical conditions peculiar to each zone in Greece, and with the political organization of each independent and closed community. The districts and their inhabitants are divided, and intercourse between them made difficult, by high mountains and mountain ranges and by the bays between peninsulas. Then there are the islands separated from the mainland by the sea.

The great zones of art during the 7th and 6th centuries B.C. are represented here by characteristic examples: 7th-century *Crete* by the limestone Auxerre 'statue' in the Louvre *6* already referred to, *Argos* by the Delphic group of Cleobis and Biton, *Corinth* by the pediment *14, 15* of the Temple of Artemis on Corfu and the Tenea Youth, the *Ionian islands* by the Apollo from *16–19; 36–38* Melos, the frieze on the Siphnian treasury at Delphi and the pediment group from the Temple of *34, 35; 48–55* Apollo at Eretria, *Eastern Greece* by the Samian Kore from the Athenian Acropolis, the Hera *66–68; 27; 32, 33* of Cheramyes, the relief from the old Temple of Apollo at Didyma, the 'Sleeping Head' from *42; 40, 41* Ephesus and the Kore from Chios from the Athenian Acropolis. The curious, provincial *70, III* style of *Boeotia*, the home of Hesiod and Pindar, is exemplified by two very typical works – the early statuette of Apollo, a votive offering presented by Mantiklos, and the limestone Head with the sharp-cut forms from the sanctuary of the Ptoan Apollo. The art of *28, 29* *Aegina* is represented by the pediment sculptures from the Temple of Aphaia; *Magna* *72–77; 82–87* *Graecia* by the metope with the dancing women from the Temple of Hera at the mouth of the *78* Sele, the Enthroned Goddess at Berlin, and the Piombino Apollo. The last two have already *97–101; 92–59* crossed the threshold that leads away from Archaic art.

The evolution of Archaic sculpture can be more clearly followed in *Attica* than in any other

Greek province. Here an abundance of large statues in marble and limestone enables us to watch the development of art from the end of the 7th century B.C. decade by decade, to distinguish the emergence of new trends and the absorption of outside influences. In Attic sculpture individual artistic personalities, such as the 'Master of the Rampin Head', stand out

11–13 from the host of other sculptors. The New York Youth was carved at the end of the 7th

20–23 century, the Standing Goddess with Pomegranate in the Berlin Museum, at the beginning of the 6th century. In its well-knit structure and distinct corporeality the latter is the earlier

32, 33 Attic counterpart of the gradually uprising, softly rounded, column-like Hera of Cheramyes

24, 25 from Samos. Around 570 B.C. there follow in Attica the Calf-Bearer and the *poros* pediment

26, I, II from the Old Temple of Athene on the Athenian Acropolis, with Hercules overcoming Triton

30, 31 in one half, and the three-bodied monster in the other. The Rider with the Bearded Head in the

39 Louvre, and the fragment of a funerary stele with the Discus-bearer date from before the middle of the 6th century. It is at this period that the long and numerous series of statues of girls donated as votive offerings to the goddess of the Athenian Acropolis begins. They are represented in this volume by two outstanding examples. From its close affinity with the figure of Leda on the Amphora of Exekias in the Vatican – which gives praise to the beautiful One-

43–45 torides – the Kore in a long peplos and chiton, a later work of the 'Master of the Rampin Head', would seem to date from about 530 B.C. The over-life size head of a statue of a youth, now in

46, 47 Copenhagen and known by the name of the 'Rayet head', a supreme masterpiece from the hand of a leading Attic sculptor of the day, must date from about the same time. The stylistic phase of those Attic vases which extol the handsome Leagros and Panaitios, is embodied in the metopes

79 from the Athenian treasury in Delphi. They belong to the last decade of the 6th century B.C. In the differentiated treatment of the marble and the extreme refinement of the whole formal

80, 81 vocabulary, the gentle Kore in her fine-ribbed green chiton and diagonal cloak represents the ultimate culmination of 6th-century Attic sculpture. The life of the mind mirrored in her pensive features presages new developments beyond the confines of the Archaic style.

The turn from the 6th to the 5th century B.C. was a period of great changes in Greek art that were of immense importance for its future development. These changes are an expression of decisive spiritual metamorphoses whose effects are visible in every sphere of art. At this period man broke away from the mythical forms of collective thinking and began to waken in a hitherto unknown fashion to consciousness of his own personality. It was a moment of universal significance when he discovered himself as an individual faced with responsible decisions in respect of the demands made by religion and the state. At the same instant he came to feel existence as a destiny from which he could not escape, with whose remorseless demands he had to come to terms. In these early years of Attic tragedy Aeschylus added to the single actor, whom Thespis had set over against the chorus, a second one, thereby preparing the ground for the action that makes up 5th-century drama. The world of sculpture now lost its colourful *insouciance*. The 'Archaic smile' gave way to a serious, often dejected expression. The figures burst the ancient bonds, emerged from the fixed framework, and broke through the law of squarely frontal presentation.

28

VII Head of the Bronze statue of a youth, found in the sea off Marathon. National Museum, Athens. cf. Plate 222

If we compare the statue of a Boy from the Athenian Acropolis, carved shortly before *89–91*
480 B.C., with the earlier figure of a Youth from Anavyssos, the new element that fills sculpture *57–61*
during the period of the Severe Style appears with perfect clarity. Whereas in the 6th-century
Youth the feet stand with both soles firmly on the ground and the body is presented in a
squarely frontal position, in the later figure a distinction is made between the leg that takes the
weight and the free leg. This movement is conveyed to the rest of the body. The sides are
displayed in mutual counterpoise. One arm and shoulder are drawn back, the head is turned
freely to the right. All the parts appear linked together in a new, organic relationship. The
figure stands confidently, as if guided from and concentrated upon an inner centre, and begins
to penetrate surrounding space.

In a few decades the way leads, in an unparalleled course of development, from this statue
of a Boy on the Acropolis to the Spear-Carrier of Polyclitus and the bronze in the Louvre, *183*
of the Youth Making a Gift, which, of our selection of pictures, serves to illustrate the
height of the Classical period of the 5th century B.C. as represented by the standing male
nude. Here the carrying and burdening parts are in harmonious equilibrium. Tension and
relaxation of tension are nicely balanced. The main stress is placed in the centre of the figure.
In a work such as this all physical, mental and psychological forces attain a state of ideal unity.

Around 500 B.C. a transformation corresponding to that which had taken place in sculpture *71*
in the round also appeared in the structure of the Greek relief. In the Aristion stele dating from
the end of the 6th century, the figure of the warrior rises in exact profile and with clearly
defined outlines from a background which, like the figure upon it, possesses an unusual degree
of dense materiality and reality. In an Archaic relief the background does not create an illusion
of space, of depth and breadth. It is the solid wall-surface that carries the figures and at the *96*
same time limits their backward extension. In the victory stele from Sunium, which is separated
from the funerary stele of Aristion by only thirty to forty years, and still more clearly in the
stele of Nisyros, the interrelation between figures and background is already different. The *133*
elements of the relief stand in a new, organic relationship to one another that accords with the
innate mobility of the figures. If figures and background were powers of approximately equal
value in the structure of the Archaic relief, in the early 5th century the figures acquire increased
importance as compared with the background. They begin to work upon the background and
draw it into their own sphere of artistic existence. In the metopes of the Temple of Zeus at *107–109*
Olympia the relief has become a living field of interacting forces that also find expression in a
new relation of the figures to one another. Their posture, their faces and their gaze disclose a
profound inner life. The figures are united by a fateful sense of belonging-together quite alien
to the works of the 6th century. In the reliefs of the Parthenon metopes and frieze the connexion *142–147; 148–171*
between the figures and their relationship to the background have become even closer and more
intense. The individual components of the relief interpenetrate one another to a still greater extent,
are yet more intimately fused. In the Parthenon frieze the background seems very largely to have
lost its material character and to have become an element in the representation.

The various art-producing regions continued to retain their own aspect during the period

31

of the Severe Style, and in some cases even beyond it, in so far as they were not, like Miletus, wrenched out of their isolation by military events, or did not, like Thasos and Aegina, lose their political independence in the mid-5th century. In about 490 B.C. the older east pediment of the 'Temple of Aphaia' on Aegina was replaced by new figures executed by a local *72–77; 82–87* sculptor. The stylistic differences between the earlier west and the later east pediments – to which attention has frequently been drawn – are symptomatic of the evolution of sculpture from the late 6th to the early 5th century. It is not primarily the external dimensions, measurable in inches, that distinguish the older pediment figures from the later. A comparison *74, 75* between the fallen warriors in the corner of the two pediments shows that the earlier figure, who is drawing an arrow from his breast, is more angular in his movements, that the relief is *84, 85* shallower and that there is less cohesion between the parts. By contrast the bearded warrior on the later east pediment, from whose powerless hand the round shield is sinking, thrusts further out into space, his body is more rounded and the parts more organically coherent. In its totality the figure is the expression of a new outlook in monumental sculpture peculiar to the 5th century. We can recognize a similar development in the composition of the later east pediment in comparison with the west pediment. Whereas the west pediment comprises a right and a left side which are separated from, rather than connected with, one another by virtue of the towering figure of Athene, which is still frontally planned, all the warriors in the east pediment are drawn together into a single whole by the striding figure of the goddess in the centre. The novel way in which the figures of the warriors are treated in the east pediment further serves to unify the composition: the outstretched position in which the one has fallen, the extended backward stumble of the other, the grasping motion of the third pair, the way the two archers face towards the middle and the attitudes of the dying men in the corners. The row of figures in the west pediment has in the east pediment become a chain, in which the component parts are indissolubly linked.

89–91 In addition to the 'Kritios boy', Attic sculpture in the Severe Style is represented in this *96* volume by the beautiful, and only slightly later, victory stele from Sunium and the small, *139* exquisite votive relief from the Athenian Acropolis with the girlish figure of the goddess of the citadel leaning on her spear in front of a pillar. The spiritualized Attic form is contrasted with the *138* more sensuous style of Ionian–island skulptors, as exemplified in the tondo from Melos *133* showing the expressive head in profile, and the sepulchral stelae of Nisyros and from the Giusti- *140, 141* niani Collection in Berlin. The richly painted terra-cotta group of Zeus abducting his favourite, *105, V; 106* Ganymede, and the splendid bronze Horse from a quadriga at Olympia demonstrate the characteristic manner in which north-east Peloponnesian sculpture was built up out of heavy, compact parts. Plastic art must have received a tremendous impetus during the period of the Severe Style in the Greek colonies of southern Italy and Sicily, a golden age connected with the position of power enjoyed by the Greek towns of southern Italy and the courts of the Sicilian tyrants. The victories of the Sicilian princes in the Pan-Hellenic contests were celebrated by no less a poet *97–101* than Pindar. We have already spoken of the Enthroned Goddess from Taranto and the Piombino *92–95* Apollo as early 5th-century works from Dorian colonial towns in Magna Graecia. They were followed in the second quarter of the 5th century B.C., from the same Sicilian, southern Italian

32

VIII   The 'Alexander sarcophagus'. From the side panel with hunting scene. cf. Plates 232 and 235

56554

56554

area, by the Delphic Charioteer, the metopes from the Temple of Hera at Selinus and the magni- *102–104, IV; 126–129*
ficent reliefs on the 'Ludovisi throne' in the Museo delle Terme. *134–137*

The supreme sculptural creation of this period, indeed one may say of the Severe Style al- *107–125*
together, is the carving from the Temple of Zeus at Olympia. These sculptures were completed
the same year – 456 B.C. – as Aeschylus died, far from his home town of Athens, at the court of
the tyrant of Gela in Sicily. The huge pediments and the metopes with the Twelve Labours of Hercules are filled with the dramatic tension and commanding ethos of his tragedies. Just as it is
typical of the pictures of the great painters of this period that they did not reproduce an action or
occurrence, but the situation immediately before or after it, so in the east pediment of the
Temple of Zeus the opposing parties confront one another during the preparations for the *110–116*
chariot race between Pelops and Oenomaus, in the calm before the storm that is about to bring *117–125*
disaster. In the west pediment the ghastly battle between the Lapithae and the Centaurs at
Peirithoös's wedding is raging on either side of the towering figure of Apollo, who gives the
Lapithae victory over the wild horse-men. In both pediments the two halves tend to form a grand,
significantly arranged and graduated composition running from the centre to the corners. The style
of the Olympic sculptures contains Peloponnesian and Ionian-island elements, which are fused
into a magnificent unity at the hands of the master who designed them. If the origin and style
of this master cannot be as unequivocally determined as is the case with 6th-century pedimental
sculptures, this is due to the greater exchange of ideas between sculptors and schools of sculpture
in the 5th century B.C. than during the Archaic period. Furthermore, the individual artist's own
style is more in evidence in the 5th century than during the earlier period.

It was above all Athens which, at the peak of its political power after the Persian War, attracted
artists from abroad and became a focal point at which they were fused together. The genius of
the Athenian Phidias outshone all other sculptors. His fame in the ancient world was based
particularly on the two colossal religious images which were fashioned out of gold and ivory around
a wooden core: Athena Parthenos and Zeus, at Olympia. They perished in late antiquity and we
can only form an idea of them from descriptions and copies. Other images of the gods by Phidias,
bronze statues of Hermes, Apollo and Athene, and also a wounded Amazon, have survived in
Roman marble copies. Apart from these statues, we can – through a rare and fortunate case of
survival – see 5th-century originals of Phidias in the Parthenon sculptures. In the metopes, the frieze *142–163*
and the pediments of the Parthenon he reached the pinnacle of his personal achievement, and at
the same time Greek sculpture entered its Classical stage. As the blossom develops from the bud
overnight, so this stage was attained in the Parthenon sculptures without any transition, even in
relation to what immediately preceded it. Everything about them is entirely original, brilliant and
magnificent – the mastery of formal and compositional problems as well as the rendering of the
mythological material and the heightened ethos of the figures. In the southern metopes the Cen- *142–147*
taurs are no longer the rough, brutish fellows we see being slaughtered by the Lapithae in the west
pediment of the Temple of Zeus at Olympia. Here they oppose the Lapithae almost on equal terms,
and are not only vanquished but also victors. Battle as such is presented in the Parthenon metopes *148–163*
in a fresh, exalted and refined light. A new feature within the framework of the Doric temple is the

35

frieze high up on the exterior of the cella. Also without precedent and without any real successor

164–169 is the theme of the procession received by the gods. The vast mythical visions on the pediments are no less unique: in the east, the miraculous birth of Athene in the presence of the great Olympian deities, on a day which Helios brings up with his quadriga on one side, while on the other Selene

170, 171 goes down with her steeds into the waters of Ocean; in the west, Athene's struggle with Poseidon for the Attic land in the presence of the gods and heroes from the Athenian citadel.

It would be a mistake to imagine that the harmony of Classical art corresponded to a tranquil outer existence or a period of peace and prosperity in 5th-century Greece. Behind the order and moderation of Classical art was a knowledge of the potentialities and limits of human nature, a clear perception that sprang from concentrated intellectual analysis of the conflict between the wishes of the individual and the demands made upon him by Religion and the State – those supra-personal powers which then enjoyed unquestioned acceptance and provided everyone with a secure framework for his own existence. Unity of form and content, the essence of Classical art, mirrors a certain idea of man which, for the Greeks at that juncture in world history, was an absolutely obligatory aim and ideal.

The equipoise of forces, as given universal expression in Polyclitus's canon and the Parthenon, was limited to a short span of time. It is true that the Peloponnesian War (431–404 B.C.), at the end of which the hegemony of Athens in Greece was broken, did not initially cause any break in artistic evolution; but already in the the first post-Parthenon generation, works like

189–191 the reliefs of the Nike balustrade, the Boy in the Piraeus Museum or the tombstone

198; 192 of Dexileos foreshadow new trends that are evident in the altered balance of the individual figure as well as in the changed relationship between figure and drapery, and between the figures and the background in relief sculpture.

Fourth-century figures are no longer self-contained in the same way as the Polyclitan bronze in the Louvre. As the result of a greater differentiation between supporting and free leg and a consequent increase in the shift of the axes of the body, these figures swing farther towards one side or the other, the centre of gravity is displaced from the middle and not infrequently a support is included in the composition, as is the case at a later stage of development, for example

211–213; 228–231 in the statue of 'Mausolus' or in the Hermes of Praxiteles. In the same degree to which they have abandoned their secure stance and inner firmness, they have, as it were, grown into surrounding space, which in the early 4th century begins to encircle and play around them as atmosphere and gradually appears in more and more distinct contrast to them.

With the figures' increasing mobility and more profound spatial evolution, the image of the human being becomes richer and more differentiated. Thus woman is rendered in all her spe-

205; 224, 225 cific femininity, as in the rare perfection of the beautiful Head from Tegea, the Demeter from

242, 243 Cnidus, or the delicate Head of a girl from Chios. The little Dionysus on the arm of the Hermes

228–231; 226 at Olympia, and the weeping boy crouching beside the hunter in the picture on the Ilissus stele, are portrayed as real children with childish forms and ways. Further, the relation between mother and daughter, father and son, husband and wife, as well as the various ages of man, are more finely distinguished. This is easily seen from the series of Attic sepulchral reliefs repro-

36

IX The 'Alexander sarcophagus'. One of the pediment reliefs with battle scene

duced here. In general, the portrayal of states of mind through expression, pose and gesture gains ever-increasing importance in the course of the 4th century B.C. According to ancient tradition, Praxiteles was a pioneer in this direction, and we find this confirmed by his surviving work as well as by sculpture produced under his influence. With the progressive differentiation of the human image, the treatment of the individual portrait also underwent a change from a more or less supra-personal reproduction of outward appearance at the beginning of the 4th century B.C., which was still rooted in the High Classic of the Parthenon period, to a more individual – one might go so far as to say more naturalistic – conception of the portrait at the end of the same century. The bronze head of an African from Cyrene, the magnificent statue of *210* 'Mausolus' and the Boxer from Olympia, shown here, are both important and typical examples *211–213; 238, 239* of Greek sculpture at this period.

The stylistic differences between the various art-producing regions, some of which may be traced to the end of the 5th century B.C., become less numerous during the 4th century. In the Greek motherland those two regions assume leadership in the field of sculpture in which the Classical form attained its maximum development: Attica, and the north-east Peloponnesus. Several names of artists and works of art from the school of Polyclitus, who was probably rather younger than Phidias, have come down to us through literature. The Polyclitan tradition is still perceptible during the second half of the 4th century B.C. in such works as the bronze Youth from Anticythera or the relief from the base of a column in the later Artemision at *218–220* Ephesus. The most famous master of Sicyonian metal-casting was Lysippus, whose extremely *223* fertile working life must have extended over more than six decades and lasted until towards the end of the 4th century B.C. Of similar importance and influence in Athens were Praxiteles, who worked chiefly in marble, and Leochares, who collaborated with Lysippus during the Alexandrian period. It is typical of the times that one of the greatest monuments of the 4th century was not publicly commissioned, but erected on the orders of a single ruling personage. This was the colossal tomb of Mausolus at Halicarnassus, the sculptural decoration on which brought together in the residence of the prince from Asia Minor four of the most celebrated Greek *214–217* sculptors of the day – Scopas, Timotheus, Bryaxis and Leochares.

Again, it is instructive to trace the changes of form that took place during the 4th century B.C. in the relief style also. Two Attic sepulchral reliefs portraying a similar scene afford an illuminating comparison: the tombstone of Hegeso dating from the end of the 5th century, and a *187* tombstone three or four decades later in date showing a Woman and her Maidservant, both of *202, 203* which are in the National Museum, Athens. In Hegeso's tombstone the inner link between the two figures is expressed through the slight inclination of the heads, the use made of the box which the maidservant is holding out to the seated woman and from which the latter has taken the jewellery, the position of the arms and the close contiguity of the hands, the framing outlines of the curved chair and the long robe falling at the maidservant's back. In the superficially similar 4th-century relief, the serving-girl stands on her own with the box in her hand; she holds it close to her, raises the lid and looks down at it. The bowed, seated mistress and the striding maidservant are so firmly enveloped in their garments that every movement of the limbs and every curve of the body comes up against the resistance of the fabric. There is no longer anything connective about the straight lines of the seat. The figures have become more independent and possess a deeper spatial volume, they stand out from the background with well-defined contours and the background itself acquires greater solidity and autonomy in relation to the figures.

As the 4th century progresses, the figures approach more and more closely to free sculpture, *226, 227* as may be seen in the sepulchral stele from the Ilissus, the tombstone from Rhamnus or the late *240, 241* fragment with the Bearded Man in a cloak. They gradually lose their connexion with the background and become isolated from it, while the background increasingly asserts its own independence and finally assumes the character of a wall that stands in marked contrast to the figures. In the end, the two elements whose active interrelationship gave life to the Greek relief of the 5th and 4th centuries, lose almost all connexion with each other. Thus it may be said that when Demetrius of Phaleron's proscription of luxury brought the carving of Attic sepulchral reliefs to an end in the last phases of the 4th century, this end had already been adumbrated by the artistic evolution of this form of sculpture.

187 Roughly a hundred years separate Hegeso's tombstone from the fragment of a late Attic *240, 241* sepulchral relief showing a Bearded Man in a cloak just referred to. This century was also a time of revolutionary changes. At its beginning the Greek city-states were still fighting for hegemony in Greece, during the Peloponnesian War, as closed political units; at its end, the individual communities had lost their independence and freedom in the struggles against Philip of Macedon and Alexander. Alexander had carried Greek culture as far as India. After his premature death (323 B.C.), Alexander's empire fell to his successors. The Greek motherland was thereafter forced to relinquish its pre-eminent role in the political and artistic domains to the courts of the Diadochi. Among the latter, the kings of Alexandria, Syria, Pergamon and Bithynia, in particular, gathered poets and scholars, painters and sculptors around them during the 3rd and 2nd centuries B.C. and commissioned work from them.

By the end of the 4th century B.C., tendencies were becoming noticeable in sculpture that can only be regarded as a reaction against preceding epochs. They did not bear full fruit until the 3rd century, the first century of Hellenistic sculpture, generally described as the period of the 'simple style' and 'closed form'. The great sweeping movement that still activates each of the *227; 228–231* figures on the sepulchral relief from Rhamnus and the Hermes of Praxiteles began to grow rigid during the last quarter of the 4th century. Instead of the clear arrangement of axes which had determined the construction of figures for so long, overlapping of the parts and opposing rhythms now became essential elements of sculpture. The inner structure of the figures became firmer, even stiff, and also more complicated. They no longer reach out into space, as they had done before, but on the contrary withdraw from their surroundings, becoming concentrated – by means of carefully thought-out poses and movements – about a newly created centre. It is no coincidence that, since the early Hellenistic period, draped statues acquire increased importance, alongside statues of naked athletes and images of unclothed Aphrodite. Drapery is now set free from the body and employed as an independent element in the composition, in which it is

40

X   Head of a philosopher, found in the sea off Anticythera. Bronze. National Museum, Athens

required to fulfil a definite structural function, serving either to support the body or to enclose it, as in the philosopher in Delphi or the statue of the priestess Nikokleia from Cnidus, which *245, 246* was carved soon after the middle of the 3rd century B.C. Here the forms of the body vanish behind the vertical folds of the finely puckered chiton, which looks like a curtain, and behind the cloak on top of it, whose thick material and folds running diagonally across the body are in marked contrast to the long undergarment. It is interesting to cast a glance back from this tightly self-contained statue, isolated from everything outside itself, to the Demeter at Venice, with its *206* relatively broad and clear structure and stance, and its comparatively simple arrangement of the peplos and cloak, in order to see the distance travelled by the development of the standing female draped statue from the mid-4th to the mid-3rd century B.C.

The Sacrificial Servant in the Museo delle Terme, which comes from a Roman villa near *247* Antium, is also very typical of the style that characterized the third quarter of the 3rd century B.C. With perfect mastery of his medium, the artist has recorded in this exceedingly charming work a fleeting situation. The girl, portrayed in the act of walking, is entirely absorbed by her task: she is taking a sacrificial implement or an offering from the round salver she holds in her left hand. All the main lines of the composition lead to this centre. In spite of the opposing directions of the movements and the overlapping limbs, garments and folds, this statue, too, gives the impression of being firmly shut off from everything outside it. The statue is clearly intended to be seen from one particular angle. Its artistic qualities are most manifest when it is looked at diagonally from its right side. The Hellenistic bronze original from which this statue of the Sacrificial Servant is derived must itself have stood in front of a wall or in a niche, a position in which free sculpture was frequently placed during the 3rd century B.C., as we know from literary sources. Thus an extract from the writings of Callixeinus of Rhodes quoted by Athenaeus (196 a and ff.) tells us that a hundred marble figures by leading masters stood in front of the rectangular stanchions of the pavilion erected for Ptolemy II at Alexandria in c. 270 B.C. And three statues of members of the Alexandrian ruling house were placed between Ionic columns in front of the wall of an Early Hellenistic nymphaeum described in a poem dating from the first half of the 3rd century B.C. The placing of statues in this position is an expression of a particular feeling for space current at that time, and also manifest in the style of 3rd-century reliefs. If a marked isolation of the figures both from one another and from the background is already evident in late 4th-century reliefs, the 3rd century goes still farther in this direction. It is characteristic of the intrinsic structure of Early Hellenistic reliefs, for example, that the individual figures support themselves against a tree, a pillar or a column, objects which operate in the composition like a piece of scenery and evoke the impression of a solid boundary or of several distinct layers of space.

In the votive relief to Cybele and Attis from Asia Minor in Venice, which belongs to the same *244* period as the Nikokleia and the 'Antium Girl', each of the two main figures is portrayed on its own and at a marked interval from the other. The deities stand in statuesque pose and dimensions in front of the wall of their sanctuary, which is broken by a lofty door with a half-open and foreshortened right leaf, through which the woman worshipper has entered the sacred precincts with a little serving maid. The figures and the background are here assigned to two different and contrasting spheres of art. This antithesis between the elements of the relief probably explains why the 3rd century B.C., compared with the Classical epoch, showed little taste for relief sculpture. By nature it was a period of statuesque free sculpture. The prerequisite for the relief style of the succeeding period was that the figure should be differently inclined towards the plane.

This mutation in the history of Hellenistic sculpture, however, means nothing else than the dissolution of 'closed form'. It must have taken place at the end of the 3rd and the beginning of the 2nd century. In our selection, two masterpieces of the highest quality convincingly demonstrate the transition from the 'closed form' and the 'simple style' of the 3rd, to the 'open form' and 'pathetic style' of the 2nd century: the 'Sleeping Satyr' from the Barberini Collection in the Munich Glyptothek and the Nike donated by the Rhodians to Samothrace as a votive offering in gratitude for their victories over Antiochus III of Syria around 190 B.C. The outline of the mighty, outstretched sleeper, sunk in oppressive dreams, originally – as restored in modern times the left arm and right leg do not occupy quite their old position – fitted into a wide parallelogram. The practice of focusing the composition on a centre, which was characteristic of mid-3rd century sculpture, has been abandoned by the artist of the later 3rd century in this magnificent figure. The sculptural form as such has also changed in comparison with older works. It has become looser, the surface transitions are more lively. Light and shade play a greater part in the modelling than hitherto. The adherence of the Nike of Samothrace to the plane is considerably greater than that of the Munich Satyr, although the Nike now seems more of a free sculpture than the Satyr, which is attached to the background formed by the surface of the rock. It appears from the circumstances in which it was found, however, that the Nike once stood on the prow of a ship in front of a wall, and was designed to be seen from one particular angle – diagonally from its left side. In the opposing lines of movement and the manner in which some of the drapery clings close to the body, while the rest is rendered in ridges and deep, shadow-filled valleys, or blows out freely in the wind, it constitutes an immediate precursor to the Great Frieze on the Pergamon Altar.

The kingdom of Pergamon was then at the height of its power, after Attalus I had repulsed repeated attacks by the Gauls. The latter had invaded Macedonia and Greece in 280 B.C., crossed the Hellespont and settled in Asia Minor, where they later became the Galatians. In the years around 180 B.C. Eumenes II (197–159 B.C.), the son and successor of Attalus I, erected the huge altar, in extent the largest connected work of art of the Hellenistic epoch, on the citadel mountain of Pergamon – a vast memorial in thanksgiving for the victories over the Gauls. In the Great Frieze, which runs round the base of the monument to a length of 396 feet, the historical event – the victorious struggle of the Pergamenes against the wild barbarian tribes – is transposed Greek-fashion into the mythical sphere as the war of the gods against the giants. With tremendous effort and unrelenting ferocity the forces of light battle with the powers of the earth. The mightily extended movements of the figures, the restless counterpoise of the bodies, the rendering of the naked torsos with their huge muscles, the loud rustle of the masses of drapery and

44

XI   Male portrait head, from Delos. Bronze. National Museum, Athens. cf. Plate 274

the emotion that blazes forth from the eyes are in keeping with the magnitude and savagery of this combat. Outwardly, the treatment of form has attained grandiose proportions, but – in comparison with the 'Antium Girl' or the 'Sleeping Satyr' – it has lost firmness, density and sculptural force.

The Great Frieze is not an ornamental trimming attached to the Pergamon Altar, but an independent component in the monument's architectural structure. The background of the relief is here identical with the rising wall of the base, in front of which the figures stand. In its artistic structure it is manifestly the diametrical opposite of the Classical relief. In the latter, in *142–147; 148–163* the metopes and frieze of the Parthenon, for example, the background participates in the life of the composition: it is flexible and binds the figures together. Here, in the Great Frieze of Pergamon, it is the rigid, impenetrable surface of a wall. How strongly the material qualities of the standing surface and background have been felt as objective and tangible components in the architectural construction, and how powerfully the ideal sphere of the relief encroaches upon the real structure of the building, is particularly evident on the inner side of the northern flank of the stairway, where a giant is winding his way up the steps of the staircase with his serpent-leg, and a second giant in front of him rests his knee and hand on the steps. Because of the impenetrability of the background, on the Great Frieze the figures have no chance to develop outwards into space or to lose themselves in the depths behind them. In the progressive action of the battle they can only expand sideways in a single plane. This adjustment of the figures to a plane is the beginning of a return to the Classical relief, the first sign of a classicizing attitude that is also visible in the way in which the master of the Great Frieze has based the widely extended group comprising Zeus and Athene and the chariot teams beside them, situated on the east side of the altar, upon the central section of the western pediment of the Parthenon showing the huge figures of Poseidon and Athene and their two rearing chariot teams.

The powerful portrait of Alexander, the ruler, from Pergamon has very close stylistic *260, 261* affinities with the leading master of the Great Frieze; similarly, the fine, vehemently mobile head of Helios from Rhodes, with its deep undercutting in the long, sinuous locks, *263* must have been produced under the direct influence of high Pergamene art. But the turbulent emotionality of the Great Frieze seems already to have been toned down in this work from the second quarter of the 2nd century B.C. From this point on, the evolution of Hellenistic sculpture no longer proceeded, as heretofore, in a single line, but in several currents nourished by various sources and tributaries. Some of them preserved and continued the Hellenistic inheritance, while others harked back to the past and employed older models for new creations adapted to their own age. The structure and rhythm of works of sculpture became more complex and less unitary. Periods during which Hellenistic 'baroque' had apparently quietened down alternated with others during which sculpture was dominated by a new outward emotionalism. During this epoch sculpture once more eloquently mirrors the spiritual state of the Greek world, which was one of general dissolution and transformation. The traditional faith in the old gods, and in the State as a political factor, were no longer able to afford man the inner stay he needed. Consequently the individual was thrown back more and more on his own resources and sought happiness in the doctrines of salvation preached by the great Hellenistic schools of philosophy, which foreshadowed the joyful tidings of the Gospel and the doctrine of redemption propounded by Christianity.

264, 265   The monumental portrait statues that follow the head of Helios in our selection, the Ruler
266, 267 in the Museo delle Terme and the figure known as Hippocrates from Cos, are both based on 4th-century works. In all probability we should see in the bronze statue of Demetrius I of Syria a Greek vassal of the Roman Republic, which was then ceaselessly advancing in the Mediterranean area. The Hellenistic ruler is similar in type to the famous 'Alexander with the Spear' by Lysippus. But the artist of the mid-2nd century B.C. has made only outward use of his Late Classical model. In comparison with the statue of Alexander the stance of the figure is vacillating, the sculptural form restlessly mobile, the face tormented by doubt. When it was first discovered, the marble statue from Cos was taken to be a 4th-century original. But if it is com-
211–213 pared with the 'Mausolus' statue, or a figure bearing an outward resemblance to it from one
227 of the 4th-century Attic sepulchral reliefs, it can be seen to lack the firmness and compactness of Classical works. The figure is not self-contained, but stands uncertainly and, spreading out its whole structure in one plane, seeks a stay on the wall in front of which it was originally set. The soft materiality of the cloak and the spirited treatment of the folds presuppose the phase of the Great Frieze at Pergamon just as much as the hesitant, questioning pose of the head and the searching, tired gaze. The disappearance of the feeling for the body's sculptural unity is blatantly manifest in the way in which the figure is cut in two by the vertical edge of the cloak, that falls down over the left shoulder, and the deep fold that continues this vertical dividing line.

270, 271   In the second half of the 2nd century B.C. the master of the Aphrodite from Melos used a large bronze statue dating from the late 4th century more independently, changing its relatively simple and lucid structure by the introduction of contrasting movements and opposing motifs, effectively transmuting the character of the whole work into an emotional and grandiose image of cool beauty. An example of a different sort of transformation is afforded by the marble
273 statue of the kneeling Aphrodite at Rhodes. Here the Late Hellenistic sculptor redesigned a mid-3rd-century composition that was closed on all sides – the famous crouching Aphrodite of Doidalses – in such a way that it offered a single face to the spectator; this he did by twisting the upper body into a single plane and altering the position of the hands so that they grasped the loosened hair. The statuette reveals how Late Hellenistic art sought to replace the inner firmness, of which the figures were becoming more and more devoid, by a new attachment to the plane. This is the meaning of the 'single-view' figures and groups which depended upon a principle of composition that was developed with ever greater artistry during the 1st century
278, 279 B.C. In the Laocoön group by the three Rhodian sculptors Agesandrus, Athenodorus and Polydorus this principle was carried to such lengths that the pictorial effect of this relief-like composition is fully effective only when the group is looked at from one definite spot. Having reached the limit of 'single-view' sculpture as exemplified in the Laocoön group with the twist of the bodies, the overlapping of the limbs, as well as the rhetorical pathos of the movements and the increased striving after purely sculptural effect, Hellenistic sculpture was incapable of

48

any further advance. Just as the ghastly fate of the unhappily entangled priest of Apollo and his two sons is portrayed by Virgil, in the *Aeneid*, as an augury of the imminent downfall of Troy, so the dying Laocoön has at the same time been regarded as a symbol of the end of Greek art.

As was only natural, the sculptor's methods of work and marble-cutting technique changed during the age of 'single-view' figures and groups as compared with earlier epochs. The sculptors of the Archaic and Classical periods worked the marble block, in which they first cut the rough outline of the figure, equally from all sides with a pointed chisel which they generally applied at right angles to the block. They worked step by step from the outside towards the centre, walking round the block and keeping the work of art as a whole in view all the time, until the contours of the figure had been reached on all sides and finally all that remained was to face the stone. This continuous chipping with a pointed chisel and hammer 'bruised' the marble and destroyed its individual crystals. The surface thus lost its transparency and appeared to the eye dull and soft. To this method of working, which was employed until well into the Hellenistic period, Greek marble sculpture largely owes its appearance of warm life, which has survived unchanged through hundreds and thousands of years. From the Late Hellenistic period onwards, when feeling for the unity of the work of art as a self-contained organism constantly diminished, it was usual to complete individual parts of a figure or group without reference to the whole, while leaving other parts untouched to be dealt with later. It was typical of Roman copyists that they reproduced the model by mechanical means, with the aid of dividers and plumb-rule. They did their best to avoid 'bruising' the marble in order to achieve a surface as smooth and transparent as possible. To this end they abandoned the pointed chisel in favour of tools like our two-bevelled chisel, with which the sculptor, as it were, peeled the stone off in layers.

The period following the Laocoön group, upon which the Graeco-Roman world bestowed a saviour from political chaos in the person of Augustus, turned more and more to the works of the 5th and 4th centuries B.C., which were already recognized as Classical and which sculptors of the day either modelled their own style upon or actually copied.

What Hellenistic portrait sculpture achieved in its progressive concern with the individual personality is clearly shown by the series of impressive heads and statues that runs from the statue of a Cynic in Delphi and the magnificent portrait of a Philosopher found in the sea off *245, 250, X* Anticythera, via the head of Alexander from Pergamon, the Ruler in the Museo delle Terme and *260, 261; 264, 265* the Cloaked Statue from Cos, to the Bronze Head from Delos. Whereas the portrait sculpture *266, 267; 274, XI* of the Classical period disclosed the essence of the personality by a general portrayal of the subject in the unity of his spiritual, psychological and physical characteristics, in Hellenism the subject's nature is presented more specifically through the unique features of his inner being and his outward appearance. From the standpoint of the modern spectator Hellenistic portrait sculpture may be regarded as the acme of Greek portraiture. In reality, however, its development mirrors particularly clearly the great spiritual process in which Greek man was gradually released from his religious, political and social attachments until he found himself in a position of isolation and loneliness.

49

250, X   Whereas in the Delphi Cynic and the Bearded Bronze Head from Anticythera – the remains of a cloaked statue dating from the second half of the 3rd century B.C. – individual features are still combined with representation of the Greek philosopher as a type, and whereas the design of these heads still follows a clearly defined system and its sculptural form still possesses firmness

274, XI and inner concentration, the Late Hellenistic Bronze Head from Delos is marked in every respect by the general atmosphere of dissolution. Compared with the earnest, inward-looking gaze of the Bearded Man, this face gives the impression of an unfulfilled, perpetually questioning doubter, whose glance wanders around in an endless search. The modelling is vacillating and unstable, the surface restless with the attempt to achieve an effect of vitality.

280, 281; 282   Finally, the Boy from Tralles in Caria and the beautiful head of Aphrodite from Satala in Armenia have been chosen to give idea of the conflicting potentialities of Greek ideal sculpture in the Late Hellenistic or the Early Roman Imperial period. Taken together, the convulsed features of Laocoön, the Boy and the bronze head of Aphrodite, with the classicistic simplicity and severity of its design and modelling, typify the profound disunity which characterized this last epoch of Greek sculpture.

PLATES

1   Standing horse, from the Peloponnesus. Bronze. Berlin

2   Warrior, from the Athenian Acropolis. Bronze. National Museum, Athens

3   Apollo, votive offering of Mantiklos. Found at Thebes. Bronze. Boston

4   Head of a griffin protome found at Olympia. Bronze. Olympia

5 Griffin protome found at Olympia. Bronze. Olympia

6 Standing female figure, known as the 'Auxerre statuette'. Limestone. Paris

7 Fragment of female figure in relief found at Mycenae. Limestone. National Museum, Athens

8   Reclining lion from Corfu. Limestone. Corfu

9   Reclining lion, head. Corfu. cf. Plate 8

10   Head of Hera. From the Heraion at Olympia. Limestone. Olympia

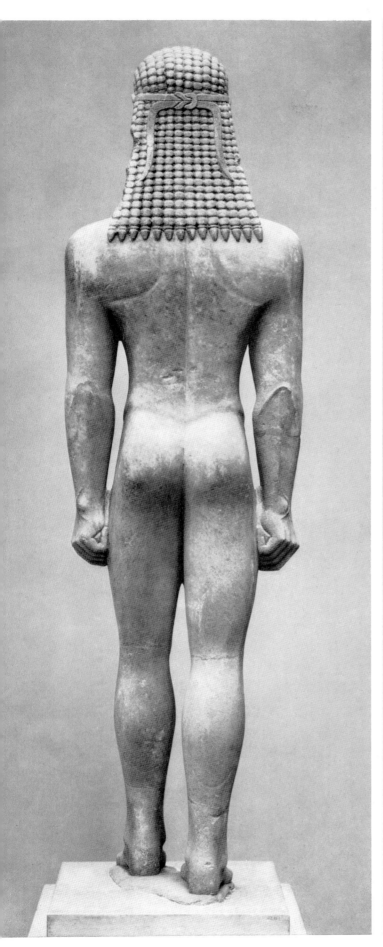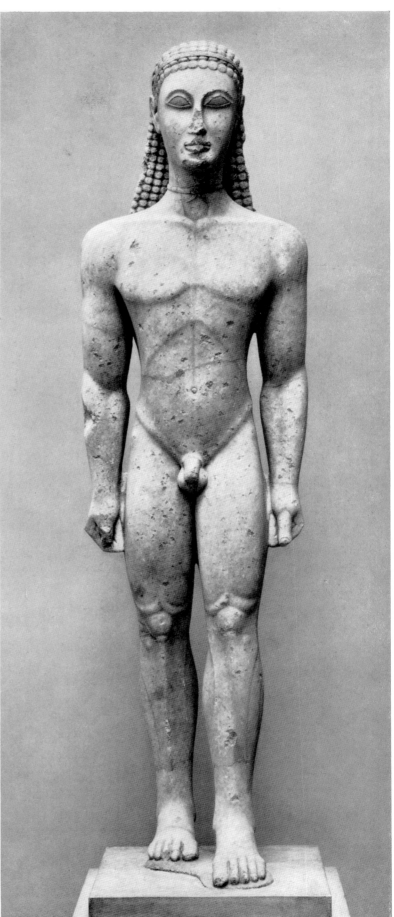

11 Standing youth, found in Attica. Marble. New York

12   Standing youth, head. New York. cf. Plate 11

13   Standing youth, head. New York. cf. Plate 11

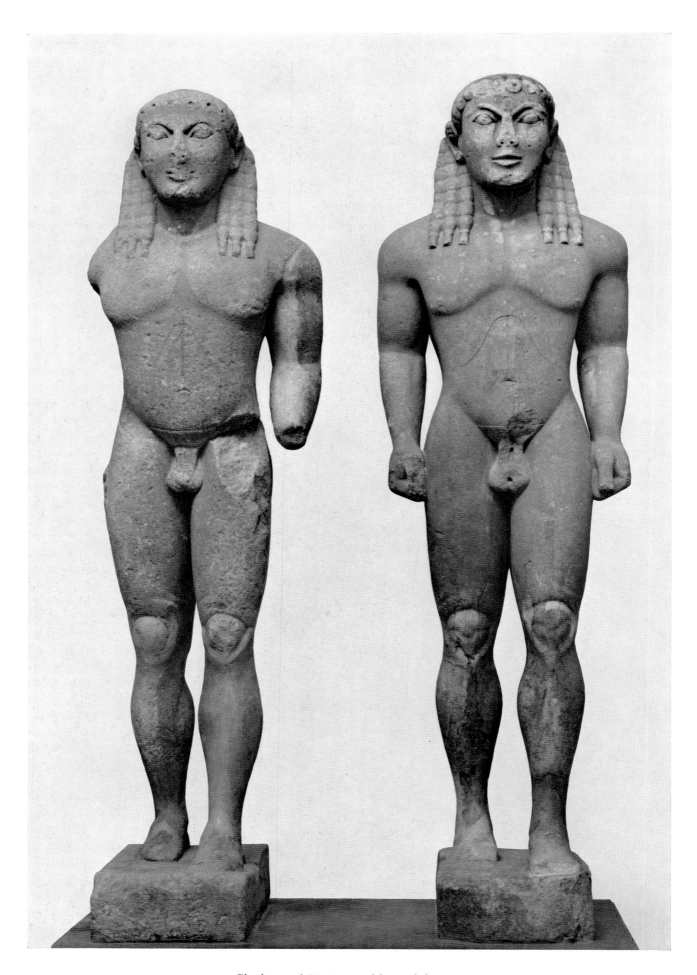

14   Cleobis and Biton. Marble. Delphi, Museum

15   Cleobis. cf. Plate 14

16 Sculpture from the west pediment of the Temple of Artemis, Corfu: left-hand lion-panther. Limestone. Corfu

17   Sculpture from the west pediment of the Temple of Artemis, Corfu:
centre section of the pediment with Gorgon. Corfu

18 Head of Gorgon. Corfu. cf. Plate 17

19   Sculpture from the west pediment of the Temple of Artemis, Corfu: Chrysaor. Corfu

20 Standing female figure with pomegranate, found near Keratea in Attica. Marble. Berlin

21 Standing female figure with pomegranate, found near Keratea in Attica. Marble. Berlin

22 Head of the standing female figure with pomegranate found near Keratea in Attica. Marble. Berlin

23   Head of the standing female figure with pomegranate found near Keratea in Attica. Marble. Berlin

24 Calf-bearer, found on the Athenian Acropolis. Marble from Mt. Hymettos. Acropolis Museum, Athens

25 Calf-bearer, found on the Athenian Acropolis. Marble from Mt. Hymettos. Acropolis Museum, Athens

26   Sculptures from the pediment of the Old Temple of Athene on the Athenian Acropolis. Limestone.
Acropolis Museum, Athens
Top: Left half of pediment showing Hercules wrestling with Triton
Bottom: One of the heads of the three-bodied monster on the right half of the pediment

27   Upper part of female statue. Marble from Naxos. Acropolis Museum, Athens

28   Head of a youth from the sanctuary of the Ptoan Apollo in Boeotia. Limestone.
National Museum, Athens

29   Head of a youth from the sanctuary of the Ptoan Apollo in Boeotia. Limestone.
National Museum, Athens

30 Rider, found on the Athenian Acropolis. Acropolis Museum, Athens, and Paris

31   Rider's head (the 'Rampin head'). Parian marble. Paris

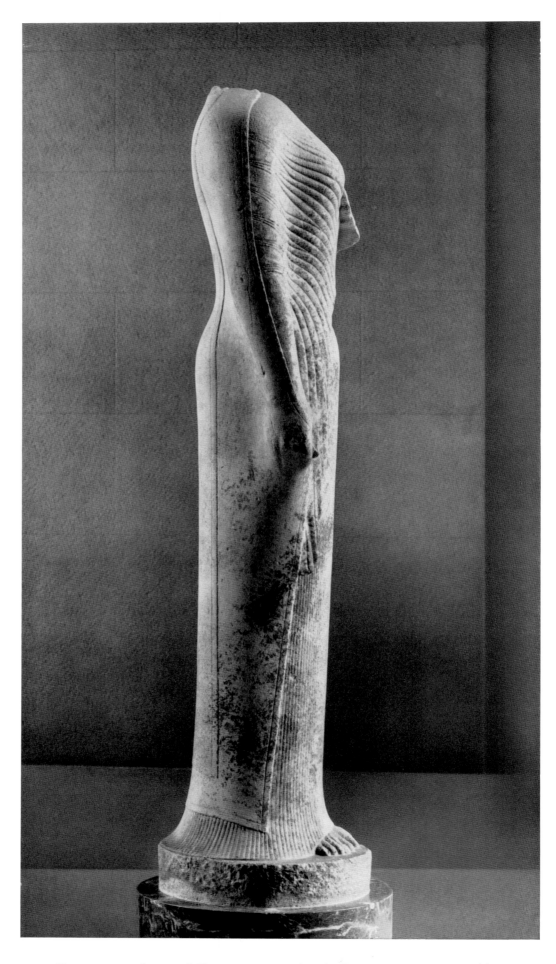

32　Hera, votive offering of Cheramyes. Found in the Heraion on Samos. Marble. Paris

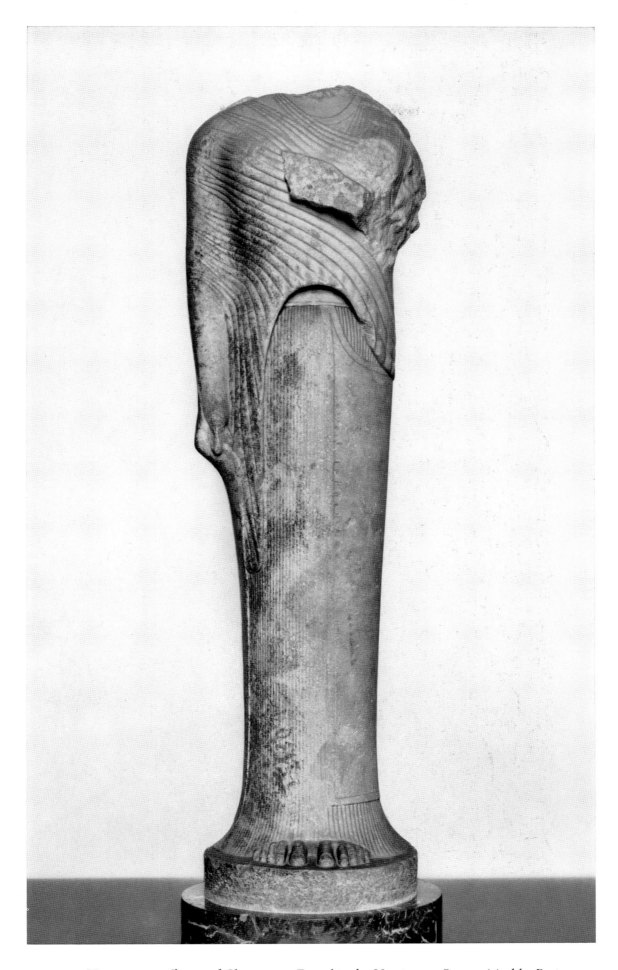

33 Hera, votive offering of Cheramyes. Found in the Heraion on Samos. Marble. Paris

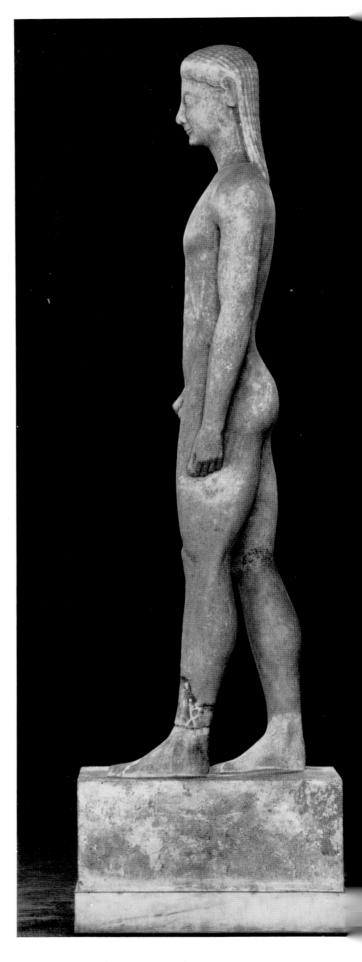

34   Standing youth from Melos. Marble from Naxos. National Museum, Athens

35   Standing youth from Melos, head. Marble from Naxos. National Museum, Athens

36   Head of the standing youth (the 'Apollo of Tenea'), found at Tenea, near Corinth. Parian marble. Munich

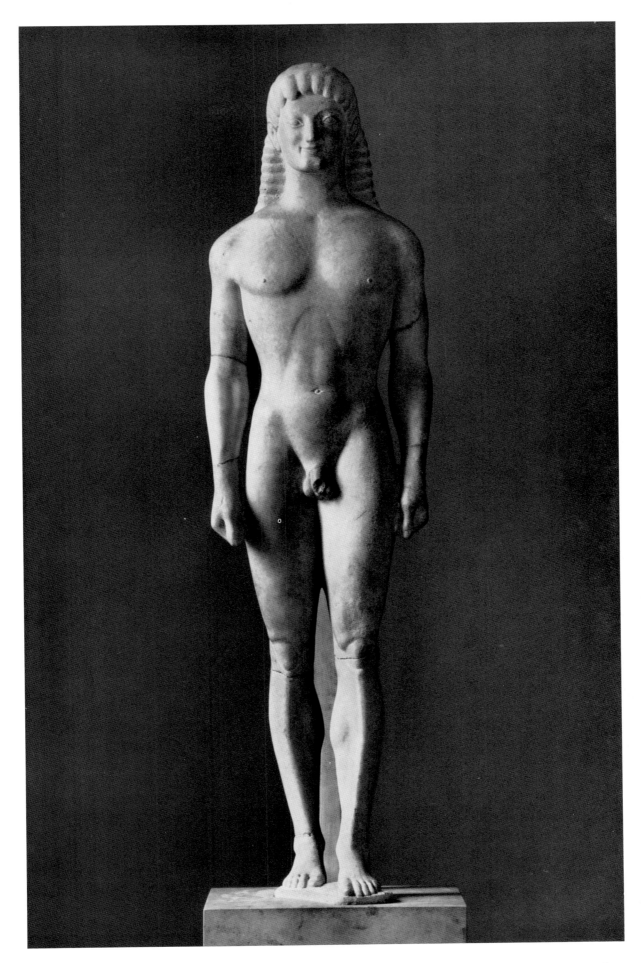

37 Standing youth (the 'Apollo of Tenea'), found at Tenea, near Corinth. Parian marble. Munich

38   Standing youth (the 'Apollo of Tenea'). cf. Plate 37. Parian marble. Munich

39   From the sepulchral stele of a discus-bearer. Found at Athens. Parian marble. National Museum, Athens

40   Head found at Ephesus. Marble. London

41   Head found at Ephesus. Marble. London

42   Female figure. Fragment of relief from the base of a pillar in the old Temple of Apollo at Didyma, near Miletus. Marble from Korossai. Berlin

43　Standing girl (kore) in chiton and peplos. Parian marble. Acropolis Museum, Athens

44 Standing girl in chiton and peplos, upper part. Parian marble. Acropolis Museum, Athens

45   Standing girl in chiton and peplos, upper part. Parian marble. Acropolis Museum, Athens

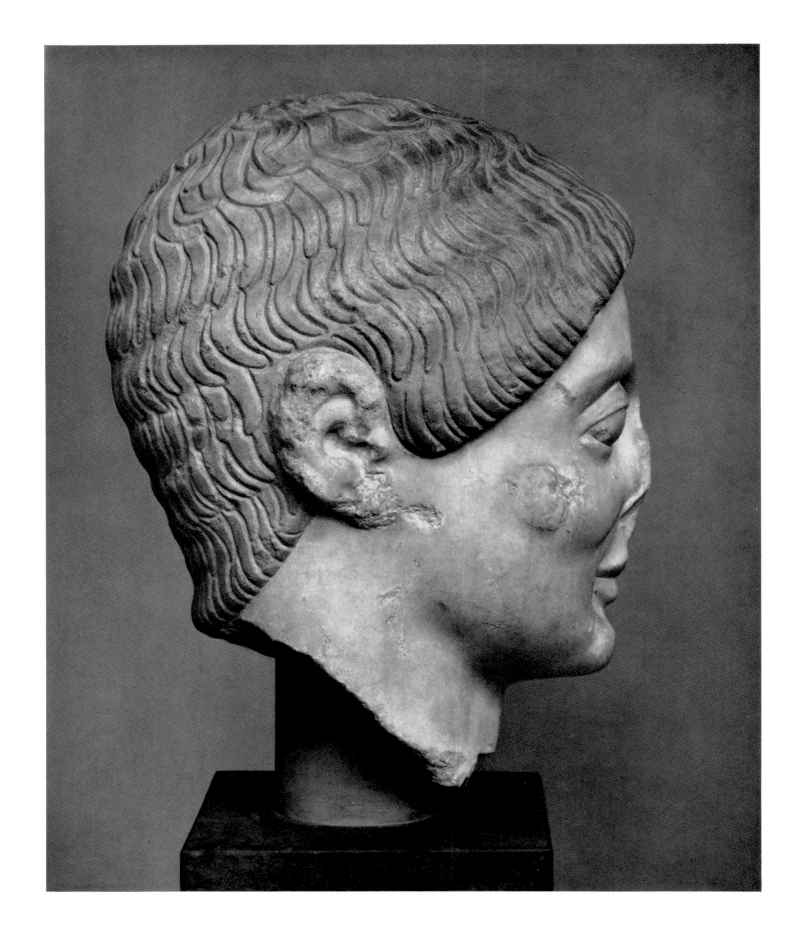

46   Head of a youth. Parian marble. Copenhagen

47   Head of a youth. cf. Plate 46

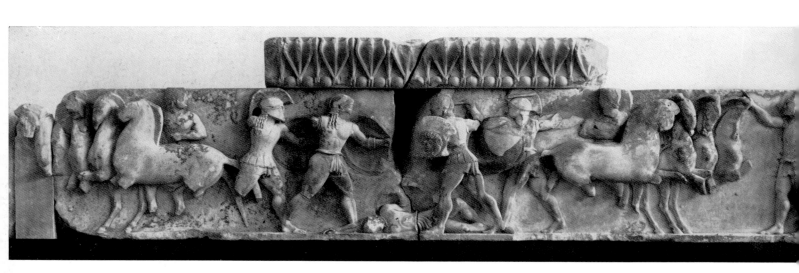

48   Sculptures from the friezes on the Siphnian treasury at Delphi. Parian marble. Museum, Delphi
Top: Council of the gods, east frieze, left half
Centre: Battle between Greeks and Trojans. East frieze, right half
Bottom: Battle of the gods against the giants. North frieze, left half

49   Sculptures from the east frieze of the Siphnian treasury at Delphi.
Aphrodite, Artemis and Apollo from the council of the gods. Marble, Museum, Delphi

50 North frieze of the Siphnian treasury at Delphi. Left half, battle of the gods against the giants

51   North frieze of the Siphnian treasury at Delphi. Right half, battle of the gods against the giants

52   From the left half of the north frieze on the Siphnian treasury.
Scene from the battle of the gods against the giants

53 From the left half of the north frieze on the Siphnian treasury.
Scene from the battle of the gods against the giants

54 From the right half of the north frieze on the Siphnian treasury.
Scene from the battle of the gods against the giants

55   From the right half of the north frieze on the Siphnian treasury.
Scene from the battle of the gods against the giants

56   Sphinx, from the Athenian Acropolis. Parian marble. Acropolis Museum, Athens

57 The youth Kroisos, found at Anavyssos, South Attica. Parian marble. National Museum, Athens

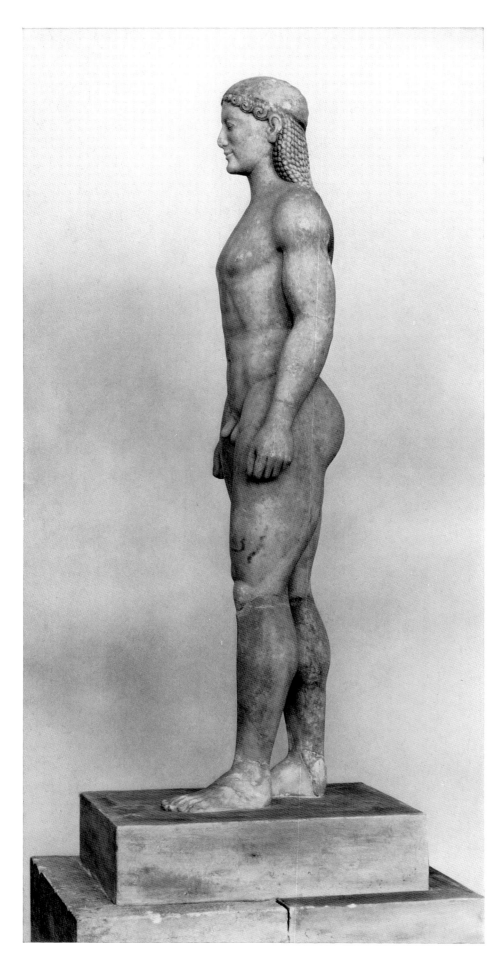

58   The youth Kroisos, found at Anavyssos, South Attica. Parian marble. National Museum, Athens

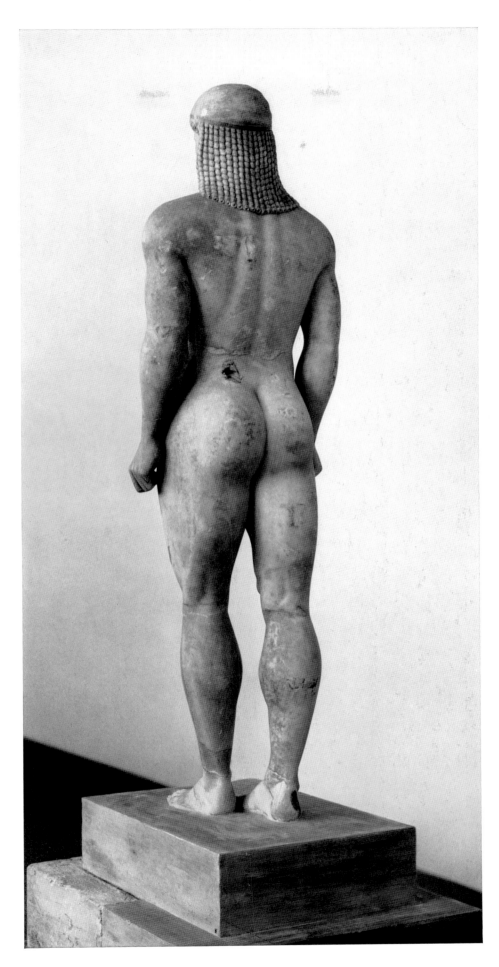

59   The youth Kroisos, found at Anavyssos, South Attica. Parian marble. National Museum, Athens

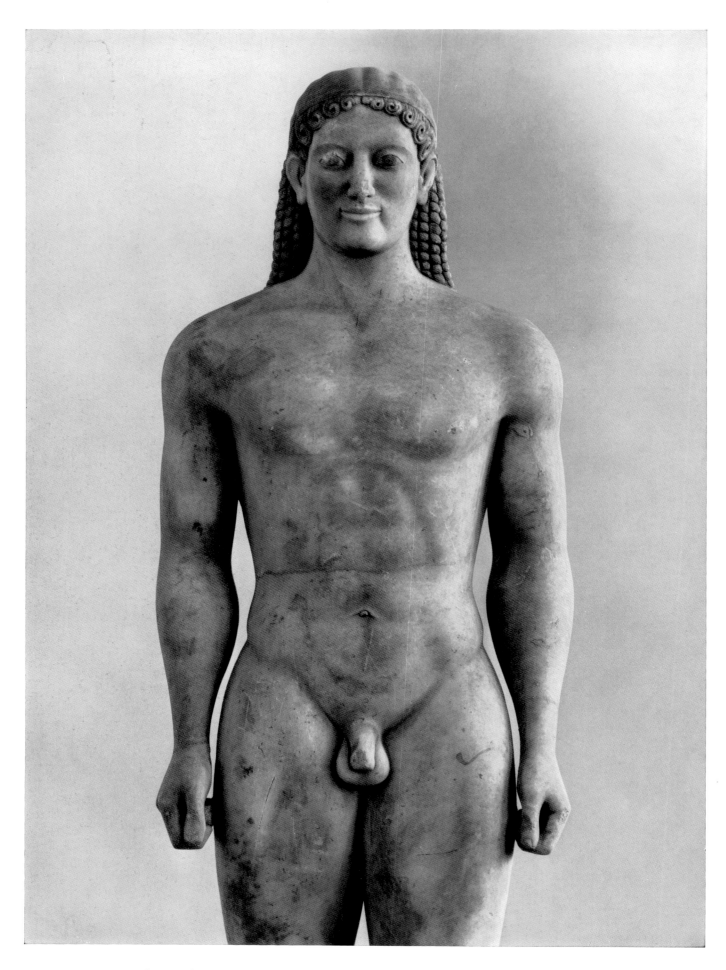

60　The youth Kroisos, found at Anavyssos. National Museum, Athens. cf. Plates 57–59

61   The youth Kroisos, found at Anavyssos. National Museum, Athens. cf. Plates 57–60

62 Reliefs from the base of a statue found at Athens. Pentelic marble. National Museum, Athens

63   Detail from the base of a statue found at Athens. Spear-thrower from the relief in Plate 62, top

64   Detail from the base of a statue found at Athens. Young people with dog and cat, left half of relief

65   Detail from the base of a statue found at Athens. Young people with dog and cat, right half of relief

66   Sculpture from the west pediment of the Temple of Apollo Daphnephoros at Eretria on Euboea.
Theseus and Antiope. Parian marble. Chalkis

67   Sculpture from the west pediment of the Temple of Apollo Daphnephoros at Eretria on Euboea.
Theseus and Antiope. Parian marble. Chalkis

68   Sculpture from the west pediment of the Temple of Apollo Daphnephoros at Eretria on Euboea.
Head of Theseus. Parian marble. Chalkis

69　From the east pediment of the Old Temple of Athene on the Athenian Acropolis: Athene. Parian marble.
Acropolis Museum, Athens

70   Girl (kore) by a master from Chios. Marble from Chios. Acropolis Museum, Athens

71   Tombstone of Aristion, from Velanidesa in Attica. Pentelic marble. National Museum, Athens

72   Head of Athene. cf. Plate 73

73   From the west pediment of the 'Temple of Aphaia' on Aegina: Athene.
Parian marble. Munich

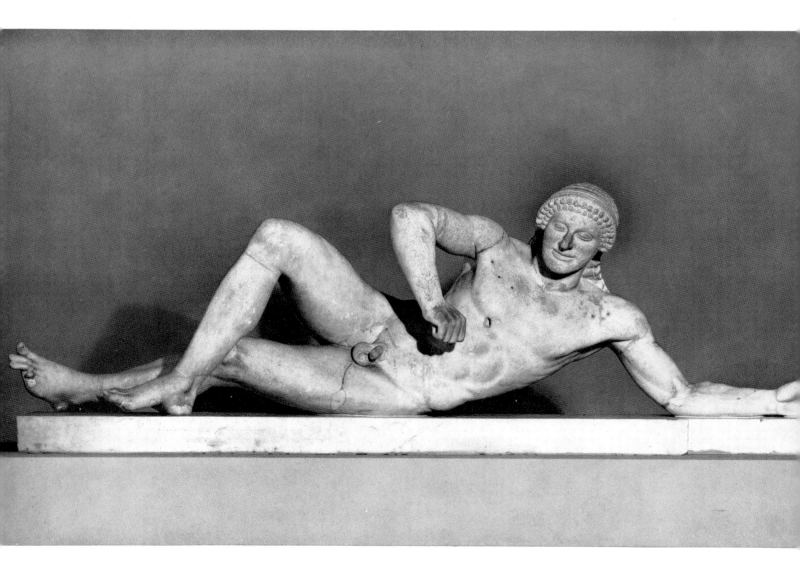

74   From the west pediment of the 'Temple of Aphaia' on Aegina: Fallen warrior.
Parian marble. Munich

75 Fallen warrior. cf. Plate 74

76   From the west pediment of the 'Temple of Aphaia' on Aegina: Lunging warrior.
Parian marble. Munich

77 From the west pediment of the 'Temple of Aphaia' on Aegina: Archer in Scythian dress.
Parian marble. Munich

78   Metope from the Temple of Hera at the mouth of the River Sele on the Campano-Lucanian border:
Two girls in ritual dance. Sandstone. Paestum

79   Metope from the treasury of the Athenians in Delphi:
Heracles slaying the hind. Parian marble. Delphi

80 Girl in chiton and cloak, from the Athenian Acropolis. Parian marble. Acropolis Museum, Athens

81   Girl in chiton and cloak, head. Acropolis Museum, Athens

82   From the east pediment of the 'Temple of Aphaia' on Aegina: Head of Athene.
Parian marble. Munich

83   From the east pediment of the 'Temple of Aphaia' on Aegina: Hurrying rescuer.
Parian marble. Munich

84   From the east pediment of the 'Temple of Aphaia' on Aegina: Fallen warrior.
Parian marble. Munich

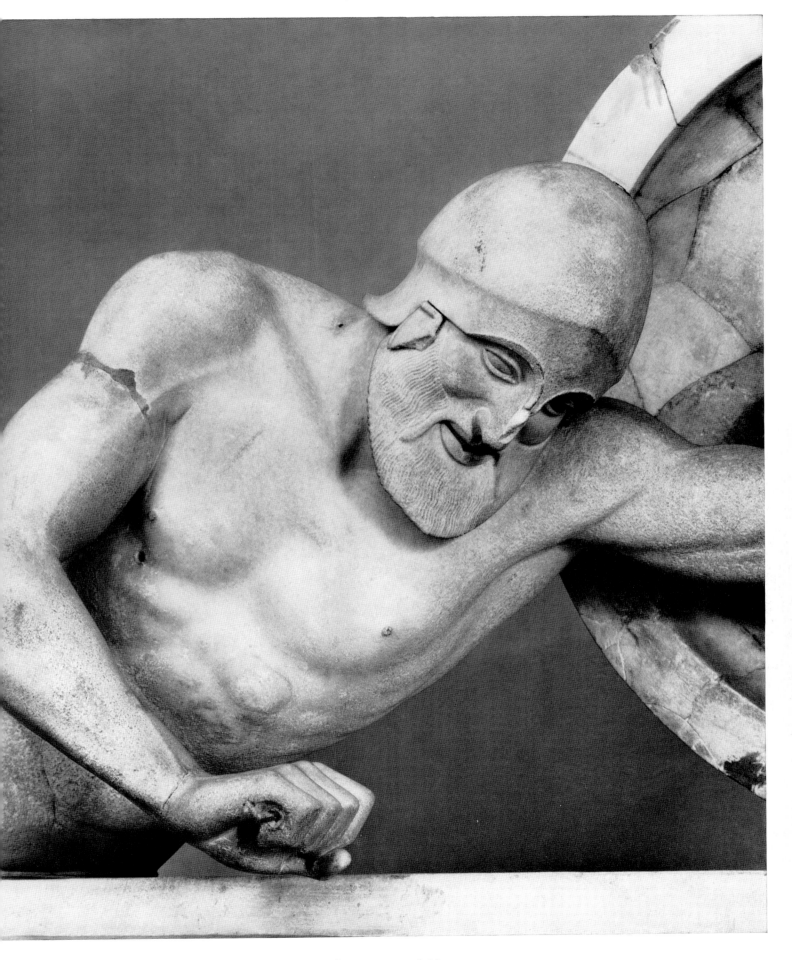

85   Fallen warrior. cf. Plate 84

86   From the east pediment of the 'Temple of Aphaia' on Aegina: Hercules as an archer.
Parian marble. Munich

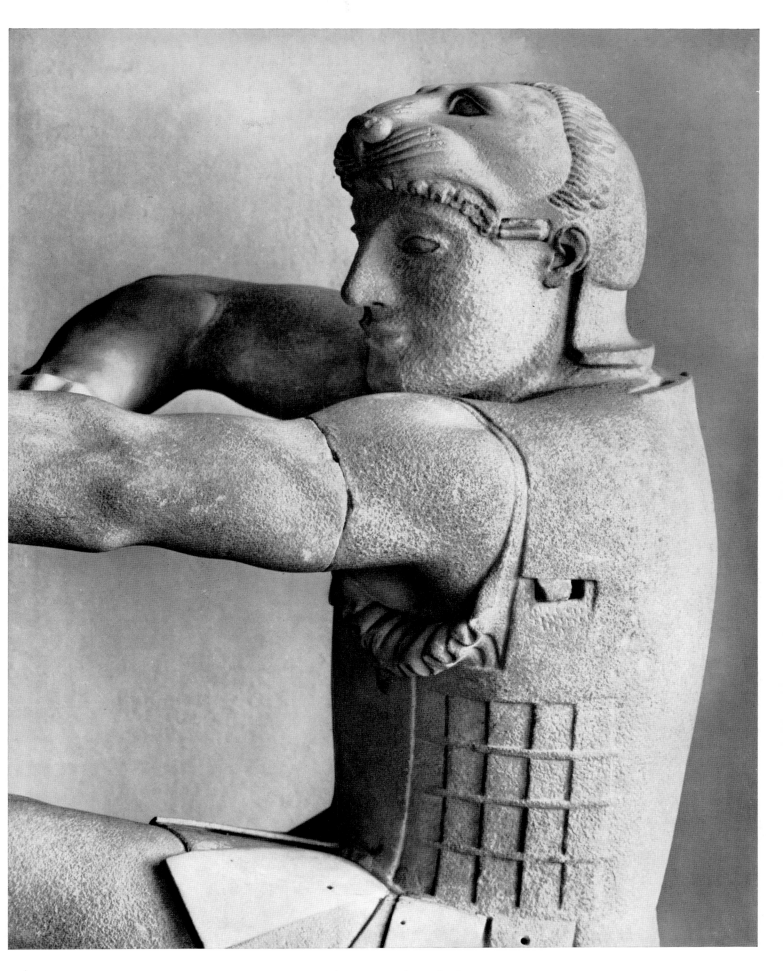

87 Hercules as an archer. cf. Plate 86

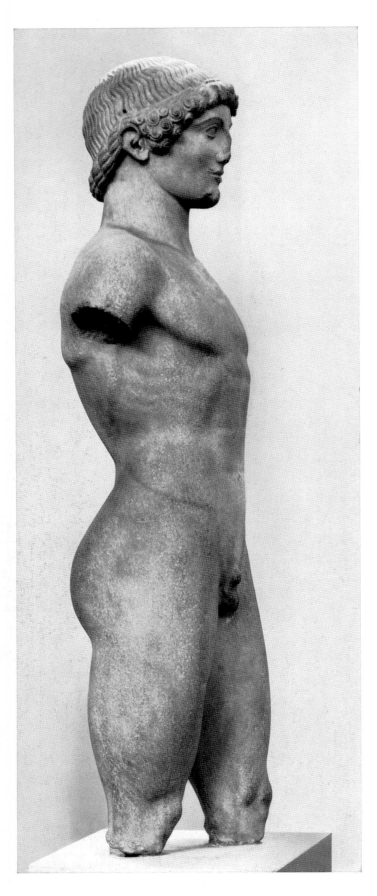
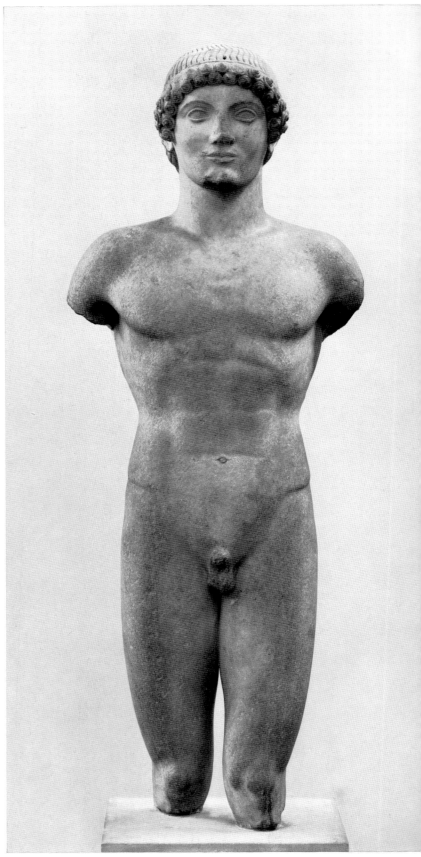

88 Youth from Lemnos, the 'Strangford Apollo'. Parian marble. London

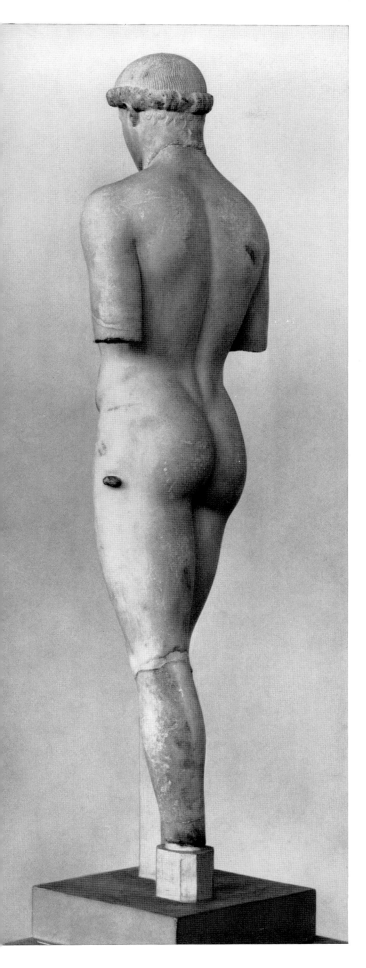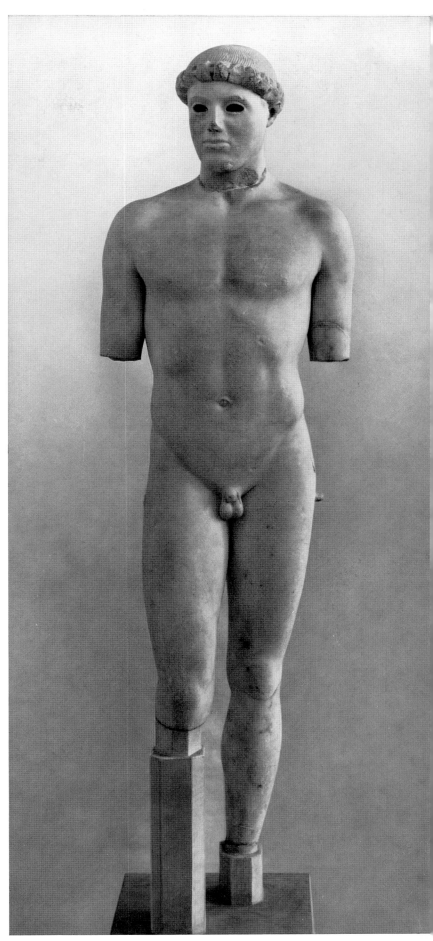

89   Youth, from the Athenian Acropolis, the 'Kritios boy'. Parian marble. Acropolis Museum, Athens

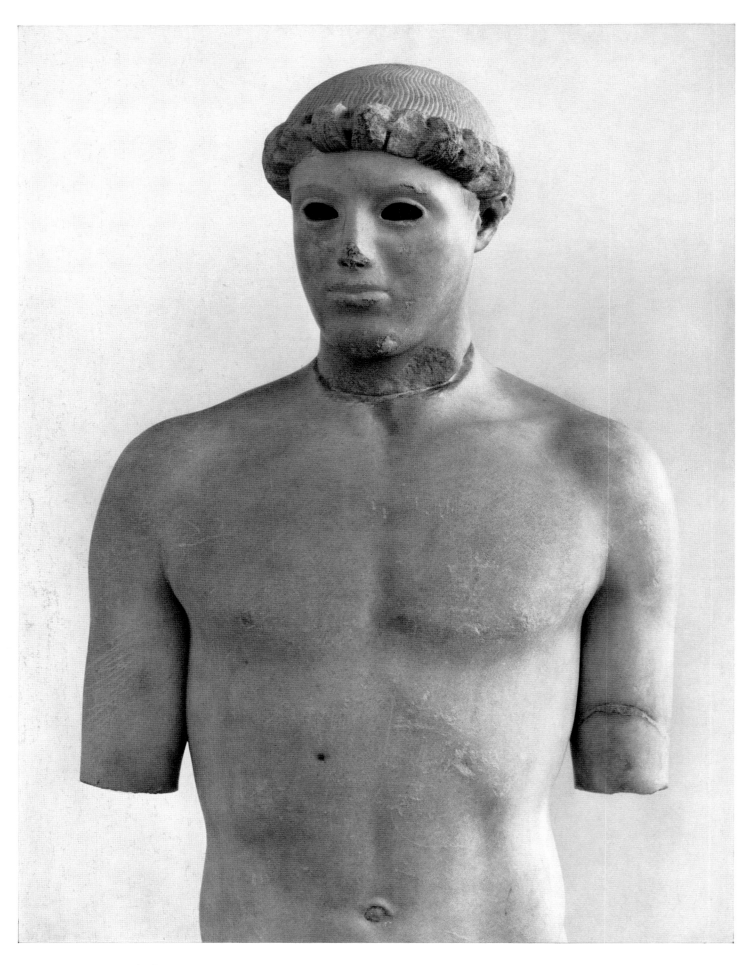

90   Youth, from the Athenian Acropolis, the 'Kritios boy'. Parian marble. Acropolis Museum, Athens

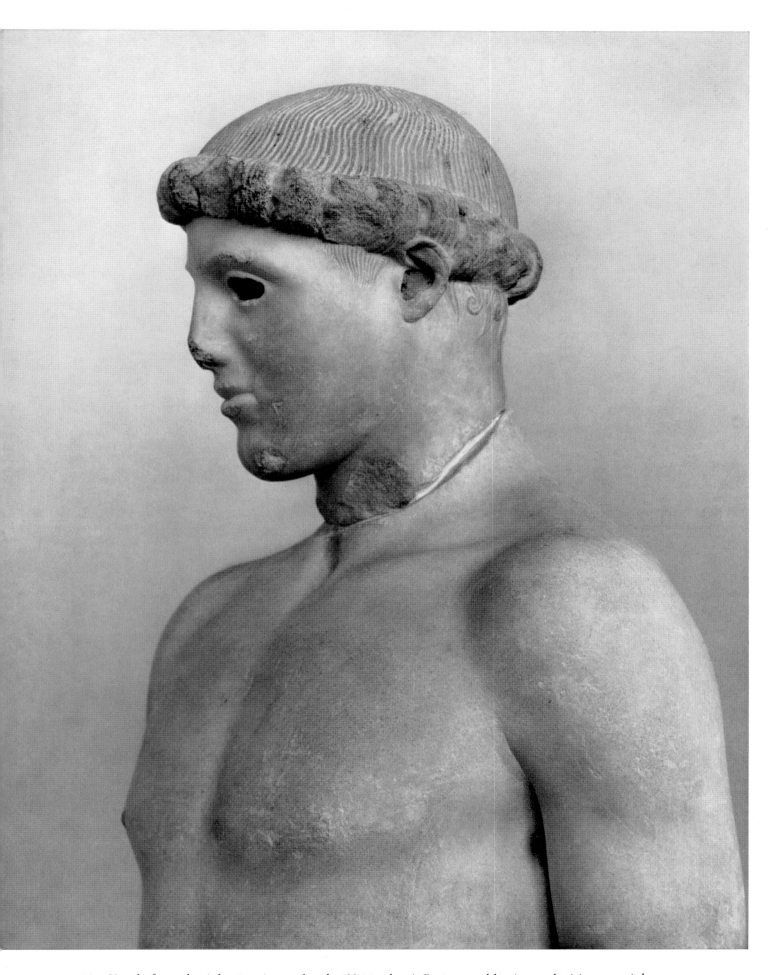

91   Youth, from the Athenian Acropolis, the 'Kritios boy'. Parian marble. Acropolis Museum, Athens

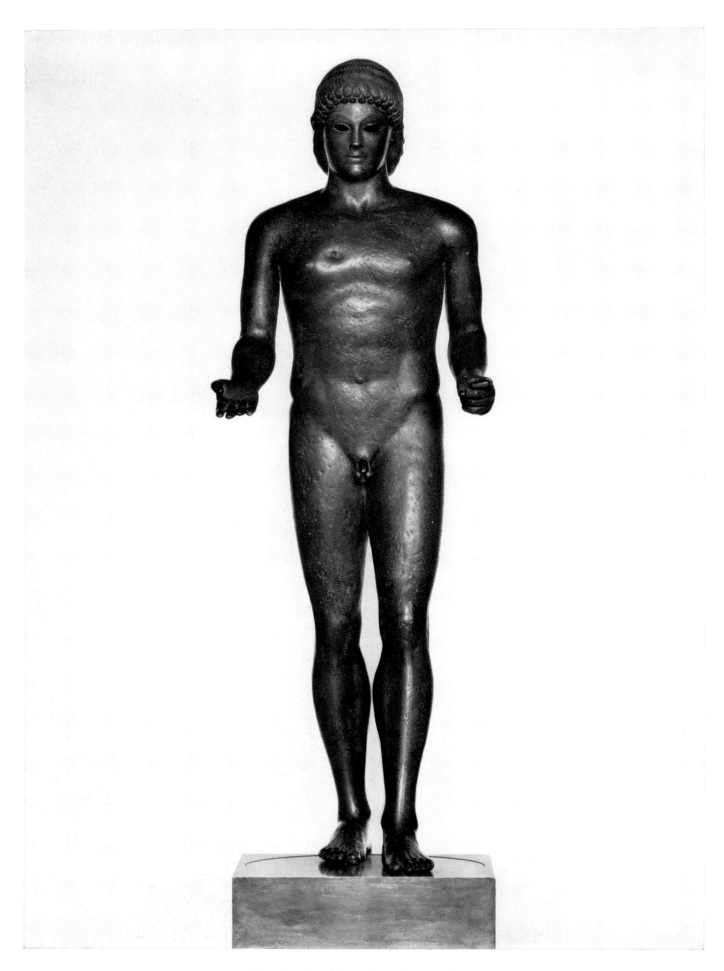

92   Apollo of Piombino. Bronze. Paris

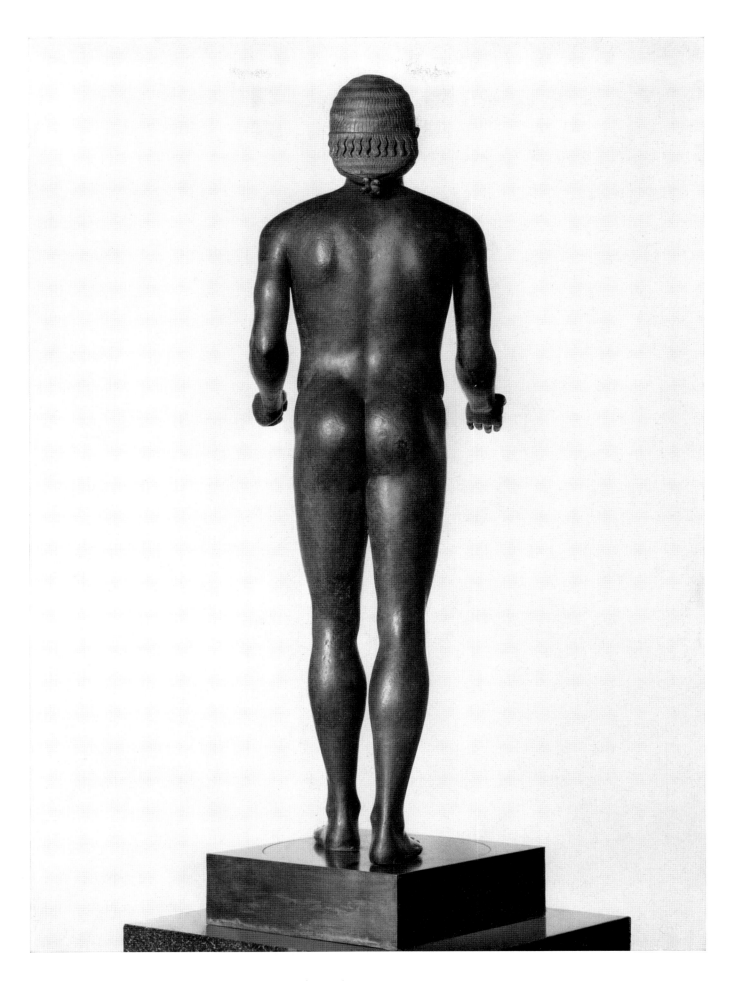

93 Apollo of Piombino, rear view. Bronze. Paris

94   Apollo of Piombino, head. Paris

95   Apollo of Piombino, side view of head. Paris

96   Votive stele of a victorious youth, from the sanctuary of Athena at Sunium.
Parian marble. National Museum, Athens

97   Enthroned goddess, from Taranto. Parian marble. Berlin

98　Enthroned goddess, from Taranto. Parian marble. Berlin

99   Enthroned goddess, from Taranto. Parian marble. Berlin

100 Enthroned goddess, from Taranto, head. Berlin

101 Enthroned goddess, from Taranto, head in profile. Berlin

102   Charioteer, votive offering of Polyzalos of Gela for Delphi. Bronze. Delphi

103   Charioteer, votive offering of Polyzalos of Gela for Delphi. Bronze. Delphi

104   Charioteer, votive offering of Polyzalos of Gela for Delphi. Bronze. Delphi

105   Zeus and Ganymede, from Olympia, detail. cf. Plate V

106   Horse from a quadriga, from Olympia. Bronze. National Museum, Athens

107   Metope from the Temple of Zeus at Olympia:
Atlas brings Hercules the apples of the Hesperides in the presence of Athene.
Parian marble. Olympia

108   Metope from the Temple of Zeus at Olympia: Hercules brings Athene the Stymphalian Birds.
Parian marble. Paris (Athene and head of Hercules) and Olympia (torso of Hercules)

109   Athene, from the metope in Plate 108

110   From the east pediment of the Temple of Zeus at Olympia, central group:
Zeus between Oinomaos (right) and Pelops (left). Parian marble. Olympia

111   From the east pediment of the Temple of Zeus at Olympia. Right-hand continuation of the central group:
Sterope (left), kneeling girl and horses from the quadriga of Pelops (right). Parian marble. Olympia

112   From the east pediment of the Temple of Zeus at Olympia: Myrtilos, Oinomaos's charioteer.
Parian marble. Olympia

113   From the east pediment of the Temple of Zeus at Olympia: Crouching youth, from the northern
half of the pediment. Parian marble. Olympia

114   From the east pediment of the Temple of Zeus at Olympia: The seer, from the northern half of the pediment.
Parian marble. Olympia

115   Head of the seer. cf. Plate 114

116   From the east pediment of the Temple of Zeus at Olympia: 'Cladeos', from the northern
corner of the pediment. Parian marble. Olympia

117 From the west pediment of the Temple of Zeus at Olympia: Lapithan woman, from the northern corner of the pediment. Parian marble. Olympia

118   From the west pediment of the Temple of Zeus at Olympia. The two three-figure groups:
A Lapith and a Lapithan woman fighting a Centaur. Parian marble. Olympia

119   From the west pediment of the Temple of Zeus at Olympia:
The Lapithan woman from the upper three-figure group shown in Plate 118

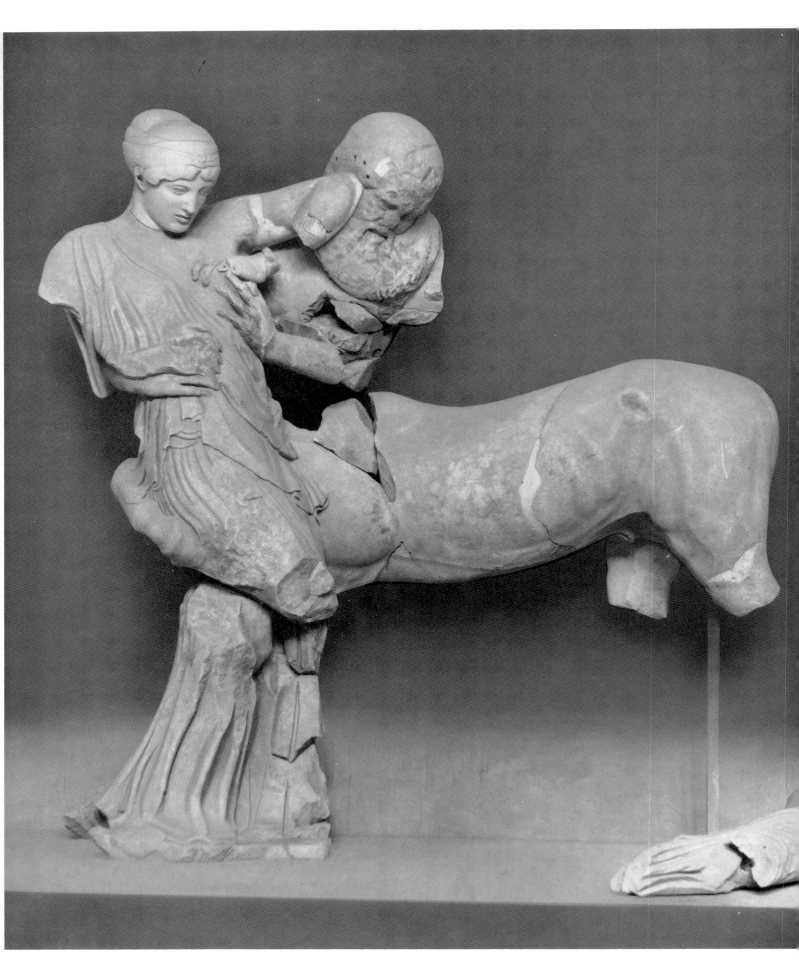

120   From the west pediment of the Temple of Zeus at Olympia: The bride of the Lapithan King Peirithoös
attacked by a Centaur. Parian marble. Olympia

121   Peirithoös's bride. cf. Plate 120

122   Apollo. cf. Plate 123

123   From the west pediment of the Temple of Zeus at Olympia: Apollo. Parian marble. Olympia

124 From the west pediment of the Temple of Zeus at Olympia : Two-figure group from the southern half of the
pediment : Lapith and biting Centaur. Parian marble. Olympia

125   From the west pediment of the Temple of Zeus at Olympia: Lapithan woman, from the three-figure group
in the southern half of the pediment (cf. Plate 118 bottom). Parian marble. Olympia

126 Metope from the Temple of Hera at Selinus: Death of Actaeon in the presence of Artemis. Tufa. Palermo

127   Metope from the Temple of Hera at Selinus: Hera unveils herself to Zeus. Tufa. Palermo

128   Head of Hera, from the metope in Plate 127

129 Head of Zeus, from the metope in Plate 127

130   Poseidon, rear view. cf. Plate 131

131 Poseidon, found in the sea off Cape Artemision. Bronze. National Museum, Athens

132 Poseidon, head in profile. cf. Plate 131

133   Funerary stele of a young man. From Nisyros. Marble from the Ionian islands. Istanbul

134   From the 'Ludovisi throne', centre panel: Birth of Aphrodite from the sea. Parian marble.
Museo delle Terme, Rome

135   Head of Aphrodite. cf. Plate 134

136 From the 'Ludovisi throne': Side panel with female flute-player. Parian marble.
Museo delle Terme, Rome

137   From the 'Ludovisi throne': Side panel with young woman taking incense from a box. Parian marble.
Museo delle Terme, Rome

138   Votive relief tondo, from Melos. Parian marble. National Museum, Athens

139   Votive relief to Athene, from the Athenian Acropolis. Marble. Acropolis Museum, Athens

140   Sepulchral stele of a girl. Parian marble. Berlin

141 Head of the girl on the sepulchral stele in Plate 140

142   From the Parthenon on the Athenian Acropolis. Metope from the south face:
Centaur triumphing over a dead Lapith. Pentelic marble. London

143 From the Parthenon on the Athenian Acropolis. Metope from the south face:
Lapith fighting with a Centaur. Pentelic marble. London

144 From the Parthenon on the Athenian Acropolis. Metope from the south face:
Centaur fighting with a Lapith who has fallen to his knee. Pentelic marble. London

145 From the Parthenon on the Athenian Acropolis. Metope from the south face:
Centaur and Lapith attacking one another. Pentelic marble. London

146   Centaur and Lapith, from the metope in Plate 144

147   Centaur and Lapith, from the metope in Plate 145

148   From the Parthenon on the Athenian Acropolis.
Frieze on the western face of the cella, seen from below. Acropolis, Athens

149   From the Parthenon on the Athenian Acropolis.
Equestrian group from the west frieze. Pentelic marble. London

150 From the Parthenon on the Athenian Acropolis. Above: Equestrian groups from the south frieze.
Centre and bottom: Equestrian groups from the north frieze. Pentelic marble. London

151   From the Parthenon on the Athenian Acropolis.
Equestrian group from the north frieze. London. cf. Plate 150 centre, left-hand panel

152   From the Parthenon on the Athenian Acropolis.
Equestrian group from the north frieze. London. cf. Plate 150 centre, right-hand panel

153   From the Parthenon on the Athenian Acropolis.
Equestrian group from the north frieze. London. cf. Plate 150 centre, centre panel

154   From the Parthenon on the Athenian Acropolis, north frieze. Acropolis Museum, Athens

155   From the Parthenon on the Athenian Acropolis, south frieze:
Festival organizer and sacrificial bull. London

156   From the Parthenon on the Athenian Acropolis, east frieze.
Bottom: Poseidon, Apollo and Artemis. Top: Poseidon and Apollo. cf. lower picture.
Pentelic marble. Acropolis Museum, Athens

157 Artemis. cf. Plate 156 bottom

158   From the Parthenon on the Athenian Acropolis, east frieze:
Festival organizer and girls, from the van of the Panathenaic procession,
left half of the panel. Paris. cf. Plate 159

159   From the Parthenon on the Athenian Acropolis, east frieze:
Girls, from the van of the Panathenaic procession, right half of the panel. Paris. cf. Plate 158

160   From the Parthenon on the Athenian Acropolis, north frieze: Water-carriers. Acropolis Museum, Athens

161 From the Parthenon on the Athenian Acropolis, north frieze: One of the water-carriers. cf. Plate 160

162   From the Parthenon on the Athenian Acropolis, south frieze. London

163   From the Parthenon on the Athenian Acropolis, north frieze:
Boy from the procession with the sacrificial bulls. Acropolis Museum, Athens

164   From the Parthenon on the Athenian Acropolis, east pediment:
Dionysus. Pentelic marble. London

165   Dionysus. cf. Plate 164

166　From the Parthenon on the Athenian Acropolis, east pediment:
The Eleusinian deities Demeter and Kore (left) and Artemis (Iris or Hebe?) (right).
Pentelic marble. London

167   From the Parthenon on the Athenian Acropolis, east pediment:
Leto (left) and Aphrodite in the lap of Peitho or Dione, her mother (?).
Pentelic marble. London. cf. Plate 167

168   From the Parthenon on the Athenian Acropolis, east pediment:
Leto. In the background right, Peitho or Dione (?) with Aphrodite.
Pentelic marble. London

169　From the Parthenon on the Athenian Acropolis, east pediment:
Horse's head from Selene's quadriga. Pentelic marble. London

170   From the Parthenon on the Athenian Acropolis, west pediment:
The 'Ilissus'. Pentelic marble. London

171 From the Parthenon on the Athenian Acropolis, west pediment:
Iris (left) and Amphitrite (right). Pentelic marble. London

172   Votive relief to the Eleusinian deities: Dispatch of Triptolemos.
Pentelic marble. National Museum, Athens

173 Triptolemos receiving the ears of corn from Demeter. cf. Plate 172

174   Dying Niobid. Parian marble. Museo delle Terme, Rome

175   Dying Niobid. Parian marble. Museo delle Terme, Rome

176   Dying Niobid. cf. Plates 174/175

177   Dying Niobid. cf. Plates 174/175

178   Nike of Paionios. Parian marble. Olympia

179   Attic funerary monument: Battle scene. Pentelic marble. Villa Albani, Rome

180   The fallen adversary. cf. Plate 179

181   Head of the rider, from the relief at Villa Albani. cf. Plate 179

182   Sepulchral stele for a youth, from Aegina. Pentelic marble. National Museum, Athens

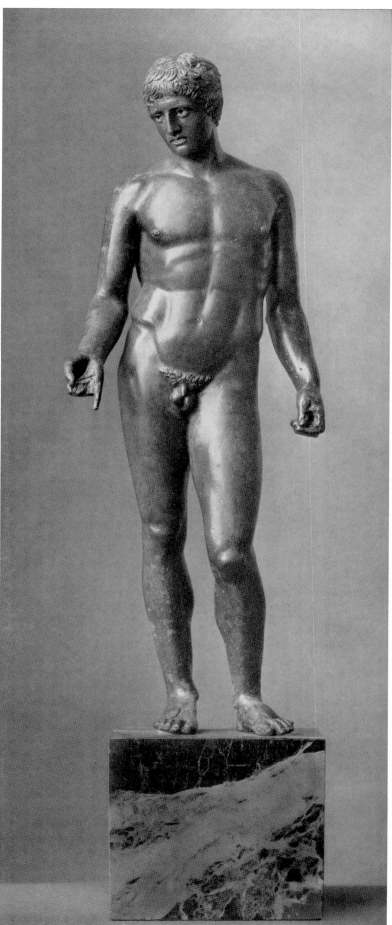

183 Youth making a gift. Bronze statuette. Paris

184   Tombstone of Chairedemos and Lyceas, from Salamis. Marble. Piraeus

185   Sepulchral relief with Timarista and Krito. Marble. Rhodes

186   Fragment of a sepulchral stele, from Athens. Pentelic marble. National Museum, Athens

187   Sepulchral monument of Hegeso. Pentelic marble. National Musem, Athens

188   Votive relief from Athens: Abduction of Basile by Echelos. National Museum, Athens
facing:
189   From the balustrade round the temple of Athene Nike on the Athenian Acropolis.
Pentelic marble. Acropolis Museum, Athens
Top: Two winged Nikes leading a bull to the sacrifice. Bottom: Athene, and a Nike decorating a Tropeion

190 From the balustrade round the Temple of Athene Nike on the Athenian Acropolis:
One of the two winged Nikes from the relief in Plate 189, top

191   From the balustrade round the Temple of Athena Nike on the Athenian Acropolis:
Winged Nike undoing a sandal. Pentelic marble. Acropolis Museum, Athens

192   Tombstone of Dexileos, from the Ceramicus at Athens. Pentelic marble.
Ceramicus Museum, Athens

193　Lycian sarcophagus. From the royal cemetery of Sidon. Parian marble. Istanbul

194　Lycian sarcophagus. Side panels: lion-hunt of the Amazons and boar-hunt

195   Lycian sarcophagus. Riders from the boar-hunt. cf. Plate 194, bottom

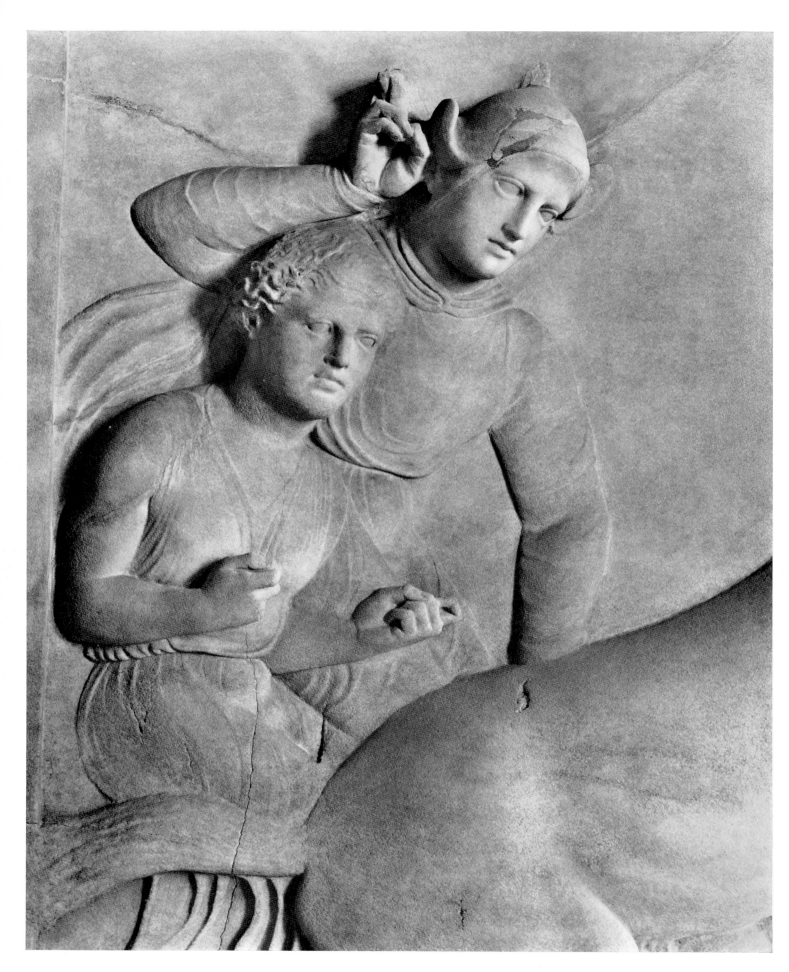

196 Lycian sarcophagus. Amazons from the lion-hunt. cf. Plate 194, top

197   Lycian sarcophagus. Amazons from the lion-hunt. cf. Plate 194, top

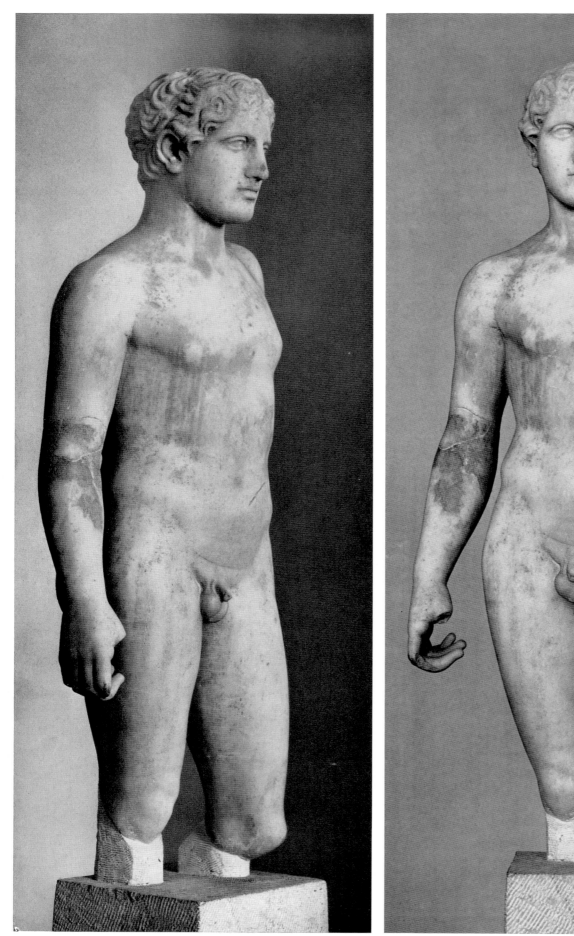
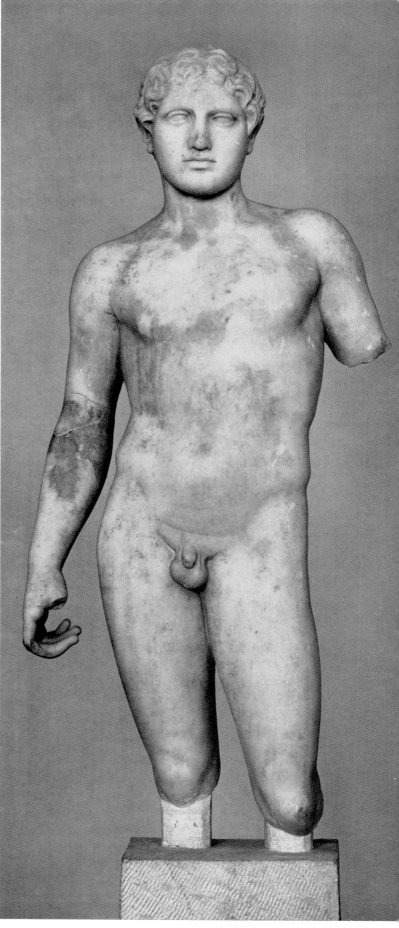

198 Sepulchral statue of a standing boy. Pentelic marble. Piraeus

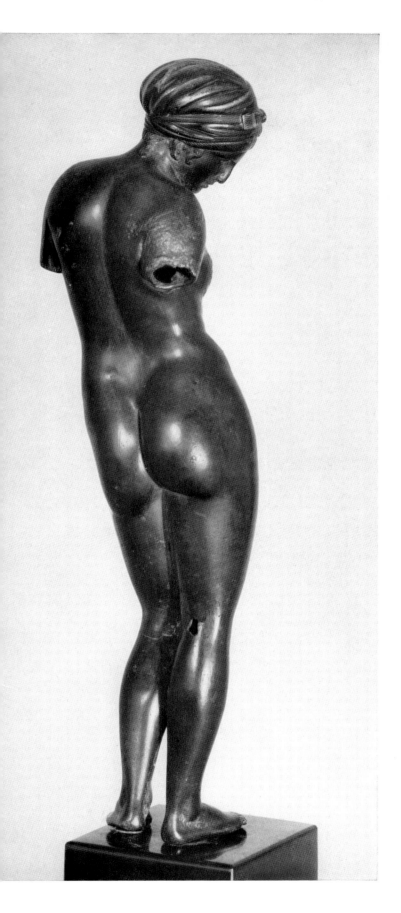

199   Standing nude girl, from Beroea in Macedonia. Bronze statuette. Munich

200   Tombstone with Ktesileos and Theano. Pentelic marble. National Museum, Athens

201   Ktesileos from the monument in Plate 200

202   Tombstone of an unknown woman with her maidservant, from Piraeus.
Pentelic marble. National Museum, Athens

203 From the monument in Plate 202

204   From an Attic funeral vase: Couple bidding one another farewell. Pentelic marble. Munich

205 The 'Hygieia', from Tegea. Pentelic marble. National Museum, Athens

206　Demeter. Parian marble. Venice

207   The 'Weeping women sarcophagus'. From the royal cemetery of Sidon. Pentelic marble. Istanbul

208   The 'Weeping women sarcophagus'. cf. Plate 207

209   The 'Weeping women sarcophagus'. Two female mourners from one of the side panels. cf. Plate 207

210   Portrait head of an African, from Cyrene. Bronze. London

211   'Mausolus'. From the Mausoleum at Halicarnassus. Marble. London

212 Head of the 'Mausolus'. cf. Plate 211

213   Head of the 'Mausolus'. cf. Plate 211

214, 215   From the Mausoleum at Halicarnassus: Greeks and Amazons fighting. Marble. London
214 and 215 top: Three panels from the frieze on the east face by Scopas   215 bottom: Panel from the south frieze by Timotheus

216 From the Mausoleum at Halicarnassus: Greeks and Amazons figthing. Marble. London
Top: From the frieze on the north face by Bryaxis. Bottom: From the frieze on the south face by Timotheus

217   From the Mausoleum at Halicarnassus: Greeks and Amazons fighting.
Two panels from the frieze on the west face by Leochares. Marble. London

218   Bronze statue of a young man, found in the sea off Anticythera. National Museum, Athens

219   Bronze statue of a young man, found in the sea off Anticythera. National Museum, Athens

220   Head of the bronze statue of a young man, found in the sea off Anticythera. cf. Plates 218 and 219

221   Head of the youth from Marathon. cf. Plates 222 and VII

222   Bronze statue of a youth, found in the sea off Marathon. National Museum, Athens

223   Base of column with relief from the later Temple of Artemis at Ephesus. Marble. London

224   Demeter, from the sanctuary of Demeter and Kore at Cnidus. Parian marble. London

225   Head of Demeter from Cnidus. cf. Plate 224

226   Sepulchral monument of a youth, from the Ilissus at Athens. Pentelic marble.
National Museum, Athens

227   Attic sepulchral relief, from Rhamnus in Attica. Pentelic marble. National Museum, Athens

228   Hermes with the Dionysus boy. Parian marble. Olympia

229   Hermes with the Dionysus boy. Parian marble. Olympia

230　Hermes with the Dionysus boy. Parian marble. Olympia

231 Head of the Hermes. cf. Plates 228–230

232   The 'Alexander sarcophagus'. Pentelic marble. Istanbul

233   The 'Alexander sarcophagus'. Alexander the Great, from the battle between Greeks and Persians. cf. Plate 234

234   The 'Alexander sarcophagus'. Side panel: battle between Greeks and Persians

235   The 'Alexander sarcophagus'. Side panel: lion and stag-hunt. cf. Plate 232

236   The 'Alexander sarcophagus'. From the side panel with hunting scene. cf. Plate 235

237   The 'Alexander sarcophagus'. From the end panels: battle and hunting scene

238   Head of a boxer, profile. From Olympia. Bronze. National Museum, Athens

239   Head of a boxer, from Olympia. Bronze. National Museum, Athens

240   From an Attic funerary relief. Pentelic marble. National Museum, Athens

241 From the funerary relief in Plate 240

242   Head of a girl, from Chios. Profile. cf. Plate 243

243   Head of a girl, from Chios. Parian marble. Boston

244   Votive relief for Cybele and Attis. Marble. Venice

245   Statue of a philosopher. Marble. Delphi, Museum

246 Statue of Nikokleia, priestess of Demeter, from the sanctuary of Demeter and Kore at Cnidus.
Marble. London

247 Sacrificial servant, the 'Antium Girl'. Marble. Museo delle Terme, Rome

248   Sleeping satyr, the 'Barberini Faun'. Parian marble. Munich

249   Sleeping satyr. cf. Plate 248

250   Head of a philosopher, found in the sea off Anticythera. Profile. Bronze. National Museum, Athens

251 Northern projection of the Pergamon altar. Berlin.
On the front: Triton and Amphitrite. On the stair side towards the left: Nereus and Doris with an adversary

252   From the Great Frieze of the Pergamon altar, east frieze:
Zeus fighting against three giants; on the right Porphyrion. Marble. Berlin

253   From the Great Frieze of the Pergamon altar, east frieze:
Athene, garlanded by Nike, battling with Alcyoneus; bottom right appears Ge (Gaia), mother of the Gigantes.
Marble. Berlin

254   From the Great Frieze of the Pergamon altar, east frieze: Hecate and her antagonist. Marble. Berlin

255 From the Great Frieze of the Pergamon altar: Artemis and two antagonists; left, the giant Otos
(right-hand continuation of the section of the frieze shown in Plate 254). Marble. Berlin

256   From the Great Frieze of the Pergamon altar, east frieze: Head of Alcyoneus. Marble. Berlin. cf. Plate 253

257   From the Great Frieze of the Pergamon altar, north frieze: Nyx. Marble. Berlin

258 From the Great Frieze of the Pergamon altar, north frieze:
The Moirae and their antagonists. Marble. Berlin

259　From the Great Frieze of the Pergamon altar, north frieze: The Lion-Goddess. Marble. Berlin

260 Head of Alexander the Great. From Pergamon. Marble. Istanbul

261   Head of Alexander the Great. cf. Plate 260

262   Winged Nike, from Samothrace. Parian marble. Paris

263   Head of Helios. Marble. Rhodes

264   Portrait statue of a ruler, probably Demetrius I Soter of Syria. Bronze. Museo delle Terme, Rome

265   Head of the portrait statue shown in Plate 264

266   Male portrait statue, known as 'Hippocrates'. Marble from Cos. Cos

267 'Hippocrates'. cf. Plate 266

268   Votive relief: sacrifice in a rural sanctuary. Pentelic marble. Munich

269   Poseidon. Bronze statuette. Munich

270   Aphrodite, from Melos. Parian marble. Paris

271   Aphrodite, from Melos. cf. Plate 270

272   Aphrodite, terra-cotta statuette. Berlin

273 Crouching Aphrodite, from Rhodes. Parian marble. Rhodes

274   Male portrait head, from Delos. Profile. cf. Plate XI

275   Head of the boxer shown in Plates 276 and 277

276 Boxer. Bronze. Museo delle Terme, Rome

277 Boxer. Bronze. Museo delle Terme, Rome

278 Death of Laocoön and his sons. Marble. Vatican Collections, Rome

279   Head of Laocoön. cf. Plate 278

280   Boy in a cloak. From Tralles in Caria. Parian marble. Istanbul

281　Head of the boy in a cloak. cf. Plate 280

282 Head of a statue of Aphrodite, from Satala in Armenia. Bronze. London

I. LATE GEOMETRIC AND ARCHAIC PERIOD
750—500 B.C.

1

A STANDING HORSE. Bronze. Light green patina, partly crusted. Height, 6.25" (16 cm.). Found on the Peloponnesus, probably at Olympia. State Museum, Berlin (Department of Classical Antiquities, Inv. No. 31317).

Solid casting. Cast in one piece with the roughly rectangular base which has an ornament of openwork triangles arranged in three rows. The horse itself is strictly stylized. All details of surface modelling have been avoided. Apparently the artist was intent on rendering the traits that characterize the horse in general and refrained for this reason from the representation of all accidental details. On the other hand, he endeavoured to stress everything that distinguishes the horse from other mammals; above all the long narrow legs, the strongly developed fore- and hind-quarters and the mane. The male parts and the long thin tail curving down right to the base, were likewise regarded as essential.

The body of the stallion is short and cylindrical, the neck which is long, broad and flat, is carried rather high. The jowls are raised slightly, with a sharp curved edge, thus setting off the head from the neck; however, the curved ears and the almost cylindrical nose merge into one another without any marked division. The head is slightly raised and the nose widens towards the muzzle. In place of the mouth there is a deep circular hole, once filled by an iron pin which is now missing – as are the eye-sockets. The outlines of legs and neck are marked by engraved lines. On the hind legs some parallel, lightly incised lines divide cannon and fetlock. The knees are marked as sharp-angled dents. The engraved zigzag pattern which appears at the base of the neck between three or four parallel lines probably represents the collar.

This statuette was a votive offering. It belongs to the Late Geometric period, as may be seen from the exaggerated stylization and from the overstressed silhouette, for in this period the strong, clear forms of the Geometric era were degenerating to a kind of mannerism. Therefore this bronze probably dates from the years following the middle of the 8th century B.C.

K. A. Neugebauer, Die minoischen und archaisch-griechischen Bronzen der Staatlichen Museen zu Berlin (1931), plate 3, No. 6. — *C. Blümel*, Sport der Hellenen (1936), p. 13, No. 20.

2

WARRIOR. Bronze. Cast solid. Height, 8.2" (20.5 cm.). Found on the Acropolis, Athens. National Museum, Athens (Inv. No. 6613).

With his right hand this warrior was brandishing a lance, the left was holding a shield. He is wearing a pointed helmet originally crowned with a crest curving forward. Below the helmet his abundant hair falls over his shoulders. His legs are long, the hips very slim; above the waist the flat thorax rises in a curve towards the broad muscular shoulders. His large, round face is characterized by the low forehead from which the nose descends dead straight between strongly marked, arched eyebrows, and by the wide mouth and pointed chin. He looks at the beholder with large wide-open eyes.

Compared to earlier statues of this type, of which the bronze statuette of a horse illustrated here (1) may serve as an example, this warrior seems much more alive. Body and limbs show a new organic unity and the modelling is more lively. Some of the traditional rigidity has given way to the rendering of bodily vigour. Dating from about the end of the 8th century B.C., this figure straddles, one might say, two eras. While transcending the limitations of the Geometric Style it has not yet attained the full monumental power of the next phase – 'Daedalic' art.

The lower right arm has been twisted. The statuette has recently been cleaned electrolytically, a process by which the bronze has regained the original light tone.

A. de Ridder, Catalogue des Bronzes trouvés sur l'Acropole d'Athènes (1896), No. 702. — *E. Kunze*, Athenische Mitteilungen 55, 1930, 156 ff., Beilage 44—45. — *F. Matz*, Geschichte der griechischen Kunst 1, 83, plate 30.

3

APOLLO. Bronze. Cast solid. Height, 8" (20 cm.). Found at Thebes (Boeotia), in 1894. Museum of Fine Arts, Boston (Inv. No. 03.997). From the Tyszkiewicz Collection.

This statuette is one of the most impressive and original early Greek bronzes that have come down to us. The posture is erect, divisions between the single parts of the body have been clearly marked; long, club-shaped thighs support a triangular thorax; the neck is very long, as is the head, which seems to rest on the long and thick plaits. The spinal line is stressed along the back, and in front the corresponding vertical of the sternum is prolonged right down to the pelvis. The hips are enclosed by a belt and the neck is adorned by a wide necklace with engraved pendants hanging down to the breast.

The long, triangular face is dominated by large, round eyes; now these are but empty holes, but originally they must have been filled by some precious shining material. On the head the figure wore a flat helmet, cast separately. The left hand is perforated; through this hole passed the bow held by the god. On the thighs there is an inscription in Boeotian script, a distich, the last dactyls of which recall Homer:

Μάντιχλος μ'ἀνέθεκε Fεκαβόλοι ἀργυροτόχσοι τᾶς δεχάτας.
τὺ δέ, Φοῖβε δίδοι χαρι Fέτταν ἀμοι [Fάν].

> 'Mantiklos dedicated me to the Far-darting God with the Silver Bow as his tithe; do Thou, oh Phoebus, graciously grant him the desired reward.'

The statuette is an effigy of Apollo, dedicated to the god by Mantiklos. It must come from Boeotia, the mountain-enclosed plain to the north-west of Attica. There tradition was always upheld. The artist who made this figure in the first half of the 7th century B.C. did indeed follow the traditional style, over-stressing even its severely geometrical approach to natural forms. Thus the whole is dominated by contrasts, of vertical and horizontal lines and of every part of the body and of every limb with the others.

W. Fröbner, Monuments Piot 2, 1895, 137 ff., plate 15. — H. Koch, Apollon und 'Apollines' (1930), 1 ff. — Dorothy Kent Hill, Journal of the Walters Art Gallery (Baltimore/Maryland) 2, 1939, 28 ff., fig. 4—5. — K. A. Pfeiff, Apollon (1943), 23 f., plate 2, fig. 1 and Beilage 1. — F. R. Grace, Archaic Sculpture in Boeotia, 49 f., fig. 65.

4

HEAD OF A GRIFFIN. The front part of a *protome*, (i.e., sculpture of head and neck only). Bronze. Height 11.5" (27.8 cm.). Found during the excavations of the German Archaeological Institute at Olympia, Winter 1937/38. Museum, Olympia, Excavation Inv. B. 145.

Bronze cauldrons adorned by such animal *protomai* were among the favourite offerings in the sanctuaries of Archaic Greece. They vary in size. Some are small, others very large with a diameter exceeding one yard. *Protomai* of griffins appear at an early date beside those of lions. Though inspired by oriental prototypes, these griffins are a Greek invention of the 8th century B.C. At first they were made of hammered sheet bronze, but from the early 7th century B.C. there appear small griffin *protomai* cast solid in one piece as well as large ones consisting of two parts, a head cast solid fastened on a neck made of embossed sheet bronze. The head of a griffin shown here is one of the largest that have come down to us. It is cast solid. The neck belonging to it is of sheet bronze and was found in a badly damaged state. It is covered by engraved scales and flanked on either side by an embossed curl. At its base appear traces of the soldering which fastened it to the cauldron. It was 18.5" (49 cm.) high; consequently the whole *protome* must have measured 31" (80 cm.). An upright support carrying a circular knob sticks out of the griffin's forehead. This protuberance has been taken to represent the upright lock of hair of oriental prototypes, which the Greek artist has transformed into this mushroom-like object. The eye-sockets were filled by some coloured material which is not preserved. The left ear is missing.

Dating from the middle of the seventh century B.C., this head is still close in style to the Geometric tradition. The sharp-edged beak curves forward with intense energy, stressed by the complementary curve of the tongue which curls upwards between the gaping jaws. Endowed with a new feeling for monumental greatness, the artist has here transformed a primeval image into a truly formidable, daemonic creature.

In addition to these examples two further griffin *protomai*, comparable in size and style, have been preserved. They were found during the earlier excavations at Olympia and probably derive from the same cauldron. One went to the National Museum in Athens, the other to the Walter C. Baker Collection in New York. (Ancient Art in American Private Collections. Cambridge, Mass., 1954, No. 198, plate LIX.)

E. Kunze, Zweiter Bericht über die Ausgrabungen in Olympia (Winter 1937/38), Jahrbuch des Deutschen Archäologischen Instituts 53, 1938, No. 3/4, 113 ff., plates 48—50. — E. Kunze, Neue Meisterwerke griechischer Kunst aus Olympia (1948), 13 f., fig. 23—24. — U. Jantzen, Griechische Greifenkessel (1955), 19, No. 77 and p. 65 ff., plates 28, 3; 29, ref. do. H.-V. Herrmann, in: Gymnasium, Zeitschrift für Kultur der Antike und humanistische Bildung 64, 1957, 377 ff., and V. Poulsen, Meddelelser fra Ny Carlsberg Glyptotek 14, 1957, 1 ff.

5

GRIFFIN PROTOME OF A KETTLE. Found during the new German excavations at Olympia. Bronze. Height 14" (35.8 cm.). Museum, Olympia, Excavation Inv. B. 945.

Unlike the monumental griffin *protome* discussed above (4) this kettle griffin is cast in a single piece on a core. The neck curves in a single splendid sweep and broadens at the base to a flat attachment piece by means of which it was fastened to the shoulder of the kettle with three rivets. The head and neck are covered with engraved scales; a large spiral curl on the neck, a smaller one behind the eyes, and the upper edges of the beak, are also finely engraved. As characteristic marks, this head also has a protuberance with knob at the end, and a wart on the forehead. The tip of the tongue and the end of the erect right ear have been broken off. The filling in the eye-sockets has not been preserved.

Compared with the enormous griffin's head in Plate 4, this *protome* creates an impression of moderation. The head does not have the same look of daemonic ferocity. The structure and contours are more compact, the modelling more concentrated. It represents a later phase and a new climax in the evolution of Greek kettle griffins, yet it is separated from the great griffin's head by scarcely a quarter of a century.

E. Kunze, Neue Meisterwerke griechischer Kunst aus Olympia, 14, No. 25. — U. Jantzen, Griechische Greifenkessel, 20, No. 81, plate 31, 2.

6

STANDING FEMALE FIGURE. Grey limestone. Height, including the square base which is 4" (10 cm.) high, 24.5" (65 cm.). Louvre, Paris (Inv. No. 3098). Formerly in the Museum, Auxerre.

The woman is standing upright with her feet together. Her left arm hangs by her side with the palm of the left hand lying flat against her hip. The right arm is bent, the hand held in front of her breast with outstretched fingers, a gesture which is thought to be that of prayer. Her long, belted garment reaches down to her feet. The curves of her breasts and hips are stressed by the heavy, clinging material which does, however, hide the body below the hips. Descending from the centre of the belt and along the lower edge of the garment are wide borders decorated with a pattern of incised squares and rectangles. The bodice has a scale-like pattern and terminates in a narrow neck-band. She wears a short cloak round her almost square shoulders. There are bracelets around her wrists. Below the straight row of curls ranged along the top of her forehead the hair curves like a bell around her pointed face and down to her shoulders, falling along her back as well as in front in thick plaits and divided into curls by horizontal grooves. Her glance is lively and her thin lips are pursed.

It is not known where this statuette was found. Its firm, compact shape suggests that it is the work of a Cretan sculptor, belonging to the middle years of the 'Daedalic style', about 650 B.C. The absence of attributes makes it appear likely that it does not represent any deity but is a votive offering.

M. Collignon, Revue Archéologique 11, 1908, 153 ff., plate 10. — *R. J. H. Jenkins,* Dedalica, 42. — *F. Matz,* Geschichte der griechischen Kunst 1, 172 ff., plate 79. — *E. Homann-Wedeking,* Die Anfänge der griechischen Großplastik, 107 f.

7

BUST OF A STANDING OR SITTING FEMALE FIGURE.
Fragment of relief found near the Temple of Athene on the citadel of Mycenae in 1897. Limestone. Height 16″ (40.2 cm.). National Museum, Athens, No. 2869.

The fragment, which may be from the metope of a Doric temple, shows a clothed female figure whose right side is covered by a veil. The head is constructed within a clearly defined hexagonal. The horizontal element is emphasized by the straight lower edge of the chin, the mouth with its forceful lips, the almond-shaped eyes under the salient brows and the two straight and parallel rows of curls over the low forehead. The thick hair taken as a whole curves over the head in a great arch and falls on both sides of the face in the coiffure that was typical of the 7th century B.C., the so-called 'tiered wig'. Despite a certain heaviness in its forms, the face with its full lips, expanded nostrils and alert expression is full of youthful vitality.

Together with the remains of other limestone reliefs of the same period, that were found with it on the citadel of Mycenae and doubtless originated from the same building, this fragment is one of the oldest monumental stone reliefs of continental Greek art. Later in date than the Cretan statuette in the Louvre (6), the head is characteristic of the late stage of the 'Daedalic style'. The relief must have been carved by a Peloponnesian sculptor c. 630 B.C.

R. J. H. Jenkins, Dedalica, 47 ff. — *G. Rodenwaldt,* Corolla Curtius (Stuttgart 1937), 63 ff. — *H. Kähler,* Das griechische Metopenbild, 100, fig. 33. — *F. Matz,* Geschichte der griechischen Kunst 1, 178 ff., plates 87—88.

8, 9

RECLINING LION. Yellowish-grey limestone from Corfu. The surface of the plinth measures 48.75″ by 16.4″ (122×41 cm.). Found in 1843 on the island of Corfu near the tomb of Menekrates. Museum, Corfu.

The lion's body is abnormally elongated. He lies stretched out, turned slightly to the right, his head raised with a threatening expression as if he were going to jump. The fierce grandeur of the animal has been brilliantly rendered. Such anatomical details as are represented have not been given prominence, as for instance the folds of the lion's skin around the joints, his shoulder-blades or the sinews visible under the skin of the front paws. Originally these may have been stressed by the colouring. The tension which pervades the lion's body down to his mighty paws is brilliantly expressed by the irate, fear-inspiring glance of his deep-set but wide-open eyes, by the frown on his forehead and the deep curving furrows on his muzzle. These surround his almost closed mouth with an effective ornamental pattern.

The strongest of animals, the archetype of savage force, this lion was set up as the custodian of a tomb, to watch over the dead man's peace and to chase away everybody who might dare to disturb him. At the same time it may, as a sepulchral monument, have embodied the power that puts an end to all life. It seems hardly likely that the Corinthian sculptor who made this lion about 625 B.C. had ever seen a real lion, but by Graecizing an oriental prototype he created one of the most impressive lion images of Archaic Greek art.

G. Rodenwaldt, Die Bildwerke des Artemistempels von Korkyra (1938), 176 f. — The same, Altdorische Bildwerke in Korfu (1938), 7 ff., fig. 3—8. — *Fr. Crome,* Löwenbilder des 7. Jahrhunderts, in: Mnemosynon Th. Wiegand (1938) 50 ff., plates 11—16. — *F. Matz,* Geschichte der griechischen Kunst 1, 205 f.

10

HEAD OF HERA. Grey limestone. Height, 21.15″ (52 cm.). Found at Olympia in 1878 during the German excavations near the temple of Hera. Museum, Olympia.

Considerably larger than life-size, this head is all that remains of a colossal cult group which stood in the old Heraion in the sacred grove at the foot of the hill of Cronos. Pausanias, the Greek writer of the 2nd century A.D., describes the group in his travelogue, but does not mention the artist's name. Hera sat on a throne with her divine consort Zeus, bearded and armed, standing beside her.

The head conveys the impression of divine majesty. The oval face of the goddess is broad and flat. Parted in the centre, her hair frames her forehead with its ornamental curls; it fell – formerly – in such broad and heavy waves behind her ears, that it weighed on the lobes, pressing them forward. A narrow hairband encircles her forehead and on the top of her head she wears a crown of leaves from which branches carrying blossoms curve downwards on both sides of her head, a fitting attribute for Hera, bride and consort of Zeus, goddess of fertility and good fortune. The mouth with its narrow upper lip, the almond-shaped eyes under the sharply edged eyelids and the eyebrows marked by incised grooves, the geometrical regularity of her curls, everything contributes to an expression of uncompromising superiority. The intensity of the glance is due to the sharply engraved circles of eyes and pupils.

The group appears to be the work of a Peloponnesian sculptor working about 600 B.C. We have no other cult image of comparable importance from this early period. The hard and dry details, technically close to wood carving, suggest that the artist may have come from Sparta. When the head was found, there were still marks of a light, reddish yellow on the hair and of dark red on the hairband.

The suggestion that the head might constitute the remnant of a reclining sphinx has also been put forward. On the other hand, its expression, coupled with the place where it was found and its size, definitely point to its having belonged to the above-mentioned cult group in the Heraion at Olympia.

G. Treu, Die Bildwerke in Olympia (= Olympia, Die Ergebnisse der Ausgrabung 3), 1 ff., plate 1. — *E. Langlotz,* Frühgriechische Bildhauerschulen, 92 f. — *P. Wolters,* Die archaische Hera in Olympia, in: Festschrift für H. Wölfflin (1935), 168 ff. — *F. Matz,* Geschichte der griechischen Kunst 1, 203 ff., plates 130, c; 131. — *D. Kent Hill,* Hera, The Sphinx? in: Hesperia 13, 1944, 353 ff.

11–13

STANDING YOUTH. From Attica. Island marble. Height, 6′6″ (199 cm.), including the plinth which is c. 2.4″ (6 cm.) high. Metropolitan Museum of Art, New York (Inv. No. 32.11.1.). Bought in 1932 from a dealer.

The youth stands erect in a strictly frontal pose with his left leg advanced. His arms are held straight along his sides with tense muscles and his fists are touching his thighs. His tresses, divided into globules, fall in a broad mass down to his shoulder-blades.

They are held in place by a fillet which encircles his forehead and is tied at the back of his head in a reef knot with long ends lying symmetrically on his full back hair. He wears a neckband tied in front in a double knot. One should picture this as being made of pure metal, perhaps gold.

The harmonious structure of this statue is based on simple but grandly conceived rules of proportion. Its design is rooted in the tradition of the Geometric style, its forms showing the artist's dedicated concentration on the most essential elements. Thus the angle formed by the lower boundary of the thorax corresponds to the central angle of the groin, the twin curves of the pectoral muscles to the lines of the clavicles bent gently upward. On the back a satisfying pattern is formed by the curves outlining the shoulder-blades and the hip-line, with the vertebral column marking its centre and the outline of the hips the contour. The bold use of stylization for rendering the essential human forms is also applied to the face of the youth. It is long and narrow, with comparatively wide, flat cheeks, wide-open eyes glancing ahead under strongly arched eyebrows and ears shaped like volutes.

This is one of the earliest among the Attic marble sculptures of young men that have come down to us. It dates from the last years of the 7th century B.C. Some scholars think it is a later work by the Athenian sculptor who made the *Dipylon Youth*, of which nothing but the head and the right hand are preserved (National Museum, Athens).

The statue is said to have come to light by the sepulchral road of Vari south of Mount Hymettos. At the time of its discovery the surface of the statue still had a hard layer of sinter attached to it, which was removed shortly afterwards. In various places, for example on the hair and the fillet, on the neck-band and the nostrils, there were traces of red paint.

Brunn-Bruckmann, Denkmäler der griechischen und römischen Plastik, plates 751 to 755. — *G. M. A. Richter*, Kouroi, 63 ff., No. 1, plates 6—8 and others. — *E. Buschor*, Frühgriechische Jünglinge, 17 ff., fig. 15—20. — *G. M. A. Richter*, Catalogue of Greek Sculptures in the Metropolitan Museum (1954), No. 1, plates 1—3. — *W. H. Schuchhardt*, Gnomon 30, 1958, 482 f.

14, 15

CLEOBIS AND BITON. Ionian-island marble. Height of the right-hand statue without base 7' (2.16 m.), with base 7'9" (2.35 m.). Height of the left-hand statue without base, but with restorations 7'2" (2.18 m.). Delphi, Museum, Inv. 467 and 980; 1524.

The story of Cleobis and Biton, sons of an Argive priestess of Hera, is told in Herodotus (I, 31). On the occasion of a feast of Hera, the oxen that should have drawn the chariot of the priestess to the goddess's shrine were missing, not having been brought back in time from their work in the fields. As time was pressing, the priestess's two sons harnessed themselves to the chariot and drew it to the shrine, a distance of 45 stadia, reckoning the stadium at 210 yards. This feat, says Herodotus, was witnessed by all those taking part in the feast. The Argive men present lauded the youths' strength; the Argive women acclaimed the mother of such sons happy. Their mother, rejoicing at her sons' deed and the approbation it had gained, approached the image of Hera and prayed the goddess to bestow upon her sons the greatest boon obtainable by men. Thereupon, her sons lay down in the shrine to sleep, and never rose again. The Argives had statues made in their likeness and consecrated at Delphi, to the honour and everlasting memory of the two brothers.

These two statues were unearthed in 1893 and 1894 in the sanctuary of Apollo at Delphi, not far from the Athenian treasury. The base of the left-hand statue came to light in 1907 in the wall of the Roman baths at the eastern gateway of the sacred precincts. Before the figures could be set up, the feet and the lower part of the legs of the right-hand one, and the left shank and the feet of the left-hand one had to be restored. Carved into the top surface of the bases, which are rounded at the front, is an inscription giving the names of the youths, the occasion of the dedication and the name of the sculptor – '. . . medes of Argos' – which is thought to stand for Polymedes or Agamedes.

The two brothers are portrayed in the customary manner applied to undraped, archaic statues of youths, the left leg set forward, the arms slightly bent at the elbow and the closed hands resting on the thighs. A curved indentation on the right shank of the left-hand figure, and the absence of developed toes in the remains of the feet that have come to light, imply that the two brothers wore high shoes. Both soles rested on the ground and the bodies were presented in a strictly frontal pose. The wide-open eyes enclosed within the almond-shaped frame of the lids and overhung by heavy, bulging brows gaze straight ahead. The hair is arranged in a horizontal row of concentric circles over the broad, low forehead; it lies close to the head in waves of fine curls. Behind the ears the fullness of the hair is held in by two circlets or bands, from beneath which three short, horizontally divided tresses protrude on either side and fall forward in front of the shoulders, while six further tresses, which are again held together by bands or circlets, lie with their ends resting on the back.

The character of the better preserved figure on the right – usually known as Cleobis – is conditioned by the architectonic structure, the thickset physique and heavy, athletic forms, which contrast somewhat with the sharply cut mouth, the clearly drawn arch of the edge of the rib-cage and the formal arrangement of the finely patterned pubic hair. It is rightly considered a typical example of Argive monumental sculpture from the early 6th century B.C. The other statue, which is less systematically proportioned and not so powerfully tensed, and which also displays a softer and more mobile modelling, is thought to be the work of a sculptor more closely bound to Ionian-island art. Though a case can be made out for the assumption that the remaining letters on the Cleobis base are part of the name Agamedes, and that this sculptor is identical with one of the two architects traditionally credited with building the oldest historical temple of Apollo at Delphi, there is as yet nothing to prove it.

Th. Homolle, Fouilles de Delphes IV, 1 (1909), 5 ff. and plates 1, 2. — *G. M. A. Richter*, Kouroi, 78 ff., No. 11, plate XVIII; plate XIX, figs. 59—64; plate XXIII, figs. 79 and 82. — *E. Buschor*, Frühgriechische Jünglinge, 35 ff. — *G. Kachnitz-Weinberg*, Die ungleichen Zwillinge, in: Studies presented to David Moore Robinson I (1953), 525 ff. — *J. Frel*, in: Studia Antiqua A. Salač Septuagenario Oblata (Prague, 1955), 160 ff. — *R. Heidenreich*, Agamedes in Delphi oder Mythos und Baukunst, in: Wissenschaftl. Zeitschrift der Fr. Schiller-Universität Jena 4, 1954/55, Vol. 1/2, 49 ff.

16–19

SCULPTURES FROM THE WEST PEDIMENT OF THE TEMPLE OF ARTEMIS, IN CORFU (KORKYRA). Museum, Corfu.

The temple of Artemis was excavated in 1910–1911. Situated to

1   West front of the Temple of Artemis on Corfu.
Reconstruction. After Rodenwaldt, *Altdorische Bildwerke in Korfu* (1938)

the west of the modern town, it was a large *Peripteros* built in the Doric style. The colonnade which surrounded the cella consisted of sixteen columns along the sides with eight columns at either end. The temple covered an area measuring 158 ft. by 75 ft., (47.89 × 22.41 m.). Each pediment was 74 ft. (22.16 m.) long and 10 ft. 6 in. (3.15 m.) high at the centre including the entablature. The temple was built of yellowish limestone and the same material was used for the reliefs, which were found upside down where they had fallen. However, the limestone used for the sculptures is of finer texture than that used for the structural parts.

The stupendous figure of a winged gorgon, 9 ft. 3.5 in. (2.79 m.) high, appeared in the centre of the pediment. Her posture – one knee resting on the ground and the other bent at right angles – was in the Archaic period the generally accepted symbol for rapid running motion. Her awe-inspiring face is seen in frontal view and her terrible grin with bared teeth and extended tongue, greeted all who approached the temple. Vipers and tresses of hair curl above her forehead and other vipers are around her neck. Her short, smooth garment was originally painted red and is belted round her hips by a couple of bearded vipers facing one another with gaping jaws. Chrysaor and Pegasus, the gorgon's two sons who, according to the myth, sprang from her head when she was struck by the sword of Perseus, stood to her right and left. They are much smaller, and of Pegasus there are only scanty remains. Next to each of them a mighty feline is crouching, a cross-breed of lion and panther. Their threatening glances were directed towards the

approaches of the temple like those of the gorgon herself. These awe-inspiring beasts were the traditional guardians, put up there to protect by their daemonic powers the cult image and the temple that contained it. This impressive central array of figures was flanked by two smaller groups, each of which represents a dramatic scene from Greek myth, subjects recurring in Greek art through centuries and inspiring some of the most outstanding works by Greek artists. To the right, Zeus is represented brandishing his thunderbolt against a giant who has sunk upon one knee. To the left is the rendering of a decisive scene from the siege of Troy: Neoptolemus slaying Priam with his lance. Under the tapering angles of the pediment lay two reclining figures of wounded or dead warriors, a giant on the right, a Trojan on the left.

The pediment lacks artistic unity as well as unity of subject matter. Following the tradition of the Archaic period, the figures and groups were lined up and have no connection with one another.

The work of a great Corinthian artist – for Korkyra belonged to Corinth, – the pediment dates from the beginning of the 6th century B.C., though the power and strength of the figures links it with the 'Daedalic style' of the preceding century.

Of the main, east pediment of the temple of Artemis only a few fragments survive, just enough for us to recognize that here too the gorgon was represented between two felines of the lion-panther breed.

Korkyra, Archaische Bauten und Bildwerke, published by *G. Rodenwaldt.* vol. I:

Der Artemistempel, bearbeitet von *H. Schleif, K. A. Rhomaios* und *G. Klaffenbach*, Berlin 1940. vol. II: Die Bildwerke des Artemistempels von Korkyra, revised by *G. Rodenwaldt*, Berlin 1938. — *G. Rodenwaldt*, Altdorische Bildwerke in Korfu (Berlin 1938), 11 ff. — *W. H. Schuchhardt*, Archaische Giebelkompositionen (Freiburg/Br. 1940), 8 ff. — *F. Matz*, Geschichte der griechischen Kunst 1, 206 ff.

20–23

STANDING FEMALE FIGURE WITH POMEGRANATE.

Found near Keratea (Attica). White Attic marble with grey-blue veins. Height, 6'5.15" (1.93 m.) (including the plinth which is 4" to 4.25" high (10 cm. to 10.5 cm.)). State Museum, Berlin, Department of Classical Antiquities (Inv. No. 1800). Bought in 1924.

According to a reliable statement this statue was found wrapped in lead; it was thus carefully preserved in antiquity, and, like the *Youth* from Tenea at Munich (34–36), probably before the Persian invasion of the 5th century B.C.

Dignified and majestic, the woman stands erect with feet slightly apart and toes pointing forward. She looks straight ahead. She grasps the pomegranate with her right hand, which is held above her lap; her left hand lies flat across her breast with the thumb pushed under her cloak. Her hair encircles her forehead in regular small curls. At the back of her head it is parted in the centre and tied behind her ears with a triple ribbon, the plait reaching down to her shoulder-blades. She wears a sleeved chiton, the pleats of which fall from the belt to the feet in straight parallel lines; between these pleats there is a smooth central space adorned by a painted meander, and an engraved meander flanked by ornamental squares surrounds her neck. About her shoulders hangs a cloak draped in six wide parallel pleats reaching down to her waist at the back, and in front from her shoulders to her thighs. On her feet she wears sandals and on her head a circular crown, the Greek *polos*, ornamented with an engraved meander around its lower edge and with blossoms and buds around the top. She wears a necklace with bud-shaped pendants, ear-rings, likewise representing buds, and on her left arm a spiral bracelet.

The powerful effect this figure exerts is due to its compact form and the firmness of its modelling. The impression of liveliness is due to the face with its eyes glancing radiantly from sharply edged eyelids, its comparatively large, flat cheeks and the firmly shaped mouth the lips of which look as if they were chiselled. The statue dates from the early 6th century B.C. Neither the feature nor the attributes – pomegranate and *polos* – make it possible to decide whether this woman is a goddess – perhaps Persephone or Aphrodite – or a human being.

There are comparatively extensive remains of the original colouring. Apart from blue, which was used sparingly, it consists mainly of red and yellow. Coloured red were the chiton, the pomegranate, the edges and tassels of the cloak, the necklace, hair-ribbons, sandals and the meander and blossoms on the crown; coloured yellow were the cloak, the stripes along the meander ornaments of the chiton, the hair, ear-rings and the bases below the soles of the sandals. The meander at the centre of the chiton was red, yellow and blue.

Jb. Wiegand, Antike Denkmäler 4, 1928, 15 ff., fig. 1—8, plates 11—18. — *C. Blümel*, Griechische Skulpturen des 6. und 5. Jahrh. v. Chr. = Katalog der Sammlung antiker Skulpturen in Berlin (1940) II, 1, A 1, plates 1—8.

24, 25

THE CALF-BEARER.

Marble from Mt. Hymettus. Height, 5'6" (1.65 m.). The torso was found on the Athenian Acropolis in 1864, the base made of *poros* (a kind of limestone) in 1887. It had the plinth with the right foot of the statue attached to it. Acropolis Museum, Athens (Inv. No. 624).

From the inscription on the rectangular plinth we learn that the statue was dedicated by one Rhombos, Bombos or Kombos (the beginning of the name is missing). There is no doubt that this was a distinguished and well-to-do citizen of Attica who offered his own likeness to the goddess. He is approaching Athene carrying a little calf, his sacrificial offering, on his shoulders. A smooth, thin cloak, closely following the outlines of his body reaches from his shoulders nearly down to his knees. It is open in front. His curls shaped like corals or pearls encircle his forehead and, starting from behind either ear, three plaits fall to his breast. The hair, the surface of which has been left rough at the top of the head to make the colour adhere, is tied with a narrow ribbon. A pointed beard encircles his face, curving around his shaved upper and lower lip. The narrow, curving mouth is firmly outlined. The large, deep-set eyes were made out of coloured stones, now missing, to render the glance more lively.

Man and beast, the donor and his gift, are closely integrated by the pattern formed by the man's arms raised to hold the feet of the calf slung over his shoulders. His hands gripping the hooves form a fitting decorative centre-piece for it.

By its clear and concise form this sculptured group, typical in its composition of the early 6th century B.C., achieves a rare and pleasing unity. An Attic sculptor, no other work by whom is so far known, carved it about 570 B.C.

There are remains of blue paint on the skin of the calf.

H. Payne and *G. M. Young*, Archaic Marble Sculpture from the Acropolis, 1 ff., plates 2—4. — *H. Schrader*, Die archaischen Marmorbildwerke der Akropolis, 278 ff., No. 409, plates 154—155. — *E. Langlotz* und *W. H. Schuchhardt*, Archaische Plastik auf der Akropolis, 3 and 4. — *W. Schiering*, Der Kalbsträger. Opus Nobile, Meisterwerke der antiken Kunst, No. 11 (1958).

26, I, II

SCULPTURES FROM THE OLD TEMPLE OF ATHENE ON THE ATHENIAN ACROPOLIS. Limestone (*poros*).

Hercules wrestling with Triton. Length 11'7" (3.535 m.). Triple-bodied monster. Length 11'4" (3.40 m.), height of foremost bearded figure 2'4.15" (70.5 cm.). Found on the Acropolis in 1888. Acropolis Museum, Athens.

The figurative arts of the 6th century B.C. betray a marked predilection for mythical tales and for the invention of mythical figures. This weird creature, that looks at us with such a lively expression, testifies to the inexhaustible imagination characteristic of this period. Three human bodies with big wings propped up on their elbows merge below the waist into a bundle of twisting snakes. The human figure farthest to the right is holding a bird in his hand, that in the centre a stream of water and the one on the left a bunch of flames. These attributes probably indicate that this three-headed being had the power to transform itself into any of the three elements it symbolizes.

The creature's three muscular bodies express boundless energy which finds a fitting climax in the gay vitality expressed by its faces. The carving is sharp and incisive, technically close to wood-

2 So-called Typhon Pediment, from the Old Temple of Athene on the Athenian Acropolis.
Reconstruction. After Buschor, *Größenverhältnisse attischer Porosgiebel* (Athens 1924)

carving. The three-headed monster filled the right angle of a pediment in the left angle of which there was a corresponding group representing *Hercules wrestling with Triton*, a monster from early Greek myth whose human thorax emerged from a fish's tail. The style points to the years around 570 B.C. The unusually good preservation of the original colouring is remarkable. The dark blue colour used for the hair has changed in some places to dark green, the snakes are a deep red and the tint of the human skin varies from yellow to reddish tones. The red eyes of the face turned towards the beholder are rimmed with black, the complexion was probably yellow, the hair and beard are dark blue, for which reason he has been nicknamed 'Bluebeard'.

Two different theories are held as to what constituted the missing centre of this pediment. According to one of these it was formed by two frightened Nereids running towards the three-headed creature to tell it of Triton's defeat. In this case the three-headed one would be Nereus, the father of the Nereids, who lived in the sea and had the power of changing his shape. This solution would need a total length of about 31 ft. 4 in. (9.40 m.) for the whole pediment. It has been thought that in this case it might have adorned the *Hekatompedon*, the early temple of Athene which had a length of about 100 ft. and stood on a site between the Erechtheum and the Parthenon. The other theory, which is held by W. H. Schuchhardt, is based on a different assessment of the probable height of the entablature belonging to the pediment. Schuchhardt thought that the centre of the pediment was taken up by a large animal group consisting of two lions devouring a bull which they had set upon. Remains of such a group have been found. In this case there would only have been space for one small figure between the central group and the three-headed one; no dramatic link between the latter and the group of Hercules and Triton, and the total dimensions of the original pediment would have been far larger – 55 ft. 2.5 in. (16.16 m.), in length and 5 ft. 8 in. (1.70 m.), in height. This suggests a temple encircled by a colonnade, the earliest building of its type to be erected on the Acropolis.

Jb. Wiegand, Die archaische Poros-Architektur der Akropolis zu Athen (1904). — R. *Heberdey*, Altattische Porosskulptur (1919), 46 ff. No. V — E. *Buschor*, „Die Wendung des Blaubarts" and „Der Dreileibige", in: Athenische Mitteilungen 37, 1922, 1 ff. and 53 ff. — W. H. *Schuchhardt*, Die Sima des alten Athena-Tempels, in: Athenische Mitteilungen 60, 1935, 86 ff. and the same, Archaische Giebelkompositionen (1940), 20 ff. — E. *Buschor*, Meermänner, in: Sitzungsberichte der Bayerischen Akademie der Wissenschaften. Philos.-histor. Abteilung 1941, vol. II, 1, p. 22. — O. *Broneer*, The Head of Herakles in the Pediment of the Old Athena Temple, in: Hesperia 8, 1939, 91 ff.

27

UPPER PORTION OF A FEMALE STATUE. Marble from Naxos. Height 21.4" (53.5 cm.). Athens, Acropolis Museum, No. 677.

Two fragmentary statues of girls found in 1886 and 1887 near the Erechtheum, in the 'Persian rubble', show that works by sculptors from eastern Greece were also consecrated as votive offerings on the Athenian Acropolis as early as the first half of the 6th century. The two statues supplement one another most felicitously as regards their preservation. The upper portion of the one statue, reproduced in our plate, may be regarded as part of a standing figure in a severe, erect pose. It was clothed in a long Ionian sleeved chiton of thin material, which enclosed the lower part of the body in narrow, parallel, vertical folds that gave it the appearance of a column, and in a short cloak held together with claps over the right shoulder and right upper arm but leaving the left shoulder and left arm free. Her right arm hung down more or less loosely, while in her left hand she holds a fruit as a votive offering in front of her chest.

The narrow head faces straight to the front and is carried on a powerful, round neck, which is framed at its base in a gentle curve by the borders of the chiton and cloak. The fine, horizontal mouth with the tender lips and the small, almond-shaped eyes lie flat in the elongated oval of the face. The long, heavy upper lids, each with an indented skin fold, lend the eyes a rather tired expression. The hair is parted in the middle and forms long, fine waves over the brow and on the head. At the back it hangs down to the shoulder blades, in a broad, full mass divided up by both horizontal and vertical lines. The hair is held together by a long, narrow headband. The headband is artistically knotted at the back, and the knot and the two equal and divergent ends rest like an ornament upon the soft mass of the hair.

The feeling for the life being expressed in this figure differs very markedly from the style of other contemporaneous works on the Acropolis. From among our illustrations we may cite for comparison the standing female figure now in Berlin, the work of an Attic sculptor and some twenty years earlier in date (20–23). Primitive vigour and an intense fullness of life seem to be bursting out of the taut, tense forms of the Berlin goddess. The artist who made the kore from the Acropolis, on the other hand, models more gently and softly. He likes curved planes and flowing lines. His ideal of beauty is more sensitive, more delicately attuned, akin to the natural life of growing things. Much of the composure and wisdom of the East seems also to have found its way into the musing face of the girl.

It was long ago recognized that this kore must be the work of a Samian artist, whether it was imported to Athens from the east or actually carved in Athens. It can only have been produced a few years prior to the Hera of Cheramyes (32, 33), a masterpiece which, in its unique perfection, surpasses in importance even the votive offering on the Acropolis.

The left elbow, intermediate portions of the left upper arm and

59

forearm and parts of the hanging hair on the left side of the figure have been recently restored. A fracture in the neck has been sealed.

H. Payne and G. M. Young, Archaic Marble Sculpture from the Acropolis, plates 18, 19. — E. Langlotz, Frühgriechische Bildhauerschulen, 115 f. and 120 ff., plate 71, d. — E. Buschor, Altsamische Standbilder, 24 ff., fig. 76, 80—83. — H. Schrader, Die archaischen Marmorbildwerke von der Akropolis, 64 f., No. 23, plate 34.

28, 29

HEAD OF A YOUTH. Whitish Boeotian limestone. Found in Boeotia in 1885, in the sanctuary dedicated to the Ptoan Apollo. Height, 13.15" (33 cm.). National Museum, Athens (Inv. No. 15).

This impressive head is considerably larger than life. It is all that remains of a statue which must have belonged to a group of early Greek works representing standing male youths (see above, plates (11–13). At the back of this head his long hair descends in beaded tresses. It is held by a broad fillet from which descends a fringe of short strands of hair, arranged symmetrically to the right and left of the central parting. The outstanding characteristics of this head are the almost triangular shape of the face and the stress laid on horizontal lines in the designing of the features, i.e. the almost straight mouth marked where the thin lips are pressed together by a sharply incised line and the neatly carved lids surrounding the long, almond-shaped eyes. Compared to earlier Attic or Ionian-island pieces, this head shows less depth and sharper outlines; it seems harder, and the incisive technique employed is reminiscent of wood carving. A marked stiffness and certain mannerisms are characteristic of the early arts in Boeotia, a region where stylistic traditionalism was tempered by receptiveness to innovations made in other regions, resulting in some interesting combinations of typically provincial traits with more lively and novel elements.

This combination of different styles makes the dating of the piece rather difficult, with the result that rather divergent suggestions have been made; however, it probably dates from the years immediately preceding 550 B.C.

The surface of the stone is somewhat corroded on the right and there are some dark stains on the left cheek and forehead.

M. Holleaux, Bulletin de Correspondance Hellénique 10, 1886, 98 ff., plate 5. — R. Lullies, Jahrbuch des Deutschen Archäologischen Instituts 51, 1936, 138 ff., fig. 1—2. — F. R. Grace, Archaic Sculpture in Boeotia, 58 ff., fig. 71—72.

30, 31

RIDER. Parian marble. Louvre, Paris, No. 3104, and Acropolis Museum, Athens, No. 590.

The British archaeologist Humfry Payne first recognized the fact that a bearded 11½"-high head (29 cm.), which had come to the Louvre from the Rampin Collection, belonged to an almost life size equestrian statue of which the torso (height 2.8"; 81.5 cm.) had been found in 1886, eleven years after the head, also on the Athenian Acropolis, and which is housed in the Acropolis Museum. In the Louvre the original head is now attached to a plaster cast of the Rider at Athens.

The horse's head is turned a little to the right, while the rider's is turned to the left and bent slightly forward in the action of riding. His hands, clenched into a fist, rest on his thighs. A diagonal hole has been bored through the right hand to take the bronze reins. Both horse and rider are powerfully and compactly built.

The rider's shoulders, back and chest are broad. The back is rather flat. The artist has shown the spine as a broad hollow, the shoulder-blades as simple curves, and the edges of the rib-cage as pointed ovals.

The expressive, lively and individual face with its sweeping eyebrows, almond-shaped eyes between sharp-cut lids, and slightly pursed, firm lips, is boldly conceived and straightforwardly carved. The head is distinguished by the highly decorative rendering of the hair, which is adorned with a fine ivy wreath. The hair is stylized in coral-shaped curls and falls to both sides from a centre parting and down at the back in regular tresses, which are full behind the ears and are cut off horizontally at the nape of the neck. Over the forehead the hair protrudes from under the wreath like thick, S-shaped strings of beads whose ends are wound into curls. Cheeks and chin are framed within the firm, plastic oval of a short beard shaved to a neat edge and rendered in the form of small beads set close together. To visualize the original appearance of the head we must imagine the addition of a painted moustache. The delicate, tapering structure of the individual forms and the artistic coiffure recall the enthroned Zeus on the poros pediment of the Acropolis showing the introduction of Hercules on Mount Olympus, which dates from about 560 B.C. This rider must also be the work of an outstanding Attic master from the period shortly before the middle of the 6th century. Other works are believed to have been carved by the same hand, the most important of them being the statue of a girl in chiton and peplos from the Acropolis (43–45).

In addition to this rider the remains of a second equestrian statue, the reverse counterpart of the first, have also been found on the Athenian Acropolis. The two figures together formed a group. Judging by the ivy wreath, they must have been two victors in horse-racing. The outward appearance, the place of dedication and the importance of the group as a work of art indicate that the pair must have belonged to the Attic nobility. It has therefore been conjectured – perhaps correctly – that the two riders were a memorial to Hippias and Hipparchus, the sons of Peisistratus.

H. Payne and G. M. Young, Archaic Marble Sculpture from the Acropolis, 6 ff., fig. 1 D-E and plates 11 a-c; 133, 3—4. — H. Schrader, Die archaischen Marmorbildwerke der Acropolis, No. 312, plates 134 ff. — E. Langlotz und W. H. Schuchhardt, Archaische Plastik auf der Akropolis, plates 5—6. — K. Schefold. Die großen Bildhauer des archaischen Athen, 41 ff.

32, 33

HERA OF CHERAMYES. Found c. 1875 in the sanctuary of Hera on Samos. Large-crystalled white marble. Height 6.4' (1.92 m.). Louvre, Paris, No. 686.

The statue grows from below with magnificent compactness. The head and left arm are missing. The right arm hangs down in a relaxed attitude, the closed hand holding the veil; the left rests on the breast. The body is draped in three garments, each clearly differentiated according to its material: a long, thin linen chiton that falls vertically to the ground in narrow, parallel folds and spreads out in a circle at the bottom showing its border; a cloak that lies diagonally in broader folds across the right shoulder and breast, with its long end at the side accompanying and emphasizing the line of the right arm; and a wide, outspread veil drawn over the head and covering the whole of the back and the right arm, a corner of which is tucked into the girdle in front under the over-fold of the cloak. Running along the front edge of the veil, and reading from the bottom upwards, is an inscription stating that Cheramyes dedicated the statue to Hera. The over-life-size dimensions, the august attitude, the clothing, and in particular the long veil have rightly been construed as signs that the figure represents the goddess Hera herself, the bride and spouse of Zeus.

The contours of the figure, the lower part of whose body is rounded like a column, are flowing and reveal an exquisite harmony of line. The firm and gentle curves of the female body are shown or hinted at beneath the richly modelled surface of the drapery. The statue takes its place as one of the peak achievements in the series of women's figures belonging to the 6th century B.C. found at the Heraion of Samos. It must have been a Samian sculptor who carved this votive offering of Cheramyes in about 560 B.C. Perhaps we possess other works by the same master in the remains of two similarly garbed figures from the Heraion. Two later votive offerings with inscriptions given by the same donor have also been found there – the statue of a woman and the fragment of a youth, both over-life-size.

P. Girard, Revue Archéologique 4, 1880, 483 ff., plates 13—14. — *E. Langlotz*, Frühgriechische Bildhauerschulen 120 ff. — *E. Buschor*, Altsamische Standbilder (1934), 25 f., fig. 86—89; 107. — *H. Bloesch*, Agalma (Bern 1943), 18 f. — *E. Buschor*, Altsamische Stifter, in: Neue Beiträge zur klassischen Altertumswissenschaft. Festschrift für B. Schweitzer (1954), 96 f.

34, 35

STANDING YOUTH. Found on Melos in 1891. Naxian marble. Height 7' (2.14 m.). National Museum, Athens, No. 1558.

This youth, a funerary monument or votive offering in a sanctuary, was carved only a few years before the funerary statue from Tenea (36–38), that is to say shortly before the middle of the 6th century B.C. But it differs markedly from the Corinthian work through features that are characteristic of another artistic province: it must have been carved by a sculptor from the Ionian islands.

The body is taller than life-size and slender. The arms with their gently closed hands hang loosely from the softly rounded shoulders with no bend at the elbows. The hair, which falls down at the back, frames the forehead in large, soft, flattened spiral curls. The body seems to be growing with something of the unconscious life of a plant. The individual parts flow into one another. The contours are unbroken, gently curving lines. The modelling is soft and sensitive throughout; the back contains no detail other than a long vertical depression to mark the spine and a hint of the shoulder-blades.

The surface of the figure, especially of the head, has been eroded by wind and rain. The right shank and foot, and the left foot and ankle, have been restored.

M. Holleaux, Bulletin de Correspondance Hellénique 16, 1892, 560 ff., plate 16. — *G. M. A. Richter*, Kouroi, 159 f., No. 72, plates 60—62, fig. 217—224. — *E. Buschor*, Frühgriechische Jünglinge, 64 f., fig. 76—77.

36–38

STANDING YOUTH. Found in 1846 over a tomb in the village of Athiki, the old Tenea, near Corinth. Parian marble. Height 5' (1.53 m.). Glyptothek, Munich, No. 168.

The statue was carefully hidden in ancient times, probably to preserve it during the Persian attacks at the beginning of the 5th century B.C. It lay on the slab of a tomb, its head protected from damage by an earthenware vessel. By virtue of its excellent state of preservation – only the middle section of the right arm has been restored – and its high quality, the statue has always been regarded as a model specimen of Archaic Greek sculpture, and in particular of the statues of youths executed in this style. Its fame is also due to the fact that very few statues of youths in the Archaic style were known when this figure came to the Glyptothek, Munich, in 1853.

The hair, which forms an arch over the brow and is held together with a fillet, falls over the shoulders in a broad mass made up of horizontal layers. The body is both powerful and delicate, with supple joints. The modelling, especially of the chest, abdomen and thighs, is both refined and lively with very gentle transitions. The gay expression of the face with its pointed profile bespeaks an untrammelled joy in life. The closest parallels to this face are the moulded heads on Corinthian vases dating from the mid-6th century B.C. A certain hardness and angularity in the representation of certain parts of the body, such as the sharp contour of the shin-bone, the solid calf muscles and the bony ankles, indicate that this figure is the work of a Corinthian artist. Some writers have seen Ionian-island traits in the slender figure and the lively modelling of the body.

A. Furtwängler und *P. Wolters*, Beschreibung der Glyptothek König Ludwigs I., 2nd edition (1910), page 49 ff., No. 47. — *H. Payne*, Necrocorinthia (1931), 237. — *G. M. A. Richter*, Kouroi, 137 ff., No. 58, plates 50—52, fig. 185—190. — *E. Buschor*, Frühgriechische Jünglinge, 46 ff., fig. 50—53.

39

FRAGMENT OF THE SEPULCHRAL STELE OF A DISCUS-BEARER. Found in the vicinity of the Dipylon at Athens in 1873. Parian marble. Height 13.6" (34 cm.), width 17.8" (44.5 cm.) (at the bottom) to 17.2" (43 cm.) (at the top), thickness 6" (15 cm.). National Museum, Athens, No. 38.

The fragment comes from a tall stele, similar to the sepulchral monument of Aristion (71). As in the latter, the figure was framed on either side by a projecting vertical fillet. The deceased must have been represented, over-life-size, as a naked athlete stepping towards the right with his left leg forward. He is shouldering a discus with his left hand, of which the palm and the thumb are visible. The smooth disc, which stands out in relief, forms an effective background to the expressive and very lively outline of the head with its powerful, salient nose, firm, sharply defined lips, beautifully curved chin and finely modelled throat. The jaw sweeps in a magnificent arc from the point of the chin to the large, full lobe of the ear, outlining the smooth, flat cheek. The eye is rendered like a lens, surrounded by clearly marked, symmetrical lids. The eye and mouth are embedded in the surrounding flesh as though in illuminated hollows. The hair clings to the back of the neck in a thick bunch sectioned horizontally and tied up at a point level with the lower edge of the discus.

The modelling of the relief is firm, sure and definite. The face, which radiates youthful vitality, is rendered clearly and with seeming simplicity, the surface being well modulated. When they still bore the original paint, the splendid profile must have stood out more distinctly from the discus, and the latter from the coloured background, than they do today.

The stele is the work of a great – but at present nameless – Attic sculptor from the mid-6th century B.C. It has been ascribed to the master of the rider from the Acropolis, the head of which is now in the Louvre (30, 31), and with the kore in chiton and peplos (43–45). But its style seems to bespeak another, no less important artistic personality.

A. Conze, Die attischen Grabreliefs, vol. 1, No. 5, plate 4. — *H. Schrader,* Die archaischen Marmorbildwerke der Akropolis, 225, to No. 312.

40, 41

FRAGMENT OF A HEAD. Marble. Height 7.5" (19 cm.). Found near the Temple of Artemis at Ephesus. British Museum, London, B 89.

It cannot be said for certain whether this head, which is probably that of a woman, comes from a statue or a relief – the face and neck being surrounded by broken surfaces. Nothing is left of the temples, ears or hair, so that the head, which was originally turned slightly to the left, has acquired a somewhat mask-like appearance – especially when looked at from in front.

The horizontal mouth is softly embedded in the broad, round face with the full cheeks and fleshy chin. The lips are fine and delicate, the wings of the short nose are thick and widely curved. The slanting eyes beneath the arched eyebrows are carved in a very peculiar manner. The upper lid protrudes in a wide arc, while the lower lid is more sharply modelled in a lively S-curve. The eyes themselves are flat and were originally painted in. Now that the paint has vanished the lids appear to be closed.

The soft, loose forms that seem to be welling up from within are typical of Eastern Ionian sculpture. This method of fashioning the eyes seems to have originated in this region, from whence it was soon adopted by other zones of Greek art. The head has been tentatively ascribed to a Milesian artist of the period shortly after the middle of the 6th century B.C. But it differs so greatly in style from the few surviving heads from the plinths of the older Artemision at Ephesus that it is very unlikely to have belonged to this temple.

F. N. Pryce, Catalogue of Sculpture in the British Museum (1928), B 89, plate 4. — *E. Langlotz,* Frühgriechische Bildhauerschulen, 107, plate 61.

42

BUST OF A WOMAN IN RELIEF. From a plinth in the old Temple of Apollo at Didyma (south of Miletus). Fine-grained marble from the islands of Korossai (Phurni) near Icaria. Height 22" (55.5 cm.). State Museum, Berlin, Department of Classical Antiquities, No. 1721.

Little has survived of the old Temple of Apollo at Didyma, which was destroyed by the Persians in 494 B.C. It was an Ionic building of very large proportions, with a double arcade of eight columns in front, which – as in the Temple of Artemis at Ephesus (see 223) – stood on high plinths decorated with reliefs. Our fragment, about 4½ feet in diameter, shows a roughly life-size clothed female figure seen from the front, as to the name and nature of which we have no reliable evidence. The neck of the dress is modelled and traces of red paint on the right side of the figure just below the throat suggest that a second garment under the first may have been indicated by paint alone. A linen head-dress forms a wide and beautifully curved arc over brow and

temples. On top of this lies a thick cord that was no doubt intended to hold the head-cloth in position. A rolled curl hangs down in front of each ear. From beneath them emerge two ribbons that fall down over shoulders and arms, possibly the end of a band of cloth that ran across the forehead – where it was only painted in – and was tied at the back. Further traces of red paint show that the figure was also adorned with a double necklace. The broad, softly rounded face with its serene and impassive expression, reminiscent of the calm, detached look of Asiatic countenances, is very characteristic of the fragment's style. The wide mouth with the narrow, sharply defined lips, and the slit eyes with their heavy lids, look as though they had been scored into the swelling, opulent forms. We must recognize in this fragment the handiwork of an Eastern Ionian artist of the third quarter of the 6th century B.C.

Th. Wiegand, Didyma. First Part: Die Baubeschreibung in drei Bänden von *H. Knackfuß* (1941), 123 f. and 196 f., plate 214, fig. F 724. — *C. Weickert,* Griechische Plastik (1946), 14 ff., fig. 6.

43–45

STANDING GIRL IN CHITON AND PEPLOS. Parian marble. Height including the inch-high-plinth 4' (1.21 m.). Found on the Athenian Acropolis, 1886. Acropolis Museum, Athens, No. 679.

This statue is distinguished outwardly, by the clothes, from the figures of girls on the Acropolis – the korai – belonging to the same period. The girl is wearing a girded Dorian peplos with an over-fold, and under this a fine linen chiton whose wide selvage is visible at the throat and whose fine, wavy folds appear beneath the peplos. The figure stands taut and erect, the feet together, the head looking straight in front and tilted a fraction to the left in conformity with the slightly raised left shoulder. The body is concealed by the heavy woollen material of the peplos but clearly perceptible in the curves and hollows of the modelling. There is something block-like about the lower part of the body, which is flat in front and rounded at the back. The right arm hangs down at the side slightly bent at the elbow, the hand rests against the thigh holding a wreath or sprig. The outstretched left fore-arm was made separately and inserted. The artistic qualities of the work are most clearly manifest in the powerful, rich forms of the head and the festal serenity of the expression of the face. The abundant hair frames the forehead in waves, lies in three curled plaits on each shoulder, and hangs down over the back in broad indented strands held together by a band. A bronze wreath encircled the hair. The ears were adorned with metal pendants. The statue is the mature work of one of the leading Attic sculptors of the period around 530 B.C. At least two other works have been attributed to the same hand – an equestrian statue from the Acropolis (the head of which is in the Louvre, 30, 31) and a female head from the same site, both of them older and dating from the mid-century.

The ancient painting on this 'kore in the peplos' is well preserved. The border of the robe at the throat is green. The lower border of the over-fold bears on a red ground a green palmette pattern and above this a pattern of green spirals. The ends of the green-striped girdle hanging down at the side are bound with two wide strips of green braid with brightly coloured rosettes. The hair, lips and iris are red, the pupils, brows and lashes black, the neck-band green.

H. *Payne* and G. M. *Young*, Archaic Marble Sculpture from the Acropolis, 18 f., plates 29—33; 38, 5. — H. *Schrader*, Die archaischen Marmorbildwerke der Akropolis, No. 4. plates 3—8. — E. *Langlotz* and W. H. *Schuchhardt*, Archaische Plastik auf der Akropolis (1938), 10—13.

46, 47

HEAD OF A YOUTH. Parian marble. Height 12.6" (31.5 cm.). Copenhagen, Ny Carlsberg Glyptotek, No. 11 (Inv. 418).

This extremely important, over-life-size head was the first piece of Greek sculpture acquired, in 1879, by Carl Jacobsen, the Danish patron of the arts who founded the Ny Carlsberg Glyptothek. It was previously owned by the French archaeologist Olivier Rayet and was found in Athens on the Sacred Way to Eleusis, between the Dipylon and the river Cephissus.

The head, which is set frontally on the thick, muscular neck, must have belonged to a funerary statue of the Archaic 'standing youth' type. The powerful impression it creates derives above all from the magnificent compactness and exceptional strength and firmness of its sculptural forms. Wide, interrelated arcs, semicircles and circles characterize its build and outline. The hair is cut short and lies in waves like a close-fitting cap round the crown of the head. The individual tufts of hair resemble flickering flames or sickles. Behind, it clings close to the head and flows in a firmly controlled curve to the nape. It frames the untroubled brow in a semicircle, which, seen from the front, combines with the cheeks and chin to form a great oval. The eyebrows curve upwards from the root of the nose and the arcs of the powerful cheekbones project sideways from the same point; brows and cheekbones combine to encircle the hollows in which lie the almond eyes covered by long upper lids. Clearly-cut furrows run down from the base of the nostrils and frame the mouth with its full, firm lips.

It was formerly held that the ears were swollen from blows and that the head must therefore belong to the statue of a boxer. But to do so is to put a false, naturalistic interpretation on the style of this sculpture. In reality the treatment of the ears is another aspect of that partly expressive, partly restrained handling of the shapes that well up from within which we see in the rest of this head and in other statues from the late Archaic period. The false impression created by the ears was reinforced by the fact that the rims are now damaged or missing.

To judge by the head, the statue to which it belonged is the work of one of the greatest Attic sculptors of the period. It dates from c. 530 B. C., the same period as the kore in the long chiton and peplos (43, 45). Stylistically, the Copenhagen head so closely resembles a mask of Dionysus from the sanctuary of Dionysus in the Attic Deme of Ikaria that these two works have been attributed to the same sculptor (cf. W. Wrede, *Athenische Mitteilungen* 53, 1928, 67 ff., plate 1 and *Beilage* XXI, 3; XXII, 2; and E. Buschor, *Die Plastik der Griechen*², 35). The individual shapes apart both head and mask project the same vital energy and sensuous joy, in a manner almost without parallel in the Attic art of this epoch. The two pieces of sculpture are likewise linked by their outstanding artistic quality. The pediment sculptures from the Old Temple of Athene on the Acropolis (26, I, II), often mentioned in the same breath as the Copenhagen head, do indeed bear a close resemblance to it but are probably not by the same hand. Remnants of red paint still cling to the hair, eyes and lips. The rest of the face, the surface of which is highly polished, seems not to have been painted.

O. *Rayet*, Monuments Grecs I, 6 (1877), 1 ff. — P. *Arndt*, La Glyptothèque Ny-Carlsberg (1912), plates 1, 2. — G. *Lippold*, Antike Skulpturen der Glyptothek Ny Carslberg (1924), 23 f., fig. 23, ref. do. E. *Schmidt*, Deutsche Literaturzeitung 1926. 2186 f. — W. *Wrede*, Athenische Mitteilungen 53, 1928, 69. — V. H. *Poulsen*, Three Archaic Greek Heads in the Ny Carlsberg Glyptotek, in: From the Ny Carlsberg Glyptothek 2, 1938, 94 ff.

48—55

PANELS FROM THE FRIEZES ON THE SIPHNIAN TREASURY AT DELPHI. Parian marble. Museum, Delphi.

The treasury erected in the sanctuary of Apollo at Delphi by the inhabitants of the island of Siphnos as a votive offering and for the storage of their bequests was built shortly before 525 B.C., as we know from Herodotus III, 57 and Pausanias X, 11, 2. It was constructed throughout of Parian marble, had a ground-plan of 18'8" × 27'7" (5.94 × 8.37 m.), and stood on a high limestone foundation at the foot of the steep and rugged Phaedriades, below the terrace of the temple, facing west. Its shape was that of a small temple with projecting side walls, decorated on the outside with a tremendous wealth of figurative and ornamental sculpture. Two female figures carried the entablature on the west front; only a few remains have survived from the pediment on this side. The east pediment shows Hercules carrying off the Delphic tripod.

A relief frieze showing mythological scenes ran round the whole building above the architrave, 25.2" (63 cm.) to 27.3" (68.3 cm.) (on the west front) high and 87'8" (29.63 m.) long. It was framed by magnificent sculptured decorative fillets, with Ionic cymas at the bottom and Lesbian cymas at the top. More than half the frieze is still in existence. Stylistically, two masters can be distinguished. One was responsible for the west and south faces showing the Judgement of Paris and the seizure of the Leucippides by the Dioscuri, the other for the east and north faces. Practically nothing now remains *in situ* save the foundations and the marble steps that carried the superstructure. The other remains are housed in the Museum at Delphi.

Plates 48—55 show parts of the east frieze with seated deities 48 top, 49) on either side of a now missing centrepiece and a battle scene (48 centre), and parts of the north frieze (48 bottom, 50—55) that ran along what was later the Sacred Way, with scenes from the war of the gods against the giants.

In the gathering of gods on the east frieze (48 top, 49), the gods on the side of the Trojans sit on the left – Ares, Aphrodite, Artemis and Apollo, who is turning round to speak to the two goddesses behind him, and Zeus. Facing them on the right are the goddesses siding with the Greeks – Athene, Hera and Hebe. The character of each one is splendidly brought out and they participate with lively gestures in the events which elicit their passionate interest.

The long panel with the fight over a fallen warrior (48 centre) shows, on the left, the Trojans (from the centre, Hector (?), Aeneas, and Glaucus, looking round, with a quadriga), and on the right, the Greeks (Menelaus with a gorgoneion as a shield emblem, an unknown man, Automedon, looking round and with a quadriga, and Nestor standing at the side with his right arm raised). Some of the figures are identified by inscriptions.

In the north frieze (48 bottom, 50—55) the gods are fighting from left to right against the giants, who are attacking from the other side. The giants are represented as heavily armed, equipped with helmets and shields, and some also with breastplates and greaves.

They fight with spears, swords, stones and boulders. At the left-hand extremity of the frieze, in the east, Hephaestus in the short chiton of the craftsman stands at his bellows; in front of him are two unnamed goddesses, perhaps Demeter and Kore. Facing them are some giants. Beyond these again, are Dionysus with the panther skin and Cybele with her chariot drawn by lions, which are attacking a giant; then come Apollo and Artemis, who are shooting bows. The fleeing giant in front of them, who is looking back over his shoulder, has a *kantharos*, or two-handled drinking vessel, worked into the crest of his helmet; the giant himself is named as Kantharos in an inscription. In front of him are a fallen warrior and three further giants. In the adjoining panel Zeus races forward on a quadriga; in front of him are Hera bending down to a fallen warrior, Athene with the aegis, Ares with helmet and shield over the prostrate body of a dead giant whose head is seen front-face; then comes Hermes with his pointed hat, a skin over his chiton and a broad sword-sheath in his left hand, turning towards onrushing giants; and finally Poseidon and Amphitrite (?), of the lower half of whose bodies only fragments remain on the edge of the panel. The background of the frieze was blue, the foot-fillet red. The hair, the crests of the helmets, the inside of the shields, and the manes and tails of the horses, were all red. Traces of red paint have also been left on some of the garments.

The liveliness and refinement of its execution, and its importance in the history of art, render the frieze on the Siphnian treasury a masterpiece of Archaic relief sculpture. The 'North-East Master', a Parian artist, must have been one of the leading sculptors of his day, full of imagination and sparkling temperament. The differences in nature and substance between the naked parts and the loose hair of the figures, the pliable stuffs of the garments, and the metal of the weapons, are brilliantly rendered. The over-all effect is one of power and vigour; at the same time it is decorative and festive, and marked by a spiritualized, sublime sensuousness.

Ch. Picard et P. de la Coste-Messelière, Fouilles de Delphes IV, 2, page 72 ff., plates 7—15. — *P. de la Coste-Messelière*, Au Musée de Delphes (1936), 237 ff. and the same, Bulletin de Correspondance Hellénique 68/69, 1944/45, 5 ff. — *E. Langlotz*, Zur Zeitbestimmung der strengrotfigurigen Vasenmalerei und der gleichzeitigen Plastik, 17 ff. — *Pauly-Wissowa-Kroll*, Realencyclopädie der klassischen Altertumswissenschaft, Supplement 4 (1924), 1252 ff., No. 29 (Pomtow). — *E. Mastrokostas*, Zu den Namensbeischriften des Siphnier-Frieses, in Athenische Mitteilungen 71, 1956, 74 ff.

56

SEATED SPHINX. Found on the Athenian Acropolis in 1882/83. Parian marble. Height of fragment 1'9.5" (0.55 m.). Acropolis Museum, Athens, No. 632.

The sphinx, an imaginary creature with the winged body of a beast of prey and a woman's head, is repeatedly found in conjunction with lions, panthers, griffins, sirens and other fabulous beings in the friezes with which the Greeks decorated their vessels and utensils during the Archaic period. The name sphinx as applied to this particular hybrid creature, and its appearance in the legend of Oedipus, first occurs in the 6th century B.C. The combination of an animal body with a human head is ultimately derived from Ancient Egyptian art, where the type is confined to beings of the male sex.

If the Greeks in the 6th century B.C. consecrated great free sculptures of sphinxes in their sanctuaries and set them up over tombs, these were to them highly demonic beings who possessed the power to ward off evil. They believed that enormous physical and mental forces were at work in these statues. The sitting sphinx that took its place among the motley plethora of 6th-century statues on the Athenian Acropolis must have had a similar significance.

The front legs and the lower part of the body with the hind legs have been lost. The surviving portion of the thin, sinewy body is modelled in spare forms. Two great wings curving in firm arcs like sickles are attached to breast and back and cover one another. Head and neck are turned to the front above the animal's body, which is seen from the side. The large face with the straight, wide mouth and the slanting eyes surmounted by heavy upper lids forms a soft, full oval. The hair surrounds the high forehead in a great arc of individual, sinuous strands and falls behind the ears to the shoulders. It is held together higher up by a broad band, from beneath which it spreads out at the back in a series of uniform pigtails that taper to a point and are modelled like thick strings of beads. Above the band the hair is summarily indicated by a few sculptured waves, and was rendered in detail with paint. On the crown of the head is a round disc with a peg-hole for a trailer of flowers such as sphinxes wore, or a *meniskos*, a metal rod that was to protect statues from being dirtied by birds.

The breast and back of the figure are painted down to the wings with a scale pattern in red, black and yellow. The same colours have been used to depict the feathers on the wings.

In date the sphinx must come between the Rider (30, 31) and the Kore in chiton and peplos (43—45). It is also the work of an Attic artist. The broad construction and the soft, full shapes of the face are doubtless attributable to the influence of Ionian island art.

H. Payne and *G. M. Young*, Archaic Marble Sculpture from the Acropolis 10, plates 5—6. — *H. Schrader*, Die archaischen Marmorbildwerke der Akropolis, No. 372, plate 164.

57—61

STANDING YOUTH. Found 1936 at Anavyssus (in Southern Attica). The base with inscription came to light in 1938. Parian marble. Height 6' (1.94 m.). National Museum, Athens, Inv. 3851.

The figure stands in the posture of the Archaic statues of youths, but in its inner mobility and the tremendous power of its limbs seems to be breaking away from the severity of the old style. The lively modelling of the athletic body, the radiant glance, the splendid coral-like shapes of the hair that falls in a curve over the shoulders, are in concord with the wealth and interplay of shapes exhibited by the interior and exterior contours. The surface is a warm, reddish-brown colour. Remains of red paint are visible on the hair, hairband and pupils. The hair on the head above the hairband is only summarily carved and was formerly completed in paint.

The statue originally stood on a three-tiered base, of which only the middle, rectangular tier, and the statue of Parian marble, have come down to us.

It bears in front the distich:

Στῆθι καὶ οἴκτιρον Κροίσου παρὰ σῆμα θανόντος,
ηὅν' ποτ' ἐνὶ προμάχοις ὤλεσε θοῦρος Ἄρης.

'Stand and mourn by the tomb of dead Kroisos, whom furious Ares snatched away from among the warriors in the front rank.'

While the Corinthian youth from Tenea, now at Munich, (c. 550 B.C.) (36—38) is still fashioned entirely in the style of the black figure vases, this Attic memorial figure of Kroisos already belongs, in its greater corporeality and more opulent modelling, to the period of the early red figure style. It must have been carved about 520 B.C.

A. Philadelpheus, The Anavyssos Kouros. Annual of the British School at Athens 36, 1935/36, 1 ff., plates 1—5. — *G. M. A. Richter*, Kouroi, 198 ff., No. 114, plates 89—90, fig. 317—321, plate 132, fig. 461—462. — *E. Buschor*, Frühgriechische Jünglinge, 106 ff., fig. 124—126. — To the base: *G. Ph. Stevens* and *E. Vanderpool*, with a supplementary remark by *David M. Robinson*, An inscribed Kouros base. Commemorative Studies in honor of Th. Leslie Shear, Hesperia, Supplement 8, 1949, 361 ff. and Bulletin de Correspondance Hellénique 79, 1955, 208 f., fig. 7—8.

62—65

RELIEFS FROM A SQUARE BASE. Pentelic marble. Height 13″ (32 cm.), sides 32″ (81 cm.) each. National Museum, Athens, No. 3476.

The base was built into an ancient wall in the cemetery in front of the Dipylon at Athens, together with two other rectangular statue-bases. It came to light in 1922. It has a depression in the upper surface for the plinth of the statue that stood on it. The underside rested on a second base. The uncarved side must have stood against a wall. On the front and two sides it bears reliefs depicting scenes from the life of Athenian youth in the late 6th century B.C.

The front face shows four youths in the starting position for various athletic exercises: on the left a runner at the start, on the right a spear-thrower who is resting the fingers of his right hand on the loop and seems to be testing the point or the balance of the spear with his left. In the centre two wrestlers are practising the holds. One of them has seized the other with both hands by the left fore-arm. The latter is defending himself against the pull by exerting a counter-pressure with his right hand against his attacker's shoulder. — On the left-hand face six youths may be seen playing a ball game in teams of three each. The game evidently consisted in one team throwing the ball as far as possible, while the other caught it and threw it as far back as they could, until one side or the other had been driven behind a fixed mark. The player on the left-hand edge of the relief is in the act of throwing the ball. — On the right-hand face of the base (64, 65) two young men are sitting in the middle, their cloaks over their left shoulders and carrying long staves such as were fashionable in Athens at that time. One of them holds a leashed dog, the other a cat on a lead, which they are setting on to one another. Behind them stand two friends, resting negligently and elegantly on their staves, and watching this entertaining and amusing sport with interest.

Of the ancient painting the vermilion ground on the right and left faces of the base is very well preserved. The bodies and cloaks are modelled with splendid vitality and great plastic beauty. The treatment of the muscles and garments and the anecdotal point of the scenes reappear in a very similar form in the mature vases of Phintias and Euthymides during the last decade of the 6th century B.C.

A. Philadelpheus, Archäologischer Anzeiger 1922, 56 ff. — *J. Mosel*, Studien zu den beiden archaischen Reliefbasen vom Kerameikos. Rostocker Dissertation, 1935 (Hildesheim 1938).

66—68

THESEUS CARRYING OFF ANTIOPE. From the west pediment of the Temple of Apollo at Eretria. Parian marble. Height 3′7″ (1.1 m.). Found in 1900. Museum, Chalkis, No. 4.

Theseus, the Attic hero of legend, has put his left arm round Antiope, the queen of the Amazons, and lifted her off the ground in order to mount his chariot with her. He is naked save for a short cloak over his shoulders. In his right hand he held the horses' reins. The radiant expression on his face seems to mirror delight at his successful feat and the approaching happiness with his beloved. Antiope, who is making no effort to resist abduction, is wearing a short chiton and over it a close-fitting leather jacket, as was customary among the Amazons. The forms are rendered with great sculptural power and a highly refined sensuous charm. The hair of the two figures is modelled with particular decorative splendour and beauty. Theseus's is rather short and lies on the head in parallel waves running from the crown; it is rolled up at the nape of the neck and frames the brow and temples with several rows of individual curls. It was surmounted by a wreath made of bronze. Antiope's long hair, rendered in extremely fine individual waves, is parted in the middle, adorned with a diadem and turned back at the nape of the neck.

The two figures were carved from a single block of marble and attached to the wall of the pediment by a great right-angled dowel at the back. Theseus's right arm was joined on. The group with the team of horses comes from the right half of the pediment (as one looks at it). In the centre of the pediment stood Athene in chiton and cloak, armed with the aegis, bearing a great gorgoneion. The upper part of her body without the head has survived (Museum, Chalkis, No. 5, height 2′5″; 0.74 m.). To the left – corresponding to the group of Theseus and Antiope – we may assume that there was Peirithoös, Theseus's friend and companion, with his team of horses. In addition, both halves of the pediment contained Amazons shooting bows, of which traces remain. One of them, in a kneeling position and bending her bow, must have been carried off from Greece already in antiquity. Her torso was rediscovered in Rome in 1888, in the former Villa Ludovisi, and now stands in the Palazzo dei Conservatori, the Hall of Archaic Sculpture, No. 12 (H. Stuart Jones, *The Sculptures of the Palazzo dei Conservatori* [1926], Plate 81).

The style of the figures points to a sculptor from the Ionian islands and a date around 510 B.C. It has affinities with the Parian 'North-East-Master' from the Siphnian treasury at Delphi (48—55). It is distinguished by its softer, fuller and more sensuously mobile modelling from the harder and more sober manner of the roughly coeval master of the west pediment at Aegina (72—77).

J. Kuruniotis, Antike Denkmäler 3 (1914), plates 27—29. — *A. Furtwängler*, Ägina, 321 ff., fig. 259—260. — *E. Langlotz*, Frühgriechische Bildhauerschulen, 157 f. — *E. Buschor*, Frühgriechische Jünglinge, 135 f., fig. 154. — The connection between the Amazon torso from the Villa Ludovisi and the Eretria pediment was first recognized — independently, it is to be assumed — by *J. Konstantinu*, Athenische Mitteilungen 69/70, 1954/55 (1956), 41 ff., and *D. von Bothmer*, Amazons (1957), 125 ff.

69

ATHENE FROM THE OLD TEMPLE OF ATHENE ON THE ATHENIAN ACROPOLIS. Parian marble. Height of the whole figure 6′7″ (2 m.). The head was found on the Acropolis in 1863, further fragments in the same place in subsequent years. Acropolis Museum, Athens, No. 631.

The Old Temple of Athene between the Parthenon and the Erechtheum was restored by the Peisistratids in about 520 B.C., and furnished with pediment figures of marble in place of the earlier ones of limestone (26, I, II). The theme of one of the two pediments, probably the east pediment, was the struggle of the Olympian gods against the giants. The surviving remnants of the pediment figures are insufficient to enable us to form a detailed picture of the composition. The pediment probably contained a total of three two-figure groups together with a fallen giant in each corner. The figures are modelled like free sculpture.

In or near the centre stood Athene in a long chiton and with a cloak over her right shoulder lunging far over to the right (as seen by the spectator). In addition to the head reproduced here, extant fragments include parts of the upper body and the aegis, the left hand, the right foot and shank with the robe and the long, hanging folds of the cloak. Over her outstretched left arm she held the aegis as a weapon in the battle, while with the spear in her raised right hand she struck at a naked fallen giant at whom her downward gaze is directed. Her helmet is encircled by a flat band containing eighteen equidistant holes in which were set bronze rosettes of apotropaeic significance. The crest of the helmet, also of bronze, has been lost, as have the rosettes. The hair frames the clear brow in firm waves. It falls in long curves over the back and is loosened under the ears into thick strands that lie in front of the aegis. The ears are adorned with round discs that used to bear a metal decoration in the centre.

The Peisistratides assigned the new pediment sculptures on the Acropolis to one of the leading sculptors in Athens at that time. The head of Athene in this plate is not seen diagonally from its right side – the view it presented to anyone standing in front of the pediment – but from its left side, which was turned towards the pediment. It is here set against the head of Theseus from the Eretria pediment (68), a later work from the same decade. Both the Ionian-island artist's soft, gentle modelling that seems to bubble up from within, on the one hand, and the Attic sculptor's firmer, more concentrated forms and more intellectually determined and compact style, on the other, are typical products of two closely neighbouring provinces of Greek art in the late 6th century B.C.

H. Payne and *G. M. Young*, Archaic Marble Sculpture from the Acropolis, 52 ff., plate 35, 1—2; 36. — *H. Schrader*, Die Archaischen Marmorbildwerke von der Akropolis; 345 ff., No. 464, plate 185 ff. – *E. Langlotz* and *W. H. Schuchhardt*, Archaische Plastik auf der Akropolis, 61 ff.

70, III
GIRL IN SLEEVED CHITON AND CLOAK. Found on the

Athenian Acropolis, 1886 (the head) and 1888 (the torso). White to milky grey marble from Chios (?). Height 22.2" (55.5 cm.). Acropolis Museum, Athens, No. 675.

The flourishing Athens of the time of Peisistratus (560–527) and his sons (527–514/10) attracted a large number of sculptors and vase painters from abroad, especially from the East, whose activities were not without influence on the evolution of Attic art. Several statues by 6th-century Ionian-island and Eastern Greek artists have been found on the Athenian Acropolis, some of them imported into Attica, some produced in Athens itself.

To judge from its material and style, this little statue of a girl came from the island of Chios. It is valuable on account of its particularly well preserved painting. The slim, delicate figure wears a girded sleeved chiton – formerly dark blue, now almost completely green from oxidization – which she is holding aside with her left hand, and a light-coloured cloak over her right shoulder which is pinned together on the right upper arm and sewn together under the arm. On the figure's right side the folds of the cloak, starting from the gather on the upper arm, are rendered by fine wavy lines, in the same way as the thin material of the chiton. Round the throat the chiton has a single-colour border, at the bottom a broad red meander border enclosed in blue (now green). The cloak is studded with a pattern of fine blue spirals and red triangles and has a violet border containing a pattern of meanders and crosses likewise enclosed between blue (now green) edges.

The outstretched hand held a bowl or a votive offering. The neck is long and rounded, the head strikingly oval, the face with the long, oval chin, wide mouth and slanting almond eyes beneath the wide curve of the eyebrows, is curiously flat. The hair above the brow is rendered in beautiful sinuous waves, and above this in thick strings of beads emerging in rows from beneath the lower edge of a tall diadem. The upper part of the diadem contains seventeen holes for the attachment of a metal ornament and is painted in front with a red palmette-lotus ornament on a blue (now green) background. Behind and below the ears five thick pigtails emerge, of which the two at the back end on the shoulders, while the three others fall in front of the shoulders over the fore-arms and along the breast. Large round discs with a red volute pattern on a blue (now green) background decorate the ears. A green and red painted band encircles the neck.

Only the major contours of the back are sculptured. Like the top of the head that protrudes well above the diadem, the rear of the figure is smooth. The details of the hair that hangs far down over the back in a solid mass, and of the folds of the garments at the rear of the figure, must have been painted in.

In comparison with the more solidly constructed Attic statues of

3   West pediment of the so-called Temple of Aphaia on Aegina. Reconstruction. After E. Schmidt, in 'Du', January 1959, 23

4   East pediment of the so-called Temple of Aphaia on Aegina. Reconstruction. After Furtwängler, *Aegina* (1906)

girls from the Acropolis with their relatively harder modelling (43–45; 80, 81), this figure is softer, more sensuous, and more decorative in the varied treatment of the drapery and hair. The features are more animated, more expressive than those of the contemporaneous Attic korai. This distinguishes the statuette, which some writers have held to be a small-scale copy of a larger work from Chios, from the more opulent Parian figures, such as the caryatids from the Siphnian treasury at Delphi – which is a few decades older – or the pediment group from Eretria (66–68), which is of about the same date.

In the winged victory from the Acropolis we have a second work from the hand of the same master (Acropolis Museum, Athens, No. 693; H. Payne and G. M. Young, *Archaic Marble Sculpture from the Acropolis*, Plates 50, 4 and 120, 3–4; E. Langlotz, *Frühgriechische Bildhauerschulen*, Plate 84, b; H. Schrader, *Die archaischen Marmorbildwerke von der Akropolis*, 118, No. 68, Plate 88).

H. Payne and *G. M. Young* l. c. 31 and plate 49, 3–5; 50, 1–3. — *H. Schrader* l. c. 91 ff., No. 43, plate 60 f. and p. 35, group A. — *A. E. Raubitschek*, Dedications from the Athenian Acropolis (1949), 14 f., No. 9 and page 484 ff.

71
TOMBSTONE OF ARISTION. Pentelic marble. Height without base 8′ (2.4 m.). Found 1839 near Velanidesa in Attica. National Museum, Athens, No. 29.

The relief shows a warrior in absolute profile clad in a short chiton falling in narrow folds and equipped with breastplate, greaves and helmet. With his raised left hand he calmly holds the vertical lance, whose butt end rests on the ground. The slight inclination of the head intensifies the compactness of the composition. The tall stele was originally crowned at the top with a palmette. Of the rich painting the red in particular has been preserved, especially on the hair of head and beard, on the armour and on the background of the relief. In addition, the armour is decorated with ornamental patterns and with a lion's head incised on the foremost armour plate over the breast, obviously in imitation of bronze armour.

According to the inscription on the base, the stele marks the tomb of Aristion; according to the inscription on the projection on which the figure is standing it is the work of Aristocles. It is one of the finest and best preserved Attic tomb reliefs from the late 6th century B.C. The rich modelling of the surface and the subtlety of all the details have been admired for generations. The closest parallel to the treatment of the drapery-folds is to be found on the mature vases of Euphronios from the period round 510 B.C. Attempts to identify other works by the hand of Aristocles on the basis of their style have so far been unconvincing. All the

same, a few years ago a fragment of a base inscribed with the name Aristocles was found in the old city wall of Athens between the Ceramicus and the Hill of the Nymphs; it obviously must come from a further work by this sculptor (cf. *E. Vanderpool*, American Journal of Archaeology, 58, 1954, 231 Plate 43, fig. 2).

A. Conze, Die attischen Grabreliefs, vol. 1, No. 3, plate 2, 1. — *H. Schrader*, Aristokles, in: Die Antike 18, 1942, 95 ff., fig. 2—4.

72–77 and 82–87
PEDIMENT SCULPTURES FROM THE 'TEMPLE OF APHAIA' ON AEGINA. Parian marble. Glyptothek, Munich.

The figures come from a Doric temple on a high mountain falling steeply to the sea on the northern headland of the island of Aegina. The temple has a ground-plan of 95′ by 45′ (28.80 by 13.80 m.), with six columns on the short sides and twelve on the long. Most of the figures were found in 1811 in the immediate vicinity of the temple. They were acquired in 1813 by the then Crown Prince Ludwig of Bavaria, restored 1815–1817 by Thorwaldsen at Rome, and entered the Glyptothek, Munich, in 1828. Subsequent excavations in the sanctuary of Aphaia on Aegina in 1901 brought to light further fragments, which provided important information concerning the arrangement of the individual figures on the pediments. These fragments remained in Greece and are now in the National Museum, Athens.

The remains of three pediments have been discovered – an older east pediment and the west pediment, dating from c. 510 B.C., and a second east pediment that is some twenty years later in date than the first. The older east pediment, of which only comparatively few relics have been found, must have been damaged soon after completion and replaced by a new pediment in about 490 B.C. In every case the subject is mythical battles of Aeginetan heroes before Troy. Athene stood armed in the centre of the pediment, to be thought of as invisible to those fighting.

The west pediment (72–77), which is divided into two almost identical halves, contains thirteen figures in all – six on either side of the central figure of the goddess (73). To right and left of the centre was first of all a warrior lunging at an already staggering opponent. These were followed on either side by a kneeling archer (77) and a warrior (76) leaning forward in the act of thrusting a spear into his fallen adversary; finally the corners were occupied by a dying man (74, 75). The main line of movement in the triangular pediment runs from the centre to the corners. The style of the west pediment is characterized by the way in which the delicate figures are arranged almost like surface ornament, and by the studied treatment of the drapery and the artistic coiffures. The plastic shapes are firmly knit and full of inner life.

The later east pediment (82–87) contains eleven figures in all, that is, two less than the west pediment. Apart from the goddess Athene in the centre (82), we can identify only the figure of Hercules in the act of firing a bow (86, 87) – recognizable by the head of the Nemean lion, which he wears on his head like a helmet. Here again the figures on each side of the pediment were arranged in the same order: right and left of the centre a warrior bearing down with sword and spear upon a sinking foe; next on both sides a rescuer (83), who is coming to the victim's aid, a kneeling archer (86, 87), and in each corner a fallen warrior (84, 85). In comparison with the figures on the west pediment those on the later east pediment are not only distinguished by their larger proportions, but are also freer in their movements, more naturally spaced, and liberated from the rigidity that characterizes Archaic figures. A more coherent current of life seems to flow through them: they are the visible expression of a new organic conception of the human body and a new approach to monumental sculpture. Attention has often been drawn to the fact that there is a certain affinity between the comparatively hard and abstract forms of the pediment sculptures of Aegina, and the style of the Peloponnesian workshops. But, great as was the mastery of these sculptors in the handling of marble, it has been pointed out that they must have been most versed in bronze-casting.

The four figures each from the west pediment and the later east pediment at Munich here reproduced are:

From the west pediment

72, 73: Athene. Glyptothek No.74 (A 19). Height 5′6″ (1.68 m.).
74, 75: Fallen warrior, from the right-hand corner of the pediment. Glyptothek No. 79 (A 33). Length 4′2″ (1.59 m.), height 1′6″ (0.47 m.). The right shank between knee and foot, and the right fore-arm, have been restored.
76: Lunging warrior from the left half of the pediment (as one looks at it). Glyptothek No. 80 (A 14). Height 3′6″ (1.43 m.). The legs have been restored.
77: Archer in Scythian dress, from the left half of the pediment. Glyptothek No. 81 (A 8). Height 3′5″ (1.04 m.).

From the east pediment

82: Head of Athene. Glyptothek No. 89 (A 65). Height 1′ (0.31 m.).
83: Rescuer from the right half of the pediment. Glyptothek No. 88 (A 82). Height 3′1″ (0.97 m.). Arm and nose restored.
84, 85: Fallen warrior, from the left-hand corner of the pediment. Glyptothek No. 85 (A 41). Length 6′ (1.85 m.), height 2′ (0.64 m.). The right leg has been restored.
86, 87: Hercules firing a bow, from the right half of the pediment. Glyptothek No. 84 (A 86). Height 2′6″ (0.79 m.). Left shank, left hand, right forearm and the front half of the right foot have been restored.

A. Furtwängler, Ägina. Das Heiligtum der Aphaia. Text und Tafeln, München 1906: summarizing: A. Furtwängler, Die Ägineten der Glyptothek König Ludwigs I. (München 1906) and G. Welter, Ägina (Berlin 1938), 64 ff. — On the reconstruction of west pediment see also E. Schmidt, Bericht über den VI. Internationalen Kongreß für Archäologie, Berlin 1939, 374 f., plate 35, a.

78

METOPE FROM THE TEMPLE OF HERA AT THE MOUTH OF THE SELE (Silaris, north of Poseidonia [Paestum]). Sandstone. Museum, Paestum.

The Doric temple in the sacred district of Hera at the mouth of the River Sele, which forms the boundary between Campania and Lucania, was uncovered by the Italian excavations between 1934 and 1940. It was a limestone building with a surface area of 127′ by 60′ (38.56 by 18.32 m.) surrounded by eight columns ont he short, and seventeen columns on the long side. The pediments had as little sculptural decoration as the temples at Poseidonia (Paestum). Only a small part of the metopes has been found. Of these, five constitute a series with a common theme, representing a ritual dance by girls or women. Four metopes show two figures each, moving in a dance step one behind the other from left to right. A fifth metope bears a single dancing woman who is looking back over her shoulder, thereby creating a link with the neighbouring metope.

The best preserved metope shows women dancing in pairs (78). Maximum height 2′10″ (85 cm.) maximum width 2′4½″ (71.6 cm.). Both women are dressed in the long sleeved-chiton with a cloak over their shoulders and have their left arm raised to the front. Their long hair is divided horizontally and vertically and adorned with a diadem. The foremost dancer has her left hand open with the palm to the front, while with her right she holds up her chiton so that the drapery shall not impede her in dancing. The second figure has her left arm stretched further out. The raised left hand is broken off at the wrist. The palm of the hand was probably turned towards the face. Traces on the broad fillet suggest that it held a flower between thumb and forefinger.

The metopes must have been carved by Italo-Greek sculptors in the last decade of the 6th century B.C. The stylistic relationship to Ionian-island and Eastern Ionian sculpture is evident in the opulent and rounded forms of the bodies, the sensuously decorative treatment of the hair and garments, and the festally joyful expression of the heads. At the same time, the heavy fluidity of the shapes betrays an affinity with the Late Archaic metopes in the temple at Selinus in Sicily.

P. Zancani Montuoro and U. Zanotti-Bianco, Heraion alle Foce del Sele I (1951), 123 ff., plate 41 ff.

79

METOPE FROM THE ATHENIAN TREASURY AT DELPHI. Parian marble. Delphi, Museum, Inv. 2027.

A bare twenty years after the Siphnian treasury was completed (48–55), the Athenians also built a new treasury at Delphi. It was constructed of Parian marble and shaped like a small Doric temple *in antis* with an approximately square cella. Like the Siphnian treasury it stood by the Sacred Way, but closer to the temple terrace, and faced east. It was excavated during the 1890's and rebuilt out of the original fragments at the beginning of the present century. The statement by Pausanias (X, 11, 5) that the treasury of the Athenians was built after the battle of Marathon is clearly based on an error. Pausanias was misled by the inscription on a plinth which projects from the south side of the treasury, but was built on later and served as a base for a group of statuary depicting arms taken as booty at Marathon. In reality the Athenian treasury must be assumed on stylistic grounds to date from the last years of the 6th century B.C. It may be linked with the victories of the Athenians under Kleisthenes over the Boeotians and Chalcidians.

The building was embellished with thirty metopes in all. The nine metopes on each of the long sides portrayed the deeds of Hercules (on the north) and of Theseus (on the south). The six metopes on the front showed Theseus fighting the Amazons; the six metopes on the west face depicted Hercules plundering the cattle of Geryon. Each metope, together with a triglyph, is carved from a single block of marble 26.8" (67.1 cm.) high and 3'6" (1.022 m.) long. Each metope is 25" (63 cm.) in length.

The over-all design of the metopes is probably that of a single artist. The execution however, is the work of many hands. Much as the individual metopes may differ, even in composition, in the size of the figures and in detail, they all share the same exuberant beauty of sculptural form, the same firmness and expressiveness of the modelling, the same clear and anatomically precise portrayal of the naked male body and the same method of treating drapery. Their style suggests a date close to that of the sculptures on the west pediment of the 'Temple of Aphaia' on Aegina (72–77) and of the vases of the mature Euphronius and the early 'Panaitios painter'.

Our picture shows one of the best preserved metopes from the north face – Hercules slaying the hind.

J. Audiat, Le Trésor des Athéniens = Fouilles de Delphes II, 1 (1933), ref. do. H. Schleif, Gnomon 11, 1935, 65 ff. — Fouilles de Delphes IV, plates 38—48. — E. Langlotz, Zur Zeitbestimmung der strengrotfiguren Vasenmalerei und der gleichzeitigen Plastik, 69 ff. — P. de la Coste-Messelière, Bulletin de Correspondance Hellénique 47, 1923, 396 ff. — K. Schefold, Kleisthenes, in: Museum Helveticum 3, 1946, 72 ff. — W. B. Dinsmoor, The Athenian Treasury as dated by its Ornament, in: American Journal of Archaeology 50, 1946, 86 ff. — H. Kähler, Das griechische Metopenbild, 102 ff., plates 42—51.

80–81

STANDING GIRL IN LONG CHITON AND CLOAK. Parian marble. Height 3' (0.92 m.). Found on the Athenian Acropolis, 1888. Acropolis Museum, Athens, No. 674.

This figure is one of the finest of the statues of girls, belonging to the mature Archaic period, which stood on the Acropolis as votive offerings to Athene. The brightly coloured painting, which in this case is well preserved, lends the statue particular value.

The body is very delicate and slender, the sloping shoulders are narrow, the neck is strikingly long. The right fore-arm, which was stretched out in front, was attached separately. The right hand no doubt held a bowl or votive offering. The thin material of the sleeved chiton covers the upper part of the body in fine, parallel wavy folds. On the lower part it falls in long curves and is held to one side by the left hand. Over the chiton is draped a cloak of heavy woollen material that is fastened on the right shoulder and hangs diagonally across the breast with an over-fold. It veils the body in long vertical folds that are tiered at the edges. The face is a long oval within the framework formed by the loose curls of the hair, which is adorned with a diadem and falls far down at the back in glorious tresses divided horizontally. Three long curly strands come forward from behind the ears on each side and cling closely to the contours of the shallow breasts. Large round discs adorn the ears.

The sculptor, one of the greatest Attic masters of the last phase of the 6th century B.C., handled his chisel with consummate artistry: the physical properties of the various garments and the different parts of the coiffure are reproduced with marvellous fidelity. The individual, pensive expression of the gentle face with the slanting eyes covered by heavy lids is typical of the period around 500 B.C., when great interest was shown in the portrayal of the special and unique quality of the individual. The mouth, which passes without any sharply defined delimitation into the soft and mobile contours of chin and cheek, no longer exhibits the old Archaic smile.

The chiton is dark green with red stripes on the braiding of the sleeves, the cloak is painted with green, blue and red rosettes and at the lower edge with a meander trimming of green and red. Traces of green have remained on the frilly over-folded border that runs diagonally across the breast. The hair is red and yellow, the brows, lids and pupils are black, the iris brown with a black margin. The blue disc on each ear bears a red rosette, the diadem a blue meander pattern with red dots enclosed between green stripes.

H. Payne and G. M. Young, Archaic Marble Sculpture from the Acropolis, 34 f., plates 75—78. — H. Schrader, Die archaischen Marmorbildwerke von der Akropolis, No. 44, plates 62—67. — E. Langlotz and W. H. Schuchhardt, Archaische Plastik auf der Akropolis, 26 ff.

II. THE SEVERE STYLE

500—450 B.C.

88

STANDING YOUTH. Supposedly from Lemnos (Anaphi), the south-easternmost of the larger Cyclades Islands. Parian marble. Height 3'4" (1.01 m.). British Museum, London, B. 475. From the collection of the Sixth Viscount Strangford, 1864.

This figure deviates from the strict system of the Archaic statues in so far as its weight is no longer evenly distributed on both legs. A slight distinction is made between the right supporting leg and the left which merely balances the figure; the arms, too, no longer lay along the sides, but were stretched out in front. But the rest of the body hardly shares in this movement and the upper part is presented in a squarely frontal posture, which gives the whole figure a certain stiffness. The modelling is executed in planes and the abdominal muscles are markedly flat. The line of the pelvis curves far back on either side and constitutes a relatively abrupt division between the thighs and the trunk. The hips are narrow and boyish, the chest and back, by contrast, muscular and powerful. The strong pectoral muscles mark a new stage in the representation of the body. The shoulders are broad. The head is perched on the thick, unjointed neck in a strictly frontal position. The wide-open eyes gaze from between firmly outlined lids, the mouth is horizontal and the lips finely curved. The hair clings closely to the head in parallel waves starting from the spine, frames the forehead and temples in two rows of large, individually distinct, tight curls, which become three rows above the ears, and is turned up over a circlet at the back.

The figure may have been carved in the period between the later east pediment (82–87) of the 'Temple of Aphaia' on Aegina (c. 490) and the boy from the Acropolis (89–91) (towards 480), but it differs from the Aeginetan and Attic works by a severity and even stiffness of posture in excess of what was usual at that period, and an emphasis on planes and lines in the sculptural treatment. Because of this, it has been associated with Boeotian sculptures.

C. Friedrichs-P. Wolters, Bausteine zur Geschichte der griechisch-römischen Plastik, No. 89. — E. Langlotz, Frühgriechische Bildhauerschulen, 185. — R. Lullies, Jahrbuch des Deutschen Archäologischen Instituts, 51, 1936, 145 f. — G. M. A. Richter, Kouroi, 228, No. 134, plate 109, fig. 377—379.

89–91

STANDING BOY. Parian marble. Height 2'9" (0.86 m.). The body was found on the Athenian Acropolis in 1865, the head in 1888, also on the Acropolis but at a different spot. But it has been repeatedly and rightly stressed that there can be no doubt as to the connexion between the two fragments. Acropolis Museum, Athens, No. 698.

The figure cannot have been standing on the Athenian citadel for more than a very short time, when the Persians destroyed the Acropolis in 480 B.C. Stylistically it belongs among the latest works from the so-called 'Persian rubble'. The boy, who has been recognized as a victor in the Panathenaea, the great festival of Athene, stands calmly and confidently. The right leg is bent at the knee, the right thigh thrust forward, the shank placed slightly to the side and to the back, so that the displacement of the weight on to the left leg is also expressed in the upper part of the body and the relation between the axes is shifted a little. The upper arms were drawn back, the left rather more than the right; the forearms were slightly raised from the elbow. The head is turned to the right. The eyes, which were inlaid with coloured material, gazed ahead self-confidently. The hair lies on the head in fine waves running from the crown of the head, and is taken up over a circlet. The down on the nape of the neck is arranged in alternating curls and straight wisps.

The modelling of the body is extremely lively. The stylistic affinity of the head to the Harmodios from the bronze group of the tyrannicides by Kritios and Nesiotes, which was erected in the market-place at Athens in 477 B.C. and has come down to us in marble copies dating from the time of the Roman Empire, led soon after the statue's discovery to its being called the 'Kritios boy' (*vide* most recently: Sture Brunnsaker, *The Tyrant-Slayers of Kritios and Nesiotes*, Lund, 1955). Whether this boy is correctly attributed to Kritios remains an open question that does not affect the importance of the work, whose beauty raises it above the conflict of opinion. The importance of this statue – executed by one of the leading Attic masters in about 480 B.C. – consists above all in the fact that it is a splendid example of the new distribution of weight which was a precondition for the perfectly poised Classical figure.

H. Payne and G. M. Young, Archaic Marble Sculpture from the Acropolis, 44 f., plates 109—112. — H. Schrader, Die archaischen Marmorbildwerke von der Akropolis, No. 299, plates 120—123. — E. Langlotz and W. H. Schuchhardt, Archaische Plastik auf der Akropolis, 42 ff. — E. Homann-Wedeking, Athenische Mitteilungen 60/61, 1935/1936, 203 f. and 212 f., remarks 2 and 3.

92–95

APOLLO. Found in 1832 in the sea off Piombino (in Etruria opposite Elba). Bronze. Height 3'9" (1.15 m.). Louvre, Paris, No. 2 (Inv. 61). Acquired in 1834.

According to the remains of a votive inscription in the Dorian dialect, which has been preserved in inlaid silver letters under the bronze's left foot, it was presented to Athene as a tithe. There can be no doubt that, despite the figure's extreme youth, it represents the god Apollo himself, for the boy held a bow and arrow in his left hand. The right hand held an offering bowl. In its frontal pose with one foot advanced the figure follows the Archaic pattern, but a slight loosening of all the parts, the slight outward turn of the left leg, and the inclination – small though it is – of the head, indicate that the bronze stands at the end of the evolution of the early Greek youth and in fact has already passed beyond the fixed severity of Archaic sculpture.

On long, thin legs there rises a relatively broad, unathletic torso, showing but little jointing, with broad, square shoulders carrying a short, heavy neck topped by a gentle, almost delicate, boy's head with a fine, pensive expression. The hair lies close to the head in waves running from the crown. In front it is rolled into two rows of curls over the forehead and it is bound into a projecting bundle at the back.

The votive inscription shows that the bronze originated within the Dorian orbit. The suggestion has been made that it is the work of a Sicyonian artist; but the disunity that arises from mingling the old-fashioned, stiff type of figure with the later mobility and from combining narrow, tall and sharply defined parts of the body with others that are heavier, softer and more flatly modelled rather suggests that we have here an example of toreutic art from a Dorian district of southern Italy or Sicily. This Greek master would then have created the image of the boy Apollo, perhaps as early as the second quarter of the 5th century B.C., in the style of mainland Greek models but under conditions of provincial backwardness and also drawing upon Italian sources.

The eyes were inserted in coloured material. The brows that rise in a wide arc from the root of the nose, the soft lips, and the nipples with their areola, are inlaid in copper.

A. de Ridder, Les Bronzes Antiques du Louvre 1 (1913), No. 2, plate 2. — E. Langlotz, Frühgriechische Bildhauerschulen, 32, No. 30, plates 1 and 19.— K. A. Pfeiff, Apollon (1943), 59 ff., plate 18. — E. Buschor, Frühgriechische Jünglinge, 154 ff., fig. 179 f.

96

RELIEF OF A BOY VICTOR. Found in the sanctuary of Athene at Sunium (Attica) in 1915. Parian marble. Height 24.4" (61 cm.), width 19.6" (49 cm.). National Museum, Athens, No. 3344.

The fragment is part of a tall, rectangular stele that was crowned at the top by a palmette ornament. The relief depicts a standing boy, approximately half life-size, and was donated as a votive offering in gratitude for his victory in a contest. With the thumb and forefinger of the right hand – a gesture that is typical of the early 5th century B.C. and occurs with great frequency during this period – he is placing on his head the victor's wreath of precious metal, which in this case was attached by pegs in large holes in the hair below the circlet. The upper part of the body is presented almost in front view, with the left arm drawn back. The sinews above the wrist are tense, as though the boy was originally holding a heavy object in this hand — most likely something connected with athletics. The head, which is turned sideways and slightly bowed, is set on a short, thick neck; the face wears a serious expression. The full, gently rounded chin curves up towards the smooth cheek. The soft, youthful mouth is slightly open, the large eye beneath its flat brow is bordered by heavy lids. Part of the hair is knotted over the forehead, the rest falls from the temple in symmetrical waves, covering the ear. Above the circlet the hair was rendered only by paint.

The thickset, quietly mobile body stood out in gentle curves from the background, on which traces of light blue pigment remain. The modelling leads in gentle transitions from areas of powerful muscle to clearly marked sinews and slender joints. The relief was carved soon after 480 B.C., a few years later than the statue of a boy from the Athenian Acropolis (89–91). At this period, due to Kleisthenes's law concerning luxuries, there were no sepulchral stelae in Attica. The soft modelling of the body is doubtless attributable to the influence of Ionian-island relief sculpture on the Attic master. The head, on the other hand, recalls in its pensive earnestness and in the construction of its individual forms the 'Blond head', which comes from an Attic statue of a victor. (Acropolis Museum, Athens, No. 689. H. Payne and G. M. Young, *Archaic Marble Sculpture from the Acropolis*, Plates 113–15. H. Schrader, *Die archaischen Marmorbildwerke von der Akropolis*, 197 f., No. 302, Plates 125–26.)

V. Stais, Deltion Archailogikon 2, 1916, Beiblatt 78 and the same, Archaiologiki Ephimeris 1917, 204 ff. — *F. Studniczka*, Archäologischer Anzeiger 1921, 326 ff. — *E. Langlotz*, Frühgriechische Bildhauerschulen, 155, No. 20; 162 f., plate 11.

97–101

ENTHRONED GODDESS. Found at Taranto. Parian marble. Height 5' (1.51 m.). State Museum, Berlin, Department of Classical Antiquities A 17 (Inv. 1761). Acquired in 1915.

The goddess sits in a solemn pose, with upright body and looking straight ahead, on a large, richly decorated throne with seat and back cushions. The sandalled feet rest on a high stool that stands on lion's claws. The fore-arms are bent forward. The right hand held an offering bowl, the left perhaps a flower or fruit. The body is draped in three garments: a long sleeved-chiton reaching down to the feet, a diagonal cloak that is held together over the right arm with six clasps and whose ends fall over the knees in zigzag folds, and a fine shawl that covers the back and parts of the arms and whose long ends fall over the seat of the throne on either side, also in zigzag folds. The tightly waved hair is parted over the centre of the forehead. It is bound up inside a cloth at the back and ends on either side in three long wavy plaits over the breast. Round the hair on the brow lies a circlet and above this a diadem with holes for the insertion of metal ornaments. The ears were adorned with pendants that were likewise of bright metal and whose glitter enhanced the luminosity of the painted colours.

The type of the enthroned goddess, and the severity of the essentially frontal composition, suggest that the statue is one of the few Greek religious images surviving from the Late Archaic period. As to the goddess's identity, she is probably Persephone or Hera, or possibly Aphrodite. The loose, material treatment of the clothing and hair, and the gently rounded face, recur in a similar form in the sculpture of Magna Graecia, early in the 5th century B.C. The statue must have been made at Taranto in about 480 B.C.

There it came to light again in 1911 in a 13-foot pit where it had been placed — probably during the wars of the Romans against Taranto in the 3rd century B.C. — as a precautionary measure.

Th. Wiegand, Antike Denkmäler 3, 1916/17, 45 ff., plates 37—44. — *F. Noack*, Archäologischer Anzeiger 1917, 119 ff. — *C. Blümel*, Griechische Skulpturen des 6. und 5. Jahrh. v. Chr. = Katalog der Sammlung antiker Skulpturen in Berlin (1940), II, 1, A 17, plates 33—39. — *E. Langlotz*, Archäologischer Anzeiger 1957, 359 f.

102–104, IV

CHARIOTEER. Found in the sanctuary of Apollo at Delphi in 1896. Bronze. Height 5'11" (1.8 m.). Museum, Delphi, Inv. 3484 and 3540.

The life-size figure belonged to a quadriga that was erected on the temple terrace at Delphi as a votive offering for victory in a chariot race. Apart from the charioteer, remains of the chariot, the shaft and the yoke, fragments of the horses' hind legs and a tail have been found. The life-size team must have been depicted at the moment of starting — as was the smaller quadriga from Olympia (106).

The charioteer was made up of seven parts, each cast separately: the feet, the lower body up to the belt, the upper body to the middle of the neck, the head, and the two arms. The victor stood in the chariot in racing garb — a long chiton belted at the waist and tied at the sleeves by bands that cross at the back — his feet pointing in the direction in which he was driving, the upper part of his body turned to the right and his head still more so. The drapery of thick cloth completely hides the body from the belt downwards beneath heavy tubular folds, giving it a curiously severe, columnar appearance. In this connexion, it is important to realize that originally the lower part of the body was largely concealed by the coach-work of the chariot. The hands held the reins, and the right also the *kentron*, the pointed rod for spurring on the horses.

A broad band with an inlaid meander pattern tied at the back adorns the hair, which lies flat on the head and neck in chiselled locks, ending in larger, more sculpturally treated curls at the temples only, where the short down of side-whiskers can be seen beneath them. The cheeks arch in a wide, gentle curve from the flat, broad eyebrows and high cheekbones across the long lower jaw to the full chin. The right side is more richly and finely modelled than the left, which, taken in conjunction with the twist of the upper body and the slightly asymmetrical construction of the face, shows that the figure was intended to be looked at diagonally from its right side. This, too, is the direction in which the eyes of coloured inlay gaze steadily above the outstretched right hand. The muscular arm and the vigorous, powerful hand are modelled in the same sweeping and gentle curves as the face.

A votive inscription on a rectangular block in the base, which likewise is in the Delphi Museum (Inv. 3517), names the donor of the quadriga as the tyrant Polyzalos of Gela (in Sicily). A sculptor's inscription by Sotades of Thespiai (in Boeotia), which has also been associated with the base of the quadriga, seems not to have belonged to it, since — apart from the difference between the characters of the scripts — the style of the charioteer is difficult to reconcile with the picture we have of Boeotian sculpture during the first half of the 5th century B.C. The heavily fluid treatment of the drapery and the austere ideal of beauty revealed in the head, suggest that the bronze's closest affinities are with Sicilian and southern Italian sculpture, such as the colossal head of a goddess in the Museo delle Terme (E. Paribeni, *Sculture Greche del V Secolo*, No. 1), the metopes from Selinus (126–129) or the great acrolithic head of Athene in the Vatican (E. Langlotz, *Frühgriechische Bildhauerschulen*, Plate 92 f.). The charioteer occupies a place among them as an important masterpiece of the period around 470 B.C. The Geloan prince must have commissioned a local artist to execute the memorial to his victory. Even if we disregard stylistic considerations, it is unlikely that an artist from the provinces should have been called in for such a representative monument.

R. *Hampe*, Text to Brunn-Bruckmann, Denkmäler griechischer und römischer Skulptur, plates 786 ff. — F. *Chamoux*, L'Aurige, Fouilles de Delphes IV, 5 (Paris 1955).

105, V

ZEUS ABDUCTING GANYMEDE. Terra-cotta. Height, including the 4.6" base, 3'7" (1.097 m.). The isolated parts of the group were found during the German excavations at Olympia in various places between 1878 and 1952. Museum, Olympia.

Because of his beauty, Ganymede, the son of a Trojan king, was abducted by Zeus who bestowed upon him eternal youth and kept him on Olympus as a cupbearer. The group shows Zeus hurrying along with the gentle boy clasped firmly in his right arm. The boy had placed his own right arm on his abductor's – the fingers of his right hand are still to be seen on the latter's wrist. In his left hand he carries a love-gift in the shape of a cock. Zeus has cast his flowing cloak about his left arm and waist. As he hastens, his left leg parts the cloak while only the toes of his right foot are on the ground. His radiant face is turned to the left in the direction of his goal. His left arm has gathered up the cloak and holds a knotted stick. The impression of swift running, and even a feeling of flying through limitless space, is enhanced by the floating posture of Ganymede, who seems to be pressing himself willingly against the god and whose legs hang free in the air. The boy looks downwards before him with a happily pensive expression. The finely divided hair shadows the face with its locks like an awning of leaves; held round the head by a circlet, it falls back and down on to Zeus's right shoulder like a wave. The god's coiffure is compacter, in keeping with the large, full face of the older man. The forehead is framed by three rows of knobbly curls and at the back the hair is turned under into a firm roll; a circlet decorated whith olive leaves runs round the head. The face is framed by the semicircle of a beard.

The configuration of the individual forms is very similar in both faces, but the expression clearly shows the difference between old and young, conscious and unconscious. The distinction is also manifest in the choice of colours. Zeus's cloak and the circlet in his hair are painted a strong brownish red, the hair of his head and beard, his eyebrows and lashes, his pupils, and the borders of his cloak (which are decorated on the outside with a pattern of winged horses), deep black with a bluish shimmer. Ganymede's brows and lashes, on the other hand, are pale brown, as is the bunch of short hair protruding from beneath the roll of hair on Zeus's neck. The cock's comb and individual feathers, and the god's lips, are dull red. All unclothed parts of the body were

probably painted yellow – Ganymede's a lighter yellow than Zeus's.

The crackle that covers the surface, especially Ganymede's head, was caused by the fact that after the group's discovery the fine outer clay unavoidably dried more quickly than the coarser centre, and cracked from the resulting tension.

The group, one of the few and at the same time one of the finest and best preserved larger Greek terra-cotta sculptures from the 5th century B.C., was modelled by a Peloponnesian artist around 470. The clay is Corinthian. It is not known whether it occupied at Olympia the position of a central acroterion on the roof of a small temple or treasury, or whether it was a votive offering standing on its own; the architectural function is the more likely one. Recent suggestions that the group represents Poseidon carrying off Pelops, or King Laios abducting Chrisippus, the son of Pelops, are improbable and have rightly been discounted.

E. *Kunze*, Zeus und Ganymedes, 100. Berliner Winckelmannsprogramm, 1940. — The same, Neue Meisterwerke griechischer Kunst aus Olympia (1948), 28 ff., fig. 63—69 and 5. Bericht über die Ausgrabungen in Olympia (1956), 103 ff., plates 54—63. — R. *Hampe*, in Gymnasium, Zeitschrift für Kultur der Antike und humanistische Bildung 66, 1959, 41 ff. — H. *Sichtermann*, Zeus und Ganymed in frühklassischer Zeit, in Antike Kunst, Biannual, Olten/Switz., 2, 1959, 10 ff.

106

HORSE FROM A QUADRIGA. Found during the German excavations at Olympia in the winter of 1938/39. Bronze, cast solid. Height 9" (22.8 cm.). National Museum, Athens.

The quadriga to which this horse belonged was the votive offering from a victor in the Olympic chariot races. Only the two hind fetlocks and hooves and the tail are still missing, otherwise it has been preserved in all its rare perfection and beauty. The firm, smooth surface has a dull, dark gleam. The powerfully built animal is wearing a snaffle and halter which are joined by narrow thongs. On the front of the breast-girth is engraved a rosette that possessed apotropaeic significance, that is to say, it warded off misfortune and brought luck. Behind the waist-girth stood an upright ring through which the reins were drawn. The left leg is thrust forward, the head turned slightly outwards to the left. Judging by the posture of the body, the slant of the ring and the position of the tightly knotted bows on the waist-girth and halter on the left side, this horse was on the extreme left of the team of four.

Although torn out of its context, the horse is a work of art with a life of its own and its expressive pose enables us to form an idea of the votive offering as a whole. The taut, gathered posture is typical of the moment of maximum concentration immediately before the start. The tense left foreleg is already advanced as though in the act of moving off. The head with the dilated nostrils, the great, wide-open eyes and pricked-up, listening ears is drawn slightly back and seems to be waiting excitedly for the reins to be released as a sign to begin the race. The splendid, regular mane curves in a tapering arc from the top of the head to the back. The thick tuft of hair over the forehead balances the tail in the composition.

With its cylindrical body, short, thick neck, and powerful head, the stallion seems to belong to a heavy breed. But the effect it creates is not one of coarseness but of fiery beauty. The simple, sweeping construction, in which individual parts are rendered with

5 East pediment of the Temple of Zeus at Olympia. Reconstruction. After Studniczka

great liveliness and combined to constitute a few large forms and surfaces, makes this magnificent animal statue a self-contained sculptural unit. It is a Peloponnesian, probably Argive, work from the period around 470 B.C.

E. Kunze and *H. Schleif*, Dritter Bericht über die Ausgrabungen in Olympia (Winter 1938/39), 133 ff., plates 59—64. — *E. Kunze*, Neue Meisterwerke griechischer Kunst aus Olympia, 31, fig. 74—75.

107–125
METOPES AND PEDIMENTAL SCULPTURES FROM THE TEMPLE OF ZEUS AT OLYMPIA. Found during the German excavations from 1875 to 1881. Height of the metopes, 5'3" (1.6 m.); length of the pediments, 87' (26.4 m.), height 10'10" (3.3 m.). Museum, Olympia, and Louvre, Paris.

The Temple of Zeus at Olympia was completed in 456 B.C. Assuming it took some fifteen years to build, it must have been started in 470. The building of this stupendous edifice was doubtless due not least to the newly established sense of the solidarity of the Greek people following the decisive battles of Marathon, Salamis and Plataea. It was a Doric temple surrounded by six columns at the ends and thirteen columns at the sides. The architecture was of limestone, finished down and painted. The sculptures were executed in Parian marble. According to tradition the architect was Libon of Elis. The colossal gold and ivory image of Zeus Enthroned, which perished during Late Antiquity, was made by Phidias, and it was chiefly through this statue – together with the only slightly older image of Athena Parthenos – that he gained his unparalleled reputation as a sculptor of religious images.

The subject of the *metopes* was the twelve labors accomplished by Hercules, the Peloponnesian legendary hero, at the command of Eurystheus. Six each were depicted high up on the front and rear exterior walls of the cella, the hall for the image in the interior of the temple. They are earlier in date than the pediments on the corresponding faces. The eastern metopes are the oldest.

The *east pediment* portrayed the preparations for the chariot race between Oenomaus and Pelops, the mythological model for

the chariot races at Olympia. According to the legend, Oenomaus, King of Pisa in Elis, was only willing to give his daughter Hippodameia in marriage to someone who had beaten him in a chariot race. Any competitor who failed to defeat him was condemned to death. Oenomaus felt capable of vanquishing any suitor with the swift steeds given him by Ares. Thirteen suitors had already lost their lives when Pelops of the tribe of Tantalus appeared. Poseidon had given him a golden chariot and horses with nevertiring wings. Hippodameia fell violently in love with Pelops and bribed Myrtilos, her father's charioteer, to take the nails out of his chariot hubs. Thus Oenomaus came to grief and Pelops became king in Elis.

In the centre of the east pediment – invisible to the other figures and towering above them – stands the tall form of Zeus. On his left hand, which held the lightning, stood Pelops and Hippodameia, on his right Oenomaus and his wife Sterope. These are followed on both sides by their quadrigas, facing the centre of the pediment. In front of Pelops's quadriga kneels a girl, in front of Oenomaus's a boy. The reins of Oenomaus's quadriga are held by the charioteer Myrtilos. Behind the quadriga of Pelops is a bearded seer, and towards each corner the crouching figure of a youth. In each of the corners is a reclining figure. Later generations of antiquity regarded these figures as symbolizing the deities of the two rivers of Olympia – the left (southern) being Alpheios and the right (northern) Cladeos. Latterly they have been interpreted as representing grooms.

The composition portrays the moment immediately before the start. A sense of tremendous and calamitous tension fills the whole pediment and joins the figures of the two halves into a powerful dramatic unity.

The *west pediment*, stylistically later than the east pediment, depicts the combat of the Lapithae with the Centaurs on the occasion of the marriage of the Lapithan King Peirithoös to Hippodameia, the daughter of the Lapithan Atrax. According to the legend, the Attic hero Theseus and the Centaurs, mythical beings half horse and half man, were invited to the wedding.

6 West pediment of the Temple of Zeus at Olympia. Reconstruction. After G. Treu

73

During the festivities, heated by wine, they sought to violate the women and boys of the Lapithae and were laid low by Theseus, Peirithoös and the other Lapithae — order and the spiritual combatting wild, unbridled instincts. In the centre of this pediment stands the towering apparition of Apollo, the god who brought victory to the Lapithae. He was framed by two mighty three-figure groups: on the left (as one looks at it), Peirithoös lunges with his sword; on the right, Theseus lunges with an axe at a Centaur, who in the right-hand group (as one looks at it) has seized a struggling Lapithan woman with his left arm, while in the left-hand group, which includes Peirithoös himself, he grasps at the bride with his right arm. Each of these groups is followed by a two-figure group of a Lapith and a Centaur, and then a magnificently interlocked three-figure group with a Centaur who has fallen to his knees in the centre. Finally each of the corners is occupied by two reclining Lapithan women.

The two pediments form a mighty contrast: in the east, brooding, ominous quiet before the catastrophe; in the west, fierce, bitter conflict at its climax. Nevertheless, the two pediments and the twelve metopes must be the work of a single outstanding master, probably a Peloponnesian, in whose style trends and influences from other Greek provinces are visible, especially Ionian-island art with its centre at Paros.

The execution of the pediments — doubtless from life-size models by the designing artist — was entrusted to four other sculptors in addition to the chief master. In the metopes, too, the hands of several executants may be distinguished.

The sculptures have been set up in the Olympia Museum in such a way that in the east pediment the figures of Oenomaus and Sterope on the one hand, and Pelops and Hippodameia on the other, have been reversed in their position beside Zeus, so that — contrary to the significance of the scene — Pelops and Hippodameia are standing in front of Oenomaus's chariot instead of their own. Among the figures of the west pediment, too, two groups in the middle have been reversed in the present arrangement in the Olympia Museum, namely those flanking Apollo. Peirithoös, with sword raised to strike the Centaur who has grasped the bride, should stand to Apollo's right; Theseus, flinging the axe at a Centaur who has seized a Lapithan woman with his forelegs, should stand to the god's left.

Plates 110–125 show the following figures (described by the letters used in the reconstructions presented in Figures 5 and 6):

East pediment

110   Centre: Zeus (G) and — wrongly placed on the god's left instead of his right — Oenomaus (F) and — on the god's right instead of his left — Pelops (H)
111   On the left-hand side of the plate, Sterope (E), who ought to be standing in the other half of the pediment next to Oenomaus. On the left-hand side of the figure (in its original position) Pelops's quadriga. In front of it the girl (K)
112   Myrtilos (C), from Oenomaus's quadriga, in the southern half of the pediment
113   Crouching youth (M) from the northern half of the pediment
114, 115   The seer (L) from the northern half of the pediment
116   'Cladeos' (N) from the northern corner of the pediment

West pediment

117   Reclining Lapithan woman (A) from the northern corner of the pediment
118   Above: Northern triad (C, D, E)
       Below: Southern triad (R, S, T)
       In both groups a Centaur is attacking a Lapithan woman and is being assailed in turn by a Lapith
119   Lapithan woman (E) from the northern triad
120   The bride (H) of Peirithoös (K) attacked by a Centaur (J)
121   The bride (H)
122, 123   Apollo (L)
124   Southern dyad: Biting Centaur (P) and Lapith (Q) in combat
125   Lapithan woman (R) from the southern triad; cf. Plate 118 below

E. Buschor and R. Hamann, Die Skulpturen des Zeustempels zu Olympia. Text and plates, 1924. The text, somewhat abbreviated and without the references, is reprinted in: E. Buschor, Von griechischer Kunst, 65 ff. See also: E. Kunze and U. Jantzen, Zu den Skulpturen des Zeustempels, in: IV. Bericht über die Ausgrabungen in Olympia (1944), 143 ff. — E. Buschor, Die Olympiameister, in: Athenische Mitteilungen 51, 1926, 163 ff. — L. Alscher, Kompositionsgesetze der Olympiameister, in: Mitteilungen des Deutschen Archäologischen Instituts 4, 1951, 65 ff. — On the metopes: H. Kähler, Das griechische Metopenbild, 61 ff.; 105 f. — Zur Atlasmetope: L. Curtius, Interpretationen von sechs griechischen Bildwerken (Bern 1947), 52 ff., Pl. 3. — On the east pediment: H. Möbius, Die Mittelgruppe des Ostgiebels von Olympia (Studies presented to David M. Robinson 1, 1953), 626 ff. On the west pediment: P. Wolters, Der Westgiebel des olympischen Zeustempels, in: Sitzungsberichte der Bayerischen Akademie der Wissenschaften, Philos.-philolog. und hist. Klasse 1908, 7. Abhandlung. — G. Becatti, Il Maestro d'Olimpia (Florence 1943).

126–129

METOPES FROM THE TEMPLE OF HERA AT SELINUS

(Sicily). Greyish-yellow limestone tufa. Height 5'4" (1.62 m.), width 4'7" (1.40 m.). Museo Nazionale, Palermo.

The Heraion at Selinus, a Doric temple with six columns on the short and fifteen on the long sides, had, like the Temple of Zeus in Olympia, at the front and rear of the *cella* six metopes, which in theme and composition must have been inter-related. The two metopes in plates 126, 127 come from the east side. They represent the death of Actaeon, and Hera unveiling herself to Zeus on Mount Ida. Recent researches suggest that the Actaeon metope was the northernmost of the row of metopes.

Actaeon, a Boeotian legendary figure brought up by Chiron to be a hunter, had dared to court Semele, the beloved of Zeus. He was horribly punished for his presumption: Artemis wrapped him in a stag's skin, so that his dogs did not recognize him and tore their own master to pieces. — On the left stands Artemis in the long chiton and peplos with over-fold, a flat cap on her head, in her hands the bow, and over her back the quiver, the upper end of which is visible above her right shoulder. The unfortunate hunter is trying to beat off with his sword the pack that has sprung upon him. The lower dog is baying at what he takes to be a wild beast, the middle one is biting it in the flank, the uppermost has sprung at Actaeon, who has caught it by the throat. Actaeon is naked save for the stag's skin about his shoulders. His short hair is curled up over a circlet. The head of the stag's skin appears behind his right hand, the tips of the long antlers reach to the topmost dog. The bronze sword-blade was superimposed on the stone. The goddess's gaze and the movements of the dogs, which are among the most lively pieces of animal sculpture of their kind, lead the eye to the head of Actaeon sinking in despair in the centre of the relief.

The other metope, which was situated more towards the centre of the *pronaos*, depicts the great moment in the life of the goddess Hera, to whom the temple was dedicated. Clad in a long sleeved-chiton of thin material, a second, belted garment reaching to the feet over this, and a wide cloak that was drawn right over her head, Hera stands erect before Zeus as a bride, and unveils herself to him for the first time. The god is leaning back supporting himself with his left hand on the rock upon which he is sitting, while he stretches out his right hand and takes Hera by the wrist, drawing his loved one ardently towards him. The divine couple gaze into one another's eyes. Zeus's body is draped in a wide cloak; his hair is bound firmly round his head in two plaits.

The metopes were carved by a Sicilian sculptor in c. 460 B.C., at the same period as the Olympian sculptures. The heads, arms and feet of the female deities Artemis and Hera are of Parian marble and have been added to the figures of limestone tufa. It has been conjectured that these parts were carved out of the finer and more precious material by Parian sculptors.

Certain details on the Actaeon metope have been restored: on Artemis, the hair and part of the brim of the cap; on Actaeon, the left foot and the male parts; on the uppermost dog, the muzzle, ears and left hind-leg; on the lowest dog, a piece in the back and the right fore-leg.

O. Benndorf, Die Metopen von Selinunt (Berlin 1873), 54 ff., plates 8—9. — H. Kähler, Das griechische Metopenbild (1949), 59 ff.; 104 f. — W. Fuchs, Zu den Metopen des Heraions von Selinus, in: Römische Mitteilungen 63, 1956, 102 ff.

130–132, VI

POSEIDON. Found in the sea off Cape Artemision (on the north coast of the island of Euboea) in 1926 and 1928. Bronze. Height 6'10" (2.09 m.), span of the arms from finger-tip to finger-tip 6'11" (2.10 m.). National Museum, Athens, No. 15161.

Of the great bronze statues of the 5th century B.C. that stood as votive offerings in Greek sanctuaries, only the charioteer at Delphi (102–104, IV) and this god from the sea have survived, apart from a few important heads. That the statue can only represent a god is evident from the over-life-size dimensions and the mighty ethos that speaks no less from the powerful body than from the head with its expression of dignified masculinity and inflexible earnestness. The outstretched arms and the position of the fingers of the right hand show that it is Poseidon, the lord of the winds and waves, the earth-shatterer and earth-preserver: with the right hand he was hurling a trident, his characteristic weapon. The left arm and hand are stretched out straight to direct the throw towards the target and balance the body thus in action. We can read in Herodotus (VII, 192) that after the shipwreck of the Persian fleet off Cape Artemision the Greeks worshipped Poseidon as the Saviour (Soter), a surname which was at that time applied primarily to Zeus. This may explain the similarity in pose between this bronze and the more common image of Zeus hurling his lightning.

The body is flexibly poised in the sweeping movement of the throw. The left foot, which is set forward, has its sole on the ground, while the right foot, set far back, touches it only with the toes. The athletically built torso is turned towards the spectator in the full glory of its magnificent and powerful modelling. The head is seen almost in profile, its gaze directed upon the adversary at whom the destroying trident is aimed. A long flowing beard frames the earnest face with its wide-open eyes, formerly inset in coloured metal, and the sharply defined brows. The hair lies close to the head in splendid waves running from the crown. Part of it is combed forward, parted in the middle, and falls far down over the forehead. Behind the ears it is plaited into two pigtails that are taken back, crossed, and joined together over the parting.

The statue must have been made shortly before the middle of the 5th century B.C. It differs from contemporaneous Attic works in the powerful build of the body, the impetus of the movement, and the expression of the head. It has been associated with Kalamis and – perhaps more justifiably – with Onatas, an Aeginetan sculptor in metal. But we have too little first-hand knowledge of either sculptor to decide with any certainty. The attribution of Poseidon to Myron, the master of the Discobolus and the group of Athene and Marsyas, has little evidence to support it.

Chr. Karusos, ῾Ο ΠΟΣΕΙΔΩΝ ΤΟΥ ᾽ΑΡΤΕΜΙΣΙΟΥ, in: Deltion Archaiologikon 13, 1930—1931, 41 ff. — H. G. Beyen, La Statue d'Artemision (1938). — L. Curtius, Interpretationen von sechs griechischen Bildwerken (Bern 1947), 69 ff. — E. Homann-Wedeking, Römische Mitteilungen 55, 1940, 204 ff. — V. H. Poulsen, Acta Archaeologica 11, 1940, 10 ff.; 41. — K. Schefold, Würzburger Jahrbücher für Altertumswissenschaft 2, 1947, 45. — G. E. Mylonas, The Bronze Statue from Artemision, in: American Journal of Archaeology 48, 1944, 143 ff.

133

FUNERARY STELE OF A YOUNG MAN. Found on Nisyros in 1910. Ionian-island marble. Height 6' (1.83 m.); width at bottom 2' (0.625 m.), at top 1'9.5" (0.545 m.). Istanbul, Archaeological Museum, Department of Classical Antiquities, No. 11 (1142).

Aristion's stele (71) is one of the last in the series of Attic grave-reliefs dating from the 6th century B.C. Soon after it was erected an anti-luxury law brought all funerary sculpture in Attica to a sudden end. This law, which is referred to by Cicero in his *de Legibus* II, 26, 24, was manifestly connected with the reforms introduced by Kleisthenes. It remained in force in Attica until the Parthenon epoch. In the other states of Greece, by contrast, the evolution of the grave-reliefs continued from the Archaic period without interruption.

Alongside new types, which made their appearance in the early 5th century, the old form of tall, single-figure funerary stele was retained into the second half of the 5th century, especially on the Cyclades and the islands in the eastern Aegean. One of the finest examples of this type is the stele from the little island of Nisyros, south of Cos. It must originally have been crowned by a sculptured ornament that was carved separately and has now been lost. This was probably a palmette fan such as tops the stele of a girl in the Giustiniani Collection, Berlin (140). Figure and ornament were combined into a compact whole, which had to be seen as such in order to evoke the artistic effect aimed at in this monument.

The relief shows a palaestrite holding a spear in his left hand, while his right arm hangs loosely by his side. Behind the left foot, which, although the weight is taken off the left leg, has its whole sole resting on the ground, stands a discus. This must have been painted, which would have caused it to stand out more strongly from the formerly red or blue background than it does now that it has lost its colour. Judging by these accessories, the youth seems to be depicted as a victor or competitor in the pentathlon, which included spear- and discus-throwing in addition to jumping, running and wrestling.

The outline of the figure is sharply defined. Whereas the lower half of the body and the slightly bent head with the long, unbroken profile and full, rounded chin are shown in complete side view, the upper half of the body is turned so as to present a three-quarter view, bringing the musculature into active play. The hair lies close to the head in wide curves resembling a stiff cap. Like the discus, the spear and other details, it was originally emphasized by the use of paint.

The Nisyros stele must have been carved during the same period as the Olympia sculptures. It has been linked stylistically with a not entirely uniform 'Northern Greek school' and also – probably more justly – compared to the palaestrite stele in the Vatican (cf. F. Magi, in *Studies presented to D. M. Robinson* I (1951), 615 ff. and plates 58–60), which is distinguished by a very similar, firmly outlined, lively and mobile modelling of the body that has already been taken a stage further and is probably the work of an Ionian-island sculptor.

G. Mendel, Catalogue des Sculptures Grecques, Romaines et Byzantines dans les Musées Impériaux Ottomans I (1912), 73, No. 11 (1142). — *E. Buschor*, Die Skulpturen des Zeustempels in Olympia, Text (1924) 36. — *M. Schede*, Meisterwerke der türkischen Museen zu Konstantinopel I (1928), 4, plate 6. — *E. Langlotz*, Frühgriechische Bildhauerschulen, 144. — *E. Pfuhl*, Jahrbuch des Deutschen Archäologischen Instituts 50, 1935, 16. — *K. Friis Johansen*, The Attic Grave-Reliefs of the Classical Period (1951), 127, fig. 62.

134–137

THREE-SIDED RELIEF, KNOWN AS THE LUDOVISI THRONE. Parian marble. Width of the front 4'8" (1.43 m.), of the sides 2'4" (0.72 m.) each. Height of the front originally about 3'6" (1.07 m.), of the sides approximately 2'8" sloping to 2' (0.84–0.61 m.). Found within the area of the Gardens of Sallust in 1887. Museo delle Terme, Rome, No. 152 (Inv. 8670).

The three reliefs are carved on a single block and consist of a wide front panel with a pediment-shaped top, and two side panels at right-angles to the front, the tops of which sloped down towards the back. It was originally held to be the throne for a religious image or the enclosure for a sacrificial pit; later it was thought to be the three-sided windbreak of a rectangular altar; the most recent theory is that the block, together with a second and corresponding block, crowned the projecting flanks of a large sacrificial altar with steps. None of these conjectures is entirely convincing.

Various explanations have also been advanced for the scene portrayed on the front. The most likely interpretation is that it represents the birth of Aphrodite from the sea. In the centre the goddess rises from the water, drawing herself up with outstretched arms by the two women who are reaching out solicitous hands to assist the miracle of her birth. They are standing on the shingle of a beach and holding out a cloth in front of the goddess's lower body, bending down towards her in their eagerness to help. They have been interpreted as two Moirae, or Fates, who together with Aphrodite Urania constituted a triad of divinities. The goddess's transfigured face is lifted towards one of the two helpers. Her long, wet hair is swept round her neck in fine waves and its ends

lie in sinuous engraved lines upon her arching breast. The thin, damp linen of her garment clings in delicate, wavy folds to the glorious forms of her body. The garments of the two women – whose vertical folds reveal the bodies beneath – are characterized by heavy materiality. According to another interpretation the scene represents a ritual bath, either of a goddess or a mortal.

The two female figures on the sides must be explained in terms of the scene on the front panel. On the left sits a young, naked flute-girl, sunk into a soft cushion, with crossed legs. Her gently modelled head with the bound-up hair is bent forward in the act of playing, her right leg hangs free to tap out the rhythm of the music. On the right an older, clothed woman sits on a cushion taking incense grains from a box in order to strew them as an offering on a tall stand with glowing coals. Like the flute-girl, her hair is tied in a cloth and she has also drawn her cloak over the back of her head for the purpose of carrying out this solemn rite. The rigidly erect posture of the draped body and the earnest expression on her finely chiselled face reflect concentration on the offering. The contrast between the two figures is manifest down to the smallest detail. Thus on the left the cushion emphasizes the swelling, unbroken curves of the naked, youthful body; on the right it repeats the play of the soft folds of drapery around the slimmer body of the clothed woman.

Both figures have their backs towards the scene on the front slab and are therefore facing the open side of the marble rectangle. The may be regarded as priestesses or servants in the cult of Aphrodite.

The bottom corners of all three sides bore an ornamentation of volutes and palmettes. This decoration seems to have been chiselled away in antiquity and replaced by similar but larger ornaments, in order to adapt the whole work to a second relief of corresponding shape and size, a counterpart known as 'the Boston Throne' that is now in the Museum of Fine Arts, Boston.

Both reliefs were produced round about 460 B.C. in Southern Italy or Sicily. The 'Ludovisi Throne' is one of the finest and most admired Greek originals that have come to light in Rome.

E. Petersen, Antike Denkmäler 2 (1891/1892), plates 6—7 and the same, Römische Mitteilungen 7, 1892, 32 ff. and 14, 1899, 154 ff. — *E. Paribeni*, Museo Nazionale Romano, Sculture Greche del V Secolo (1953), 12 ff., No. 3. — *E. Langlotz*, Das Ludovisische Relief (Mainz 1951). — *W. Hahland*, Bauform und Größenverhältnisse des Aphroditealtares Ludovisi in: Österreichische Jahreshefte 40, 1953, 27 ff. — *E. Simon*, Die Geburt der Aphrodite (1959). – On the genuineness of the Boston counterpart, see *H. Möbius*, in: Charites, Studien zur Altertumswissenschaft. Festschrift für E. Langlotz (1957), 47 ff.

138

FRAGMENT OF A VOTIVE RELIEF WITH A FEMALE HEAD. Found on the island of Melos, in the vicinity of the ancient city, in 1937. Parian marble. Maximum height 13" (32.5 cm.), maximum width 13.5" (33.5 cm.). National Museum, Athens, No. 3990.

This fragment is part of a circular marble disc, convex in front and with a diameter – judging by the existing edge – of about 18" (45 cm.). The back is flat and smooth. Exactly in the centre is a hole 1" deep by means of which the tondo was attached to a background. The surviving section represents the lower part of a female head and neck facing right. The beautiful, expressive profile shows up clearly and distinctly against the background. Brow and nose form a single straight line. The lips, which are parted to form an acute angle, are joined to the gently dilated nose and the strong, rounded chin by firm curves. The full hair, bound up in a cloth, hangs far down at the nape of the neck. In front of the small and delicate ear, which bears a round ornament, on the temple and above the brow the hair was of metal and attached.

In form and style the tondo has as yet no parallel in Greek sculpture. Hence all conjectures as to the significance and purpose of the relief, and as to the nature of the missing parts, are purely hypothetical. It probably represents a goddess. The most likely identity is Aphrodite. But it might also be a local Melian goddess, a nymph or a heroine. If the surviving outer edge is extended to form a full circle, it does not leave sufficient space on the right side for another head of the same size. It is impossible to say whether this part of the relief was occupied by an attribute, a smaller figure, an ornament or an inscription. The relief may have stood on the top or the front face of a tall stele, or have been attached to the wall of a sanctuary.

The soft modelling links the head stylistically with Ionian-island works such as the stele of a girl from the Giustiniani Collection in Berlin (140, 141), but divorces it from the relatively heavier and more compact formal vocabulary of the roughly coeval reliefs on the 'Ludovisi Throne' (134–137). The tondo must have been carved by an Ionian-island, possibly Parian, artist in about 460 B.C.

C. J. Karusos, An Early Classical Disc Relief from Melos, in: Journal of Hellenic Studies 71, 1951, 96 ff., plate 37. — W. H. Schuchhardt, Griechische Plastik der klassischen Zeit (Sammlung Parthenon, 1954), 8, plate 12.

139

VOTIVE RELIEF TO ATHENE. White Parian or Pentelic (?) marble. Height 21.6" (54 cm.). Acropolis Museum, Athens, No. 695.

This small, delicate relief was found in 1888 on the Athenian Acropolis, south of the Parthenon, in a wall of *poros* that was connected with the Parthenon terrace. It seems to have been buried under the earth a few years after it was made.

Athene, in a youthful, maidenly shape, stands with bowed head in front of a rectangular pillar. The weight of the body rests on the right leg and on the spear in her left hand. She is holding the spear-point downwards at a slant and leaning her body, which is tilted slightly forward, and her head, which is seen in profile, against this support. Her left foot, which does not carry any weight, is set back and touches the ground only with the ball and toes; both feet are seen in side view. Her right hand rests on her hip, with fingers extended. The goddess is dressed in the so-called Attic peplos, open on the right side, held together on the shoulders with two clasps, and belted on top of the overfold. It follows the small, bud-like forms of the bust, which is seen almost in front view, but veils the lower part of the body in long parallel folds that make of it an elongated rectangle. Athene is armed with neither aegis nor shield, and apart from the spear has only a Corinthian helmet with a double crest. Her hair emerges from under the helmet in simple, narrow waves.

The beautiful face with its high, symmetrical profile, big, full cheeks and heavy, rounded chin wears an earnest and thoughtful

expression. Although it cannot be called melancholy or sad, this expression, together with the figure's pose, led to its being called the 'Mourning Athene' and to the supposition that the goddess was gazing at a tombstone. This interpretation is no more satisfactory than others, suggesting that Athene is keeping watch beside a boundary stone, that she is standing by a stele bearing an edict in her capacity as guardian of the law, or that the stone in front of her is a pillar on which the inventory of her sanctuary was set out in painted letters. Another interpretation has been put forward based on the style and date. The work is one of the finest Attic votive reliefs from the years before the middle of the 5th century B.C. At this period the fortification of the Acropolis carried out under Kimon was completed by the construction of the great south wall. For this reason the relief may have been construed as a votive offering made by the craftsmen to the goddess of the citadel on completion of the new fortifications of the Acropolis. Latest research has interpreted the pillar in front of Athene as the marker, customary in those days, for the start and finishing-point of the races in the stadium, and the relief as depicting the dedication of a victorious athlete to the goddess.–At the time of the discovery of the relief there were still signs of painted decoration on the upper fillet and traces of blue paint on the background.

H. Bulle, Der Schöne Mensch im Altertum, 2nd edition (1912), 578 f. and 707 f., Text to plate 273. — E. Langlotz, Frühgriechische Bildhauerschulen, 156, No. 35; 163, plate 100. — H. Thiersch, Nachrichten der Gesellschaft der Wissenschaften zu Göttingen. Philos.-Histor. Klasse 1928, No. 2, 194. — G. Lippold, Text to Brunn-Bruckmann, Denkmäler griechischer und römischer Skulptur, plate 783 1939. — J. Chamoux, L'Athéna Mélancolique, in: Bulletin de Correspondance Hellénique 81, 1957, 141 ff.

140, 141

SEPULCHRAL STELE OF A GIRL. Parian marble, Height 4'8" (1.43 m.). State Museum, Berlin, Department of Classical Antiquities K 19 (Inv. 1482). Acquired from the Giustiniani Collection, Venice, in 1897.

Within the tall, rectangular field of the stele, which tapers slightly towards the top, a girl is represented in a long garment open at the side and overlapping at the breast – the peplos of heavy woollen cloth – which is held together on the right shoulder with a clasp. The hair is gathered into a bun at the back and encircled several times by a wide ribbon. The figure wore a metal ornament on the ear. In her left hand she holds a deep, round box or pot – whose overlapping lid is standing on the ground – and has taken from it with bowed head jewellery or frankincense as an offering. The monument is crowned by a splendidly spreading palmette fan. Two volutes are curled above the spandrel, growing out of a calyx of acanthus leaves. The image of the girl, represented in one of the activities of her life, is instinct with quiet sorrow and profound melancholy that bespeak renunciation and separation. The type of relief and the sculptural style, the soft and heavy quality imparted to the drapery, and the luxuriant, vegetal growth of the ornamentation indicate that the monument is the work of a mid-5th-century artist from the Ionian islands.

C. Blümel, Katalog der griechischen Skulpturen des 5. und 4. Jahrhunderts v. Chr. in Berlin (1928), K 19, plates 27—28. — E. Buschor, Athenische Mitteilungen 48, 1933, 44 f., Beilage 17. — O. Walter, Österreichische Jahreshefte 39, 1952, 118 ff. — J. Kleemann, Der Satrapen-Sarkophag aus Sidon. (1958), 83 f.

III. CLASSICAL PERIOD

450—300 B.C.

142–171

SCULPTURES FROM THE PARTHENON ON THE ATHE-
NIAN ACROPOLIS. British Museum, London; Acropolis
Museum, Athens; Louvre, Paris.

The Parthenon, the greatest Doric temple of the Virgin Athene
(Parthenos), built throughout of Pentelic marble, rises in the
north-east upon solid rock, in the south upon a foundation that
is up to thirty-three feet high. It faces east and covers an area of
about 102×229 feet (31×69.50 m.) at the level on which the
columns stand. The entablature was carried by eight columns at
each end and seventeen on each side; the columns were 34′8″
(10.50 m.) high including the capital. The architect was Ictinus, who
later built the Telesterion, in which the mysteries were celebrated
at Eleusis, and the Temple of Apollo at Phigalia. The Parthenon
was begun in 448 B.C., the image of Athene, modelled by Phidias
in gold and ivory over a wooden core, consecrated in 438. Work
on the friezes and pediment sculptures was completed in 432.

Ninety-two metopes were placed over the entablature between the
triglyphs, fourteen on the ends and twenty-three on the sides, each
of them 4′8″ high and 4′2″ wide (1.34×1.27 m.). On the east face
they depicted the war of the gods with the giants, on the west the
war of the Greeks with the Amazons, on the north the destruction
of Troy, and on the south the battle between the Lapithae and the
Centaurs on the occasion of Peirithoös's wedding. While the relief
figures on the east, west and north metopes were intentionally broken away when the Parthenon was turned into a Christian church
in Late Antique times, the metopes on the south face escaped this
fate – obviously because this was regarded as the rear of the
building. The middle part of the southern metopes was destroyed
later, when a powder magazine exploded in the Parthenon during
the siege of the Turks by the Venetians in 1687. The remainder of
the southern metopes, together with the major part of the frieze
and most of the surviving pediment figures, were brought to London
at the beginning of the 19th century by Lord Elgin, the British
ambassador to the Sublime Porte. Since 1816 they have been
exhibited in the British Museum. One of the most beautiful southern
metopes is still in its original position on the south-west corner
of the temple.

The metopes (142–147) were carved during the forties of the 5th
century B.C.; stylistically they are the oldest part of the whole
figurative decoration on the Parthenon, in form and content early
testimonies to Greek sculpture's attainment of Classical maturity.
In the southern metopes each rectangular field is filled by a single,
closed composition of two figures – a Centaur fighting a Lapithan
man or woman combined in ever new and often magnificent
poses.

The relief frieze (148–163) – 3′7″ (1.06 m.) high – ran to a length
of about 530 feet (160 m.) high up along the exterior wall of the
hundred-feet-long cella with the vestibule (pronaos) in the east and
the chamber that adjoined it in the west, which was carried by four
Ionic columns and to which was attached the rear hall (opistodomos).

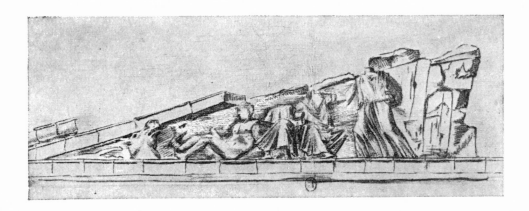

7 and 8   Drawings of the east pe-
diment of the Parthenon made by
Jacques Carrey in 1674.
Bibliothèque Nationale, Paris

78

9 and 10 Drawings of the west pediment of the Parthenon made by Jacques Carrey in 1674. Bibliothèque Nationale, Paris

The theme of this frieze is the solemn procession of the Athenians to the great four-yearly feast of the goddess of the citadel, in the course of which the latter was presented with a new ceremonial robe. The portrayal of the festal procession begins at the south-west corner of the temple. Here the riders take up their positions, the cavalcade sets out and continues in the south and along the west face to the north. On both sides a quadriga joins the procession, followed by youths making music and carrying vessels on their shoulders, youths leading sacrificial animals, and marching girls. In the east, on the front face of the temple, the twelve great Olympian gods await the procession, seated. In the centre between them a priest is folding the peplos for Athene, aided by a ministrant; beside him a priestess is taking their chairs away from two girls, in order to lay the robe on them. At the side of the gods stand ten worthy men in cloaks, the heroes of the Attic phylae (communities).

The sculptural decoration is crowned by the pediments, huge mythological visions. They treat of two central themes from the myth of Athene as the goddess of the Attic province. On the east pediment (164–169) the centre was taken up by a portrayal of Athene's birth from the head of Zeus in the presence of the Olympian gods. In the left-hand corner (as one looks at it)

Helios rose with his quadriga, in front of him were Dionysus (reclining), Demeter and Kore (sitting) and Eileithyia, goddess of childbirth, hastening away from the centre. In the right-hand corner Selene went down with her quadriga into the waves of Ocean, at her back was the group of the so-called 'dew sisters' (Aphrodite in the lap of Peitho or Dione, her mother?) and Leto (sitting).

The subject of the west pediment (170, 171) is Athene's struggle with Poseidon for the land of Attica. Athene's gift was the olive tree, Poseidon made the salt spring bubble up. Below the ridge the two hostile deities were depicted brandishing their weapons – Athene a spear, Poseidon a trident – and moving away from one another to each side with their heads turned towards the centre. To right and left their teams of horses are rearing, reined in by Nike and Amphitrite. Gods and heroes of the citadel are lined up on either side as far as the corners.

Because of the damage, especially to the centre of the pediment, the names of the individual figures and their position on the pediments are only partially established. Old drawings made by Jacques Carrey, a painter in the retinue of the French ambassador in Constantinople, the Marquis de Nointel, in 1674, shortly before the team of Athene on the west pediment crashed to the ground after the Acropolis was taken by the Venetians in 1687, enable us to form an idea of the composition.

The sculptural decoration of the Parthenon rises in three huge tiers. It embraces the whole cosmos as it appeared to the 5th-century Greeks: on the metopes, the deeds of the mythological heroes; on the frieze, the existence of men in conjunction with their heroes and gods; on the pediments, the rule of the gods themselves. As the purest and most magnificent realization of the Greek ethos it represents for us the climax of Classical art. In idea and design, which must have been planned down to the last detail, the Parthenon sculptures are the work of a single brilliant master – Phidias, whom Pericles appointed supreme overseer of the buildings on the Acropolis and who was regarded by the ancient world as the greatest sculptor of statues of the gods. Recent study of the style of the Parthenon sculptures, while it has generally confirmed their artistic unity, has also made it plain that in addition to the chief master a considerable number of sculptors of varying calibre took part in the execution of the immense work and had a certain amount of scope for the development of their own approach. Alongside nameless craftsmen, modern research sees the style of such masters as Myron, Kolotes and Alcamenes in individual metopes, sections of the frieze, and figures on the pediments.

A. H. Smith, The Sculptures of the Parthenon (1910). — M. Collignon, Le Parthénon (1914). — G. von Lücken, Die Entwicklung der Parthenonskulpturen (1930). — B. Schweitzer, Prolegomena zur Kunst des Parthenonmeisters I. — Zur Kunst des Parthenon-Meisters II. — Pheidias, der Parthenonmeister (Jahrbuch des Deutschen Archäologischen Instituts 53, 1938, 1 ff.; 54, 1939, 1 ff.; 55, 1940, 170 ff.). — E. Langlotz, Phidiasprobleme (1947). — E. Buschor, Phidias, der Mensch (1948). — G. M. A. Richter, Three Critical Periods in Greek Sculpture, 1 ff. — K. Jeppesen, The Pedimental Compositions of the Parthenon (Acta Archaeologica 24, 1953, 103 ff.) — F. Brommer, Studien zu den Parthenongiebeln I und II, in: Athenische Mitteilungen 69/70, 1954/55, 49 ff., and 71, 1956, 30 ff. — E. Berger, Parthenon-Ostgiebel. Vorbemerkungen zu einer Rekonstruktion (1958).

172, 173
VOTIVE RELIEF TO THE ELEUSINIAN DEITIES: THE DISPATCH OF TRIPTOLEMUS. Found at Eleusis in 1859. Pentelic marble. Height 7'11" (2.40 m.), breadth 5' (1.52 m.). National Museum, Athens, No. 126.

By virtue of its size alone, this relief occupies a place of its own among votive reliefs from the 5th century B.C. The figures are far larger than life-size. On the other hand, the maximum depth of the relief work is relatively small – scarcely 2" (5 cm.). Thus the effect created is similar to that of a large figure-painting.

The picture represents a scene from the myth of Eleusis, a favourite theme in Attic vase-painting of the Classical period. Triptolemus is receiving from the hand of Demeter the ears of corn with which to bring agriculture and prosperity to mankind, while Kore, Demeter's daughter, adorns him with a wreath. The boy in the centre stands erect in simple, noble modesty. His hair, parted at the side, falls in long waves. He is naked save for string-topped sandals and holds in his left hand that hangs at his side a cloak, one end of which passes over his right shoulder while the other spreads out behind him and reaches to the ground. His gaze is directed towards the ears of corn which the great goddess is placing in his hand. Demeter is a tall, matronly figure in a long chiton of heavy woollen cloth that drapes the lower half of her body in broad, vertical folds. Across her shoulder she also wears a short cape. Her wavy hair is loose, in her left hand she holds a sceptre.

By contrast, Kore is portrayed as a youthful, girlish figure, lighter and more relaxed in posture, in a long chiton of thin linen and a cloak. She wears her hair put up at the back. In her left hand she holds a torch. Her fine maidenly head is lowered towards the centre. She is looking at the wreath which she is placing on the boy's head. Her arm, neck and ear ornaments were of metal and attached.

An earnest, solemn atmosphere pervades the whole picture. A certain rigidity and primness, also in the treatment of the folds suggest that the relief was the work of an Eleusinian sculptor having close affinities with Attic art of around 430 B.C. The sublime, hieratic character of the representation, and certain features of the composition, the posture of the figures and the treatment of the drapery, which were already antiquated at that period, are doubtless to be explained by a specific tradition connected with the sacred art of Eleusis.

The work is one of the few Greek votive reliefs that were copied in antiquity. Fragments of a marble copy of the same dimensions dating from the imperial era, ostensibly from the Forum Romanum, are now in the Metropolitan Museum, New York (G. M. A. Richter, Catalogue of Greek Sculptures [1954], No. 34, Plate 32 a also W. H. Schuchhardt, Gnomon 30, 1958, 487).

J. N. Svoronos, Das Athener Nationalmuseum (1908) 1, 106 ff., No. 126, plates 24—25. — E. Buschor, Athenische Mitteilungen 53, 1928, 50. — J. Dohrn, Attische Plastik vom Tode des Phidias bis zum Wirken der großen Meister des IV. Jahrhunderts v. Chr., 40 ff.

174–177
DYING NIOBID. Parian marble. Height 4'11" (1.49 m.). Found at Rome in 1906. Museo delle Terme, Rome, Inv. 72274.

Leto had two children by Zeus – Apollo and Artemis. Niobe, of the accursed race of Tantalus, exulted over Leto in blind presumption because of her great number of children, and so called down upon herself the goddess's implacable wrath. The mortal's sacrilegious boast was followed by the punishment of the gods: Niobe's seven sons and seven daughters succumbed to the arrows of Apollo and Artemis. The legend, which already appears in the Iliad and was later given its customary literary form by Ovid, is one of the major themes of the Classical art of the 5th century B.C.

The group to which the Daughter of Niobe in the Museo delle Terme belonged consisted of the unhappy mother's fourteen children and the two gods who were executing judgement upon them. In addition to this figure two further ones from this group have come down to us: a Niobid sunk upon his knees, and Apollo shooting with a bow. The loveliest is the Niobid with the pure, firm mould of a body that has just blossomed into womanhood. The girl was striving to escape the punishment of the gods. Her long dress, fastened over the shoulders with clasps, must have slipped down as she ran. She was holding it up with her hands when the fatal arrow struck her in the back. She clutched at the wound with her right hand – and the heavy garment fell down in front. She collapses, her head falls back, her open mouth gives vent to wailing cries and her eyes and face already bear the stamp of death. The girl's tragic fate and the beauty of the modelling have won for this figure the deepest interest and admiration ever since it was found at Rome fifty years ago in what used to be the Horti Sallustiani, the Gardens of Sallust. Dating from shortly after the middle of the 5th century B.C., it differs from contemporaneous Attic works by a certain heaviness that is reminiscent of Peloponnesian sculpture. In the fullness and materiality of the formal vocabulary it also has affinities with works from the Ionian islands.

G. Lippold, Text to Brunn-Bruckmann, Denkmäler griechischer Plastik, plates 706—709. — *W. Kraiker*, Römische Mitteilungen 51, 1936, 125 ff. — *V. H. Poulsen*, Kunstmuseet Aarsskrift 25, 1938. 141. — *E. Paribeni*, Museo Nazionale Romano, Sculture Greche del V Secolo (1953), No. 4. — *W. Fuchs*, Athenische Mitteilungen 71, 1956, 70, Note 20. — On the two other figures of the group cf. *E. Langlotz*, Ein neuerworbener Niobidentorso, in: Berliner Museen, Berichte aus den ehemaligen Preußischen Kunstsammlungen. New Series 7, 1957, 2 ff., and *S. Stucchi*, Statua di Apolla Saettante dalle Rovine del Tempio Sosiano, in: Bollettino della Commissione Archeologica Comunale di Roma 75, 1953—55, 3 ff. with Pl. 1—6.

178

NIKE OF PAIONIOS. Found during the German excavations at Olympia in 1875. Parian marble. Original height of the figure, including the base, 7'1" (2.16 m.), to the tips of the wings which are now lost, about 9'6" (2.90 m.). Museum, Olympia.

This image of the goddess of peace once stood before the east face of the Temple of Zeus at Olympia on the top of a triangular pillar almost 30 feet (9 m.) high and tapering slightly towards the top. A round shield hung on each side of the pillar close below the figure. A two-line votive inscription was engraved on the front of the pillar at a height of rather more than 6 feet (2 m.) above the ground, and below this, in smaller letters, an artist's inscription. They state that the Nike was offered to the Olympian Zeus by the Messenians and Naupaktians as a tithe of military booty and that it is the work of Paionios of Mende (in Chalcidice), who had also made the acroteria on the Temple of Zeus with which he had won a contest for sculptors. Glittering gold Nikes formed the central acroteria above the pediments of the Temple of Zeus. Thus the marble goddess of victory on the pillar is both a great public monument and a personal thank-offering from Paionios for his victory in the competition.

Nike was portrayed in flight with long, outstretched wings whose tips pointed upwards; the attachments of these wings are still in place on the shoulders. She is on her way down from Mount Olympus to bring victory, but is still hovering between heaven and earth. Her feet are not yet on the ground: only the left one, which is thrust slightly forward, seems to be feeling for a solid resting place. The stone upon which the figure is standing with slanting soles represents air or a cloud, through which an eagle, the bird of Zeus, is darting horizontally with outstretched pinions. The impression that the figure was soaring in space was enhanced by the tall, narrow triangular shape of the pillar, which from a distance resembled a mere shadowless surface rather than a cube that had to bear a weight. The position of the arms and the arrangement of the drapery still further heightened the impression of floating. With both hands – the left extended to the side and the right lowered diagonally – Nike held her broad cloak, which billowed out behind her in the wind and bore her like a sail. The garment covering her body seems to consist of two parts that are open at the sides and girt about the waist with an overfold. They are held together by a brooch on the right shoulder. The left breast is uncovered. The front section of the garment falls diagonally across the upper part of the body in a curve from the right shoulder to the left hip; the back section is drawn forward under

the left arm. The fabric is pressed close against the body by the wind blowing towards the flying figure, so that the powerful, rounded forms of the body appear through the garment in places as though exposed. The right leg is entirely covered by the fabric; the left, on the other hand, thrust out between the two halves of the garment, is exposed from the thigh down. Behind the figure the garment is blown sideways against the tauter cloak in broad, sweeping folds to form a shell-like curve.

The image of Nike, standing aloft against the sky, was brought to final perfection by the addition of colour. The drapery, from which the left leg and the naked part of the bust stood out in light tones, was red. The black hair was encircled by a gleaming gold band. The stone beneath the feet must also have been painted to represent air.

According to the historical context indicated by the votive inscription, and also for stylistic reasons, the Nike at Olympia must certainly have been erected in the period immediately following the Peace of Nikias (421 B.C.). In its weightless flight, the compactness and harmony of the composition and the close relationship between body and drapery, this statue is as typical of its period as the Nike of Samothrace (262), thrusting firmly into the wind and full of passionate movement, is typical of the 'baroque' phase of Hellenism at the beginning of the 2nd century B.C.

G. Treu, Die Bildwerke von Olympia in Stein und Ton (Olympia, Ergebnisse, vol. III) 182 ff., plates 46—48. — *F. Studniczka*, Die Siegesgöttin (1898), 16 ff. — *R. Harder*, Paionios und Grophon: Zwei Bildhauerinschriften, in: Neue Beiträge zur klassischen Altertumswissenschaft. Festschrift für B. Schweitzer (1954), 192 ff.

179–181

ATTIC FUNERARY MONUMENT. BATTLEFIELD SCENE. Pentelic marble. Length 7'6" (2.28 m.), height 5'10" (1.80 m.). Found at Rome c. 1764. Villa Albani, Rome, No. 985.

The relief, which came to Rome from Greece already in antiquity, is distinguished among Attic sepulchral reliefs of the 5th century B.C. not only by its size and shape, but also by its unusual subject, a battle scene. A young rider in a short, belted and heavily folded chiton and a cloak fastened under the throat and flapping behind him in the wind, has jumped from his horse. The animal, halted in its wild gallop, rears up. He holds it by the reins with his left hand and strikes with his sword at his adversary, who is lying on the ground, now unarmed, trying to protect himself from the blow with his left arm under his short cloak. Reins and sword were modelled in bronze.

It is thought that this relief was not the tombstone of an individual, but rather a large official monument to the dead erected by the Attic state at the beginning of the Peloponnesian War. The struggle is relentless, but the horrifying nature of the events is ennobled by the lofty conception of war. The two foes, the victor and the vanquished, are united by the same humanity.

The balanced, harmonious effect of the monument is due not least to the artistic composition. The diagonal of the horse, which is galloping in the direction of the fallen warrior's gaze, is intersected at right angles by the left arm and the axis of movement of the rider, by the upper body of the fallen warrior, and the erect tail of the horse. To these diagonal axes are added vertical and horizontal ones of equal importance. But nowhere is the framework of the picture touched or disturbed. All the movements are subordinated to a circle that begins at the right hand of the rider, passes through the ends of the flapping cloak, the head and the bent forelegs of the horse, and leads back to the rounded torso of the fallen warrior and to his eyes.

The relief, one of the most important portrayals of combat that has come down to us from antiquity, must have been produced under the direct influence of the Parthenon sculptures by one of the leading Attic sculptors of the day. That it was created within a short time of the Parthenon frieze is suggested by the independence of the drapery in relation to the body, the pictorial nature of the composition, and a more consciously organized relationship between figures and background.

The nose and lower lip of the attacking warrior, part of his left forearm, the ear and eye of the horse and a small piece between its nostrils and its eye, have been restored in modern times.

A. Conze, Die attischen Grabreliefs, No. 1153, plate 247. — W. Helbig, Führer durch die öffentlichen Sammlungen klassischer Altertümer in Rom (3rd edition) (1913), No. 1861. — H. Diepolder, Die attischen Grabreliefs des 5. und 4. Jahrhunderts v. Chr., 16 f., plate 9. — E. Buschor, Kriegertum der Parthenonzeit (1943), 39.

182

SEPULCHRAL STELE FOR A YOUTH. Found on Aegina 1829. Pentelic marble. Height 3'7" (1.09 m.). National Museum, Athens, No. 715.

The high, rectangular relief panel is terminated at the top by a narrow raised fillet that was once decorated with painted ornamentation and above this by a broad projecting beam, bearing a magnificent, dense frieze of flamboyant palmettes and lilies above flat volutes in finest marble work. The erect figure of the youth with outstretched arm fills the entire panel and touches all four edges. The body is seen from front view, the fine, formerly garlanded head with the short, curly hair, full lips and large eye is turned to its right and seen in profile. The right hand is raised, palm outwards, in a gesture which is not found in any other Greek funerary relief of the Classical period. It might be understood as a signal of farewell, with which the youth appears for the last time and simultaneously withdraws into the beyond. The left hand, hanging at his side, holds a bird – the dead boy's favourite animal. The youth is wearing a cloak that leaves the right side of the upper body free, crosses it in a beautiful curve, and is taken round the back so that one end, on which the selvage is clearly visible, falls over the left shoulder. To the left of the relief a little naked boy with long, soft hair parted in the centre – the youth's servant – stands in pensive melancholy. He is leaning against a pillar on top of which a beast of prey, probably a cat, is sitting with its head turned straight to the front. It seems to be one of those monuments with lions, sphinxes and sirens that frequently stood over tombs. Above the cat is a bird-cage, the bars of which were painted in. From the beginning, viewers of this interesting funerary relief have been reminded of the Parthenon frieze and this important master is thought to have developed his style as a result of collaborating on the Parthenon sculptures. It is also reasonable to suppose that there are other works by his hand among those that have come down to us, although this has not yet been definitely proved. He bears a close affinity to the master of the Apollo panel from the east frieze of the Parthenon (156, 157), whom scholars have good reason to identify as Alcamenes, a pupil and

rival of Phidias. A notable common characteristic shared by the seated Apollo and the figure of the youth on the sepulchral relief is the manner in which the cloak frames the upper part of the body. The stele differs from Alcamenes's Attic art, however, in the rendering of forms. The modelling of the Aeginetan relief is softer and places greater emphasis on the sensuous values of the body and drapery. The style resembles that of the stele of a girl from the Giustiniani Collection at Berlin (140, 141) and of the Dying Niobid in the Museo delle Terme (174–177), which belong to Ionian-island art. The choice and arrangement of the plant motifs and the mobile growth of the leaves in the ornamental frieze points to the same conclusion. The sepulchral relief must also be the work of an Ionian-island sculptor, who created this masterpiece soon after the completion of the Parthenon sculptures, in about 420 B.C.

A. Conze, Die attischen Grabreliefs, vol. 2, No. 1032, plate 204. — H. Diepolder, Die attischen Grabreliefs des 5. und 4. Jahrhunderts v. Chr., 14, plate 6. — W. Kraiker, Römische Mitteilungen 51, 1936, 138 ff. — N. Himmelmann-Wildschütz, Ein klassischer Mädchenkopf, in: Marburger Winckelmannsprogramm 1956, 4. — K. Schefold, Agorakritos als Erbe des Pheidias, in: Robert Böhringer — Eine Freundesgabe (1957), 551 f. — As to place where the stele was found cf. Welter, Archäologischer Anzeiger 1938, 533 f.

183

YOUTH MAKING A GIFT. Bronze. Height 8.4" (21 cm.). Louvre, Paris, No. 183.

Next to Phidias, Polyclitus of Argos is the greatest sculptor of the mature Classical style of the 5th century B.C. He worked chiefly in bronze, but according to tradition he also created – in the years following 423 B.C. – the great image of Hera of Argos, which was of gold and ivory. What distinguished his work from that of other 5th-century artists was the well calculated relationship of all parts to the whole. His figures possessed a distinct rhythm that was expressed in their inner and outer equilibrium. Polyclitus not only put the rules of his art to the test in statuary, but also set them down in a treatise of his own bearing the title Canon, of which fragments have come down to us through indirect sources. He gave a practical demonstration of the theoretically established proportions of the body in a model figure bearing the same name as his treatise. It was regarded by posterity as a norm and standard.

Not one work by Polyclitus has come down to us in the original, yet we are able to form an accurate picture of his major works – such as the Discus-bearer, the famous Doryphoros (spear-bearer), the Diadumenos (victorious athlete fastening the diadem upon his brow) and the Wounded Amazon – from copies made during the period of the Roman Empire. His style is mirrored in various bronze statuettes, of which the Youth Making a Gift in the Louvre is one of the finest. The weight of the body rests on the right leg, the left is free of weight and placed to one side. The relation between the two halves of the torso is shifted to correspond with this pose. The head is tilted to the right, the side of the carrying leg, and looks down at a votive bowl the youth held in his hand. The right arm is raised just enough for its outline to correspond to that of the firm supporting leg. The left arm, hanging in a relaxed way, repeats the contour of the left leg that is placed to the side; the left hand held a staff.

The whole body is included within a fine curve that rises from the unweighted leg, and its structure is moulded and balanced down to the last detail. Every movement begins at the middle of the body and radiates outward. This is also the position of the decisive horizontal in the construction of the figure, on which, at a point outside the body, the axes meet that lead through the eyes and hands. The sculptural construction of the body simultaneously makes clear the action that draws the head and the right hand holding the bowl into relation with one another. The statuette epitomizes the harmonious concord of all physical and mental forces in the shape of an athletically formed youth at the height of the Greek Classical style.

The hair is finely chiselled. The eyes are inlaid in silver, the nipples in copper.

A. de Ridder, Les Bronzes Antiques du Louvre 1 (1913), No. 183, plate 19. — A. Furtwängler, Meisterwerke griechischer Plastik, 492 f., plate 28, 3. — C. Blümel, Der Diskosträger Polyklets (90. Berliner Winckelmannsprogramm, 1930), 6 ff., fig. 1. — E. Langlotz, Die Darstellung des Menschen in der griechischen Kunst (Bonn 1941), 20 fig. 9.

184

TOMBSTONE RELIEF OF CHAIREDEMOS AND LYCEAS,
from Salamis. Marble. Height 6' (1.81 m.), width 3'7" (1.02 m.). Museum, Piraeus.

Greek funerary reliefs of the Archaic period generally bore only one figure, like the stele of Aristion (71), the likeness of the deceased, usually in a high rectangular field. In the early 5th century a new type of relief made its appearance alongside the old and acquired great importance during the succeeding period: the first figure was joined by a second, so that the two faced one another in a mutual relationship. This new type of composition was the precondition for the two-figure groups and family groups comprising several figures seen on Greek sepulchral reliefs of the Classical period.

The tall relief panel closed at the top by a fillet, which was found on Salamis in 1915, differs from other tombstone reliefs of its time by the fact that the two figures do not face each other but are represented as walking in the same direction along a broad common supporting plane. Their names are written on the fillet above their heads. The life-size, athletic figure in ideal nakedness, Chairedemos, carries on his left arm the round shield and in his hand a spear whose ends were painted; his folded cloak hangs over his left shoulder. The upper part of his body is shown almost from the front. Behind him, half hidden by the shield, goes Lyceas, seen more from the side, in a short belted chiton, also with a round shield on his left arm. He is carrying his spear over his shoulder with the right hand.

Whereas on Greek sepulchral reliefs of the 5th and 4th centuries a distinction is made between the dead and the living through the position in which they face one another, the two warriors on this tombstone are represented as belonging to the same sphere by being shown moving in the same direction. It has thus rightly been inferred that the relief on the tombstone must be for two warriors who fell in battle. It also differs from Attic sepulchral reliefs of its time, of the late 5th and early 4th centuries, through the nakedness of one of the warriors. His well built and fully moulded body was obviously modelled on a bronze from the workshop of Polyclitus. It is directly reminiscent of the latter's Doryphoros or Spear-carrier, which has only survived in Roman copies.

A second sepulchral stele by the master of the funerary relief from Salamis, who must have been a Peloponnesian sculptor or an Attic sculptor under Peloponnesian influence, is extant and now in the Museum at Worcester/Mass. It comes from Megara and depicts a single warrior turned to the right (American Journal of Archaeology 41, 1937, 6. Fig. 1).

A. Phourikis, Ephimeris Archaiologiki 1916; 4 ff., plate 2. — G. Karo, Archäologischer Anzeiger 1916, 141 ff. — H. Diepolder, Die attischen Grabreliefs des 5. und 4. Jahrhunderts v. Chr., 21, plate 16. — N. Himmelmann-Wildschütz, Studien zum Ilissosrelief (München 1956) 19 f. — J. Dohrn, Attische Plastik vom Tode des Phidias bis zum Wirken der großen Meister des IV. Jahrhunderts v. Chr., 164 ff.

185

SEPULCHRAL RELIEF SHOWING TIMARISTA AND KRITO.
White, large-crystalled marble. Height, including the acroterion 6'7" (2 m.), width 3'2"–2'10" (0.94–0.86 m.). Archaeological Museum, Rhodes, Inv. 13638.

The monument was found in 1931 during the Italian excavations at Kamiros on Rhodes. It must have been carved there at the end of the 5th century B.C. The distance that separates Rhodes from Attica, at that time the centre of Greek funerary sculpture, explains certain differences of form, subject and style that distinguish this memorial from Attic sepulchral reliefs of the same period. The relief panel tapers slightly towards the top, where it is terminated by a projecting arch that curves over the figures like a roof and is crowned in the centre by an acroterion – originally, no doubt, painted with a palmette. The two figures stand on a groundline that slopes down from left to right. Timarista is shown on the right, standing erect and seen almost in front view; her left leg is placed well to the side, her head is turned towards the girl Krito, whom she embraces with her arm; her hand rests on Krito's neck. Timarista is dressed in a fine linen chiton, over which she wears a belted peplos with an overfold and a veil round her head. Krito – in a long chiton and cloak – has stepped towards her with bowed head; her left hand rests on the older woman's shoulder, her right is raised in greeting. This hand of the gentle, vital younger girl forms the focal point of the relief between the two heads.

It is a picture of tender and cordial affection, and at the same time of a last meeting and farewell between two people who differ from one another not only in age and height, posture and dress. As to its meaning, there can be little doubt that the right-hand figure represents the deceased. She has been given a heroic aspect by her solemn, upright stance, by the veil, the expressive pose of the left arm and hand that hang down at the edge of the relief, and by a feeling of withdrawal and distance, almost as though she already belonged to the next world. Possibly the figures are those of mother and daughter.

Stylistically the sculptor was dependent upon Attic models. Nevertheless, the manner in which the drapery is rendered – some of it as heavy cloth, some of it as a thin fabric with fine folds – as well as the arched top above the figures seems to suggest the presence of an Ionian-island or Eastern Greek element.

The girl's hair was roughened to receive paint.

Clara Rhodos 4 (1931), 37 ff., fig. 10—11, plates 1 and 5, 1 (1931), p. 31 ff., fig. 17, plates 4—7. — K. Lehmann-Hartleben, Ein griechisches Grabrelief, in: Die Antike 7, 1931, 331 ff., plates 31—33.

186

FRAGMENT OF A SEPULCHRAL STELE.
Found during ex-

cavations in the Piraeus in 1837. Pentelic marble. Height 4'8"
(1.44 m.). National Museum, Athens, No. 716.

The relief, of which a section showing the heads of two figures
is illustrated, is broken diagonally across from top left to bottom
right and only about half of it is extant. It had the rectangular
shape customary in Attic sepulchral reliefs during the late 5th and
early 4th centuries B.C. It was finished off at the top by a shallow
pediment that rested directly upon the antae at the sides without
any intermediate horizontal member. On the left sat the dead
woman, doubtless clad in a long chiton and cloak like the figure of
Hegeso (187), holding in her hands a small box containing her jewellery. Only the head, covered at the back with a cloth like a veil,
remains of the upper part of this figure. The long hair is parted
in the middle and plaited into a thick pigtail which is wound round
the head. Facing her stand two figures looking down at the seated
woman with bowed heads: a youthful female figure in chiton and
cloak and a handsome, bearded man in a cloak that leaves the chest
bare. In his raised left hand he held a knotted stick. His right hand
is stretched out to the seated woman with the palm open to the
front in a gesture expressive of deep emotion. The female figure
in front of him has thrown one end of her cloak over her left
forearm. Her left hand rests on her hip, her right draws the cloak
over her right breast with a beautifully gentle movement.

The relief portrays a family group comprising the dead woman
and her close relatives – perhaps a mother with her grown-up
children, or her son and his wife, or her daughter and her husband.
To judge by the relaxed movements and contours of the figures
with their beauty of line, the richly curving folds of the drapery
and the finely animated faces, the relief must have been carved
by an Attic artist at a date not much later than the tombstone of
Hegeso, i.e. in the early years of the 4th century B.C. An Ionian-
island influence may be seen in the low, superimposed and elongated folds of the softly modelled drapery.

A. Conze, Die attischen Grabreliefs, vol. 1, No. 293, plate 69. — *H. Diepolder*,
Die attischen Grabreliefs des 5. und 4. Jahrhunderts v. Chr., 20 f. plate 14.

187

SEPULCHRAL MONUMENT OF HEGESO. Pentelic marble.
Height 4'11" (1.49 m.). Width 3'2" (0.95 m.) below, 3' (0.92 m.)
above. National Museum, Athens, No. 3624.

The beauty and harmony of this Attic sepulchral monument have
been admired ever since its discovery, in 1870, in its old position
in the cemetery before the Dipylon at Athens. As is often the
case with Greek funerary reliefs of the Classical period, the two
figures are depicted within an architectonic frame. The triangular
pediment is decorated in the centre and at the sides with upward-
pointing acroteria that once bore painted palmettes. On the horizontal transom that carries the pediment, above the seated figure –
the deceased – her name is inscribed: Hegeso, of Proxenos (wife or
daughter).

She is seated in a chair with her legs so stretched out in the large,
rectangular field that she fills the space between the two uprights:
her back touches the right-hand pillar, the tip of her left foot on
the low stool reaches to the left-hand pillar.

Over her long sleeved-chiton she has cast a broad cloak that drapes
the lower part of her body and lightly covers her shoulders. One
end is drawn under the left arm and falls down from the chair
below the left elbow. The wide overlap swells out in close folds

over her lap. The loosely waved hair is held in front by three
ribbons and taken up at the back under a fine veil. In her hands
she held a necklace that was rendered in paint. Hegeso has taken
it from a jewellery case held out to her by her maidservant. The
girl wears a long, ungirded garment. The calm eyes of the women
meet at the mistress's raised right hand that holds the necklace,
linking them in the activity which bound them together during
Hegeso's lifetime.

The group is wonderfully integrated, held together at the sides by
the curving chair-back and by the long fall of the drapery from the
serving-girl's shoulders, as well as being framed by the verticals and
horizontals of the architecture. The broad sweep of the arms is
carried across from one figure, via the jewellery box, to the other,
joining the two figures into a single unit. Hegeso's right hand, bent
upright from the wrist, forms a strongly marked focal point of the
whole relief.

The character in the faces of the two figures sets them close in
time to the Parthenon frieze, but the carefully planned composition, the way these figures are beginning to free themselves
from the background, and the 'rich' treatment of the drapery, show
that the monument can have been carved only during the last
years of the 5th century B.C. A still later date can scarcely be
justified, on stylistic grounds.

A. Conze, Die attischen Grabreliefs 1, No. 68, plate 30. — *E. Buschor*, Erläu-
ternde Texte zu Bruckmanns Wandbildern alter Plastik (1911), No. 1. Reprinted
in: *E. Buschor*, Von griechischer Kunst. Munich 1956, 145 ff. — *H. Diepolder*,
Die attischen Grabreliefs des 5. u. 4. Jahrhunderts v. Chr. 27 f., pl. 20. —
J. Dohrn, Attische Plastik vom Tode des Phidias bis zum Wirken der großen
Meister des IV. Jahrhunderts v. Chr., 96 ff.

188

VOTIVE RELIEF WITH ECHELOS AND BASILE. Found in
the New Phaleron, between Athens and Piraeus, in 1893. Pentelic
marble. Width 2'10" (0.88 m.), height 2'5" (0.76 m.). National
Museum, Athens, No. 1783.

This relief comes from a broad stele, formerly standing free on a
pillar, the opposite side of which also bears a relief. The two
rectangular panels are topped by a shallow pediment with acroteria,
the ornaments on which were executed in paint. According to the
inscription on the reverse face, the stele was an ex-voto offering
to Hermes and the nymphs. This face, not illustrated here, shows
in one row two bearded male figures, one of which is characterized
as a river god by short bull's horns, and three nymphs. Facing
them is a slim, youthful female figure.

On the face shown here a quadriga is galloping up a strip of rising
ground. It is driven by a young man dressed only in a short cloak
held together at the breast by a clasp and flapping out behind him.
He has his left arm round a girl in chiton and cloak who is
standing with knees flexed for balance on the moving chariot and
leaning back against the youth. With one hand she grasps the
raised edge of the chariot front, with the other she holds aside her
cloak. The names Echelos and Basile are cut in the fillet above
the heads of the two figures. These are an Attic hero and heroine
whose significance is roughly that of Hades and Persephone.
Echelos abducted Basile and is now bringing her up out of the
Underworld into the light again. Hermes is hastening up the slope
in front of the quadriga, also identified by an inscription above
his head. In his right hand he holds the *kerykeion*, in his raised
left hand he seems to have had a torch, which was painted in, with

which to light the way out of the darkness for Echelos and the quadriga.

The style of the relief points to an Attic sculptor from the turn of the 5th to the 4th century B.C.

J. N. Svoronos, Das Athener Nationalmuseum 1, 120 ff., No. 1783, plate 28. — *R. Kekulé von Stradonitz*, Echelos und Basile (65. Berliner Winckelmannsprogramm, 1905) 9 ff., plates 2—3. — *O. Walter*, Ephemeris Archaiologiki 1937, I, 110 ff. —*H. K. Süsserott*, Griechische Plastik des 4. Jahrhunderts v. Chr. (1938), 99 ff. — *J. Dohrn*, Attische Plastik vom Tode des Phidias bis zum Wirken der großen Meister des IV. Jahrhunderts v. Chr., 34 and 36.

189–191
RELIEFS FROM THE BALUSTRADE ROUND THE TEMPLE OF ATHENA NIKE ON THE ATHENIAN ACROPOLIS. Pentelic marble. Acropolis Museum, Athens.

On the high, fortified outcrop of rock with a vertical drop on three sides to the south-west of the Athenian Acropolis, outside the propylaea of Mnesikles, stood the sanctuary of victorious Athene (Athena Nike). On this eminence, the so-called Nike Pyrgos, a small Ionic temple facing east was begun by the architect Kallikrates in 448 B.C. but not completed until after the Peace of Nikias in 421 B.C. In the west it extends as far as the extreme edge of the Pyrgos and its southern wall runs parallel with the southern edge of the latter and a few yards away from it. In the north the Pyrgos runs from the western corner of the temple diagonally north-east, where a stairway is cut into it leading from the approach to the citadel to the place of sacrifice in front of the temple.

It was probably not until after Alcibiades's victories over the Peloponnesians in 410/09 B.C. that, for reasons of safety, the Nike Pyrgos was provided with a balustrade of marble panels 3 ft. 6 in. (1.06 m.) high. These were smooth on the inside and bore reliefs on the outside. On the top of the parapet was a grille of metal rods. In the south, west and north the balustrade was set right on the edge of the cliff. In the northeast there was a short fourth side running along the stairway from the ascent to the citadel as far as the north-east corner of the temple. About a third of the relief panels are extant in the form of fragments that have been found at intervals from 1835 onwards on the Acropolis and its southern slope.

The subject of the frieze is the celebration of a victory. Winged Nikes are erecting trophies and moving in procession with sacrificial bulls from the north and south sides towards the west, the main side of the balustrade, in the centre of which a seated Athene is receiving the two processions. To the right and left of Athene, Nikes are standing decorating a trophy. Further seated Athenes were represented at the western corners of the north and south sides, who, by the twist of their torsos and one arm, carried on the movement of the Nikes approaching from the east and led the procession on towards the victorious Athene on the west face. On the short eastern side the figures moved with the steps of the stairway from the corner towards the altar. The leading Nike repeats the movement of the stairs and seems to be climbing up to the temple with the visitor.

The whole composition has often been compared to the Parthenon frieze, on which the seated gods in the east receive the procession approaching from both sides. The design of the frieze is the work of a single Attic master, in whom some claim to recognize the hand of Agorakritos, a pupil of Phidias. The execution was probably in the hands of six different sculptors. In comparison with

the Parthenon frieze the figures are here more markedly detached from the background. Body and drapery have acquired greater independence and are more clearly differentiated from one another in their sculptural treatment. The movements of the individual figures, which achieve an effect of depth without being superimposed one on the other, have a rare beauty and perfection of balance and flow in an unbroken rhythm from one figure to the next. The rich play of the drapery is splendidly decorative.

The illustrations show the four best-preserved panels.

189 above and 190: From the north face of the balustrade (Acropolis Museum No. 11. Height 3'5" (1.05 m.), width 4' (1.23 m.). Two winged Nikes are leading a bull to the sacrifice. The left-hand figure is pulling back the recalcitrant animal on a rope, planting her left foot firmly against a rock. The right-hand Nike, in front of the bull, was doubtless trying to restrain it with her right hand by grasping its horn.

189: below: Western panels from the south face of the balustrade (Acropolis Museum No. 1: height 3'1" (0.94 m.), width 2'5" (0.77 m.) and No. 2: height 2'11" (0.90 m.), width 1'5" (0.45 m.). A helmeted Athene in a long chiton is seated on a rock resting her right arm on her upright shield. The cloak she has cast about her lower body is spread over the rock and the edge of the shield. The upper part of her body was covered by the aegis; on the ground beside her the remains of a trophy, which a Nike with raised arms is decorating, are still visible.

191: Right half of a panel from the south face, on which two Nikes were shown beside a trophy (Acropolis Museum No. 12. Height 3'6" (1.06 m.), width 1'8" (0.52 m.). A Nike taking off her sandals in order to bring the victory offering barefoot. In the movement of untying the sandal her garment has slipped from her right shoulder. The upper part of her body shows through the thin material of the chiton as though exposed. Her cloak is carried from the left forearm right round the figure. It falls round the lower part of the body in sweeping folds, which are long and deep, creating broad valleys of shadow from which the ridges stand out in bright light.

The panels with the seated Athene and the Nike in front of her decorating the trophy are the work of the same master as the Nike removing her sandals. He is the most important artist represented on the frieze. Two different sculptors can be distinguished in the panel on the north face showing the Nikes leading the bull to sacrifice. Each of them was responsible for one of the Nikes, which differ from one another in the particular relationship of body to garments, in posture, and in the style of the drapery.

R. Kekulé, Die Reliefs an der Balustrade der Athena Nike (1881). — *R. Heberdey*, Die Komposition der Reliefs an der Balustrade der Athena Nike, in: Österreichische Jahreshefte 21/22, 1922/24, 1 ff. — *R. Carpenter*, The Sculpture of the Nike Temple Parapet (1929). — *J. Dohrn*, Attische Plastik vom Tode des Phidias bis zum Wirken der großen Meister des IV. Jahrhunderts v. Chr., 24 f. and 64 ff. — *K. Schefold*, Agorakritos als Erbe des Pheidias, in: Robert Böhringer — Eine Freundesgabe (1957), 570 ff.

192
TOMBSTONE OF DEXILEOS. Found in front of the Dipylon at Athens in 1863. Pentelic marble. Height with the base 5'8" (1.75 m.). Ceramicus Museum, Athens.

The slightly concave front face of the rectangular base, in which the relief was inserted, bears a four-line inscription in the large, clear letters of the early 4th century B.C. It states in brief and simple words that the tombstone was erected for Dexileos of

Thorikos, a young warrior who fell at Corinth in 394 B.C. at the age of twenty. He had particularly distinguished himself in the battle along with four other riders.

The square panel, which is only topped by a projecting pediment with acroteria while the sides are unframed, shows a young warrior galloping over his naked adversary – who has fallen to his knees – and thrusting vigorously down at him with his spear. In his left hand he holds the reins. He is wearing a short, belted chiton, a sword-belt diagonally across his chest and a cloak that is held together by a clasp on his right shoulder and that billows out behind him in broad folds. His foe is supporting himself with his left arm, round which is wrapped a small cloak, on his great round shield. He is striving to protect himself from the spear-thrust with the sword in his right hand; the sword sheath is visible on his left hip.

The pose of the warrior fallen to his knees with the outstretched right leg and the foreshortened left shank is borrowed from a famous creation of Phidias's day. The profound vision of combat evident in the portrayal of victor and vanquished still bears the stamp of the mature Classical style of the 5th century B.C. In this respect Dexileos's tombstone has affinities with the equestrian relief in the Villa Albani (179–181). In its pictorial composition, however, in the stress on parallel and intersecting diagonals, in the twist of the bodies out of the background into the relief plane, in the liberation of the figures from the ground and in the emphasis on psychic values it differs appreciably from the art of the Parthenon and proves itself a typical monument of the beginning of the 4th century B.C.

Bridle, reins, spear, the wreath round the rider's head and his adversary's sword-belt were of bronze. The top of the pediment contains a row of six holes at irregular intervals as though for the insertion of metal objects, perhaps rods as a protection against birds or to hang wreaths and fillets on.

A. Conze, Die attischen Grabreliefs, vol. 2, No. 1158, plate 248. — *E. Pfuhl*, Archäologischer Anzeiger 1932, 1 ff. — *J. Dohrn*, Attische Plastik vom Tode des Phidias bis zum Wirken der großen Meister des IV. Jahrhunderts v. Chr., 128 ff.

193–197

LYCIAN SARCOPHAGUS. Parian marble. From the Royal Cemetery at Sidon. Length 8'4" (2.535 m.), width 4'6" (1.365 m.), height 9'9" (2.965 m.). Istanbul, Archaeological Museum, Department of Classical Antiquities, No. 63 (369).

The shape of the high lid, the sides of which in cross section first rise steeply, then curve over and meet in the central axis, is of Lycian origin. It has given its name to a whole type of Greek sarcophagi from Asia Minor. The ogival lid of this sarcophagus is undecorated on the rounded long sides and plain apart from two lifting bosses, in the shape of lions, resting on rectangular bases. One end of the lid is ornamented with a pair of griffins springing at each other, the opposite end with two seated sirens facing away from one another and out from the pictorial plane; the pairs of two figures are set on either side of a central support. The ridge is crowned on both sides with a palmette fan that rises out of volutes resting on acanthus leaves.

The rectangular chest of the sarcophagus stands on a low quadrangular base and ends at the top in a fine bead moulding and egg-and-dart moulding. It bears bold and spacious reliefs on all four faces. The two long sides show hunting scenes. On one side five

youthful riders leap forward – three from the left, two from the right – and hurl their spears at a charging wild boar in the centre. The other side shows Amazons on two quadrigas at full gallop; those not holding the reins are flinging their spears at a crouching lion. The almost square reliefs at the ends portray two similarly composed groups: two Centaurs fighting with the invulnerable Lapith Caeneus, and two Centaurs fighting over a deer – themes which, like the griffins and sirens on the ends of the lid, are taken from the repertoire of funerary subjects.

The riders hunting the boar are inescapably reminiscent of the cavalcade of riders on the Parthenon frieze (149–154), just as the reliefs depicting Centaurs on the ends of the sarcophagus chest are inconceivable without the south metopes of the Parthenon as a model. The quadrigas, too, recall Attic works, for example the votive relief with Echelos and Basile (188) at Athens. Like this relief, the Lycian sarcophagus must have been produced some time after the Parthenon frieze, probably in the early 4th century B. C., around the period of the Dexileos stele (192). The reliefs on the sarcophagus are, however, distinguished from Attic works by characteristic features to be explained by the artist's oriental origin. On the sides the spatial depth of the reliefs and the powerful foreshortening are striking. The sculptural forms are more flexibly treated than in Attic work; they have not the same concentration and tension. Despite all the quality of execution, the figures do not possess the intense spiritual expressiveness and inner fulfilment with which we are familiar in the Parthenon frieze.

Contrary to other sarcophagi from the Sidonian Royal Cemetery, only remnants of the original paintwork remain on the ornaments and relief figures; the paint is relatively better preserved on the lid than on the chest itself.

O. Hamdi-Bey and Th. Reinach, Une Nécropole Royale à Sidon (Paris, 1892), 209 ff., plates XII–XVII. — *F. Winter*, Archäologischer Anzeiger 1894, 10 ff. — *G. Mendel*, Catalogue des Sculptures Grecques, Romaines et Byzantines dans les Musées Impériaux Ottomans I (1912), 158 ff., No. 63 (369).

198

STANDING BOY. Pentelic marble. Height 33.6" (84 cm.). Museum, Piraeus.

Whereas we possess a comparatively large number of statues of youths dating from the 6th century B.C., which stood on graves as effigies of the deceased and as memorials, only a few corresponding sepulchral statues have come down to us from Classical times. In the 5th and 4th centuries B.C., tombstones carved in the round must have diminished in number and importance as compared with funerary reliefs. We occasionally come across statuette-sized sepulchral figures of this kind, shown at the top of a tall pedestal, in representations on the white background of ointment vessels for the dead dating from the second half of the 5th century.

The withdrawn, curiously 'twilight' attitude of the body and expression of the face with the large eyes under heavy lids and the slightly drawn-down corners of the mouth – as though the boy had turned away from this world to which he had ceased to belong – render this figure reminiscent of those on Attic funerary reliefs and indicate that this is no ordinary votive statue but a sepulchral one. It is designed to be seen from the front. Very little weight rested on the left leg; the left foot was placed far back and to the side. The movement initiated by the free leg was not, however, imparted with the same vigour to the upper part of the body. The head with the full, rounded lower face rests almost squarely on the rather broad and short neck, turned only slightly to the left. The right arm is hanging slightly forward – the right hand may have held a scraper or a vessel – the left upper arm is drawn back. This gives a certain hesitancy to the rhythm of the figure, which distinguishes the statue from works of the late 5th century B.C. and, together with the boyish, almost childlike conception, the delicate modelling of the body, the soft forms of the face and the rendering of the hair in mobile tufts, suggests a date in the early 4th century B.C.

The spirit and style of the work make it very likely that the sculptor, who was certainly an Attic artist, also produced sepulchral reliefs, which must be recognizable among those that have come down to us.

W. Kraiker, Ein griechisches Knabenbildnis, in: Die Antike 14, 1938, 196 ff., plates 18—20.

199

STANDING NUDE GIRL. Found at Beroea in Macedonia. Bronze, hollow cast. Height 10" (25 cm.). Museum antiker Kleinkunst, Munich, Inv. 3669. Purchased from a dealer in 1909.

To depict Aphrodite completely nude did not accord with the idea of the goddess of love held during the 5th or even the early 4th century B.C. Erotic tendencies, which would have been fostered by Aphrodite's nakedness, were still alien to the conception of her nature current at that time. Praxiteles, in his famous Cnidian Aphrodite, was the first to venture upon the step to total nudity. Thus the bronze statuette at Munich, insofar as it was thought to date from the turn of the 5th to the 4th century B.C., was taken to be, not an image of the goddess herself, but a mythological figure, a servant in the cult of Aphrodite, or a hetaera.

The weight of the delicate figure with its beautiful lines rests on the right leg, while the left is unweighted and placed to one side, so that the axes of the body are tilted. The fine curve of movement, which rises from below, is taken up and carried on by the turn of the head and by the lowered eyes. The upper body is slender, the hair bound with a coif. The arms, which are now missing, were cast separately and attached. The figure probably leant against a pillar with the hand of her outstretched left arm. In her right hand the girl doubtless held a mirror into which she gazed, a pose that harmoniously rounded off the composition.

The rhythm, the lively modelling and the girl's calm pensiveness, account for the special charm of this precious and much admired statuette. It has recalled works issuing from the school and followers of Polyclitus, and the suggestion has been made that it may have been produced within the sphere of Argive art. Latterly, however, the number of experts who regard the provenance of the bronze in a different light has increased. The long, slender upper part of the body with its narrow shoulders, the contrariety of its movements, the marked turn of the head, the naturalistic representation of the body coupled with the inner animation of the figure, as well as the relationship between the statuette and the surrounding space – all this, they claim, points to a phase postdating the late 5th and early 4th centuries, and cannot be interpreted as deriving from before the beginning of the Hellenistic period. Furthermore, the way the hair is tied in the head-cloth differentiates the bronze from all High Classical examples and warrants dating it to the first half of the 3rd century B.C.

J. Sieveking, Münchner Jahrbuch für Bildende Kunst 5, 1910, 1 ff. — E. Buschor, Festschrift für P. Hensel (1923), 231. — W. H. Schuchhardt, Die Antike 12, 1936, 84 ff. — A. Greifenhagen, Das Mädchen von Beröa. Opus Nobile, Meisterwerke der antiken Kunst, No. 9 (1958). — N. Himmelmann-Wildschütz, Eine römische Bronze in Oxford, in: Marburger Winckelmann-Programm 1958, 6, Note 6. — J. Charbonneaux, Les Bronzes Crecs, L'Oeil du Connaisseur (1958), 109.

200, 201

ATTIC TOMBSTONE. Found at Athens. Pentelic marble. Height 3' (0.93 m.). National Museum, Athens, No. 3472.

The inscriptions on the horizontal beam over the figures state that the tombstone was erected for Theano, the wife of Ktesileos of Erythrai. She sits erect on a stool whose strong, straight legs have been turned on a lathe. Her left foot is set on a low foot-rest. She is dressed in a long, thin sleeved-chiton and a cloak draped round the lower part of her body. She has also a cloth over her back, one end of which she holds in a bundle with her left elbow, while she draws the other end, whose corners lie upon her left thigh, forward over her shoulder with a delicate movement of her right hand. Her loose, wavy hair is tied with a broad band, her ear embellished with a large, round disc. Before her stands her husband – a handsome, bearded man in a wide cloak that leaves his chest bare. He has crossed his left leg over his right and is leaning forward supported by a stick placed under his left arm-pit. His hands are clasped in a gesture that may express submission to his fate. His grave eyes rest upon the seated woman in front of him.

Although this relief is separated by only two or three decades from the tombstone of Hegeso (187) it differs in a number of characteristic features from the older work, which was still directly influenced by the Parthenon sculptures. The close compositional link between the two figures, which the artist stressed in Hegeso's tombstone by means of the box held by both the figures, the movements of the arms and hands and the inclination of the heads towards the centre, is no longer present in this relief. The figures are kept apart by the difference in scale and the wide, blank area of background between them. Each has gained more independence. At the same time they possess increased mobility and have been set more free from the background, which – like the figures – has acquired greater autonomy. The position of the woman's head, raised and gazing into space, and the twist of her torso away from the side view and towards the front, make her figure seem remote from that of the man standing in front of her.

The slant of the footstool to the picture-plane and the oval formed by the man's arms are devices employed to achieve the new type of spatial effect aimed at in this relief. The relationship between body and drapery likewise differs from that current during the period of Hegeso's tombstone. Although, in general, the fabric here still follows the forms and movements of the figures, it is more sharply differentiated from the unclothed parts of the body and, in the hang of the garments and the play of the folds, is beginning to live a life of its own as decoration.

S. Papaspiridi, Guide du Musée National d'Athènes. Marbres, Bronzes, Vases (1927), 138 f., fig. 22. — H. Diepolder, Die attischen Grabreliefs des 5. und 4. Jahrhunderts v. Chr., 28, plate 22. — J. Dohrn, Jahrbuch des Deutschen Archäologischen Instituts 70, 1955, 62 f., fig. 3.

202, 203

ATTIC TOMBSTONE OF AN UNKNOWN WOMAN WITH HER MAIDSERVANT. Pentelic marble. Found in the Piraeus. Height 4' (1.21 m.). National Museum, Athens, No. 726.

The relief, characteristic of its time, resembles in type the tomb-stone of Hegeso (187) of approximately four decades earlier: on the right is a seated woman, the deceased, and in front of her stands a serving-girl holding a box. But how differently has the 4th-century artist treated the same compositional elements!

The mistress is seated on a chair with no back-rest, lost in thought, her back curved, her head pensively bowed. Here, too, the feet rest on a small stool, but this is placed at an angle, the left foot is drawn back, the right thrust far forward, so that the robe is drawn taut between the shanks in long folds. The left forearm is held close to the body, the right elbow is supported on the left hand and the right hand grasps the cloth round the shoulders with a graceful movement. The loosely waved hair is combed back at the side and taken up over a circlet.

The essential difference from the tombstone of Hegeso lies in the fact that there the maidservant is handing the box to her seated mistress, who is taking the jewellery from it, and that this action, the movements of the arms and the common activity link the two figures together; whereas here the serving-girl stands on her own, with very little weight on her free right leg, holding the box with one hand and raising its lid with the other. As she does so, she looks down at the box. The close connexion between the figures has been abandoned in the later relief. Each of the two figures is rendered separate and compact by the drapery drawn taut around the powerfully built bodies with their emphatically rounded forms, and this tendency to independence and separateness is enhanced by the circling lines of movement. The figures move more freely in space and stand out more distinctly from the architectural background of the relief, which does not bind the group to the same extent as in Hegeso's tombstone but rather provides a foil to it.

A. Conze, Die attischen Grabreliefs, vol. 1, No. 69, plate 31. — *H. Diepolder*, Die attischen Grabreliefs des 5. und 4. Jahrhunderts v. Chr. 31 f.; 35, plate 26.

204

COUPLE SAYING FAREWELL, from an Attic funeral vase. Found on Salamis. Pentelic marble. Height of the figures, 14.2" (35.5 cm). Glyptothek, Munich, No. 498. Acquired in 1910.

Slender earthenware vessels on a round base, with a long neck and a curved handle, bearing coloured painting on a white ground, were used in Attica during the 5th century B.C. in the cult of the dead. They were called *lekythoi* and their purpose was to contain the oil with which the dead person was anointed. After the final unction the jar was placed in the grave with the dead or set up on top of the tomb. From this developed the custom of copying the earthenware vessels on a larger scale in marble, decorating them with reliefs instead of painted pictures, and erecting them as a monument.

The vase shown here is an Attic funerary *lekythos* of this type. The *lekythos* was originally about 4'3" (1.30 m.) tall. Only the middle part, height 2'5" (0.74 m.), is extant. Two figures are portrayed on the same base-piece: a bearded man in a cloak resting on a (painted) staff held under his left arm-pit, and a young woman in a long chiton and cloak with a veil over her head. They are shaking hands. Are they greeting or taking leave of one another? Are they man and wife or father and daughter? Whom does the monument commemorate? We shall find no unequivocal answer to these questions, because the artist of the relief and his age did not intend to characterize the figures in detail or give an exact account of what was happening. They were concerned, rather, to immortalize the close unity of two people. Nevertheless, the figures seem to stand between two worlds and to belong to both at once: they are united in life and death. The young woman with the veil pausing in her walk must be the deceased, who here takes leave of the man, while he gazes at her.

The splendidly rhythmic figure of the woman, the head of the bearded man, and the style of the drapery, recur in a similar form on a decree stele dating from 375 B.C. The Munich *lekythos* must have been fashioned at this period or a little later.

P. Wolters, Münchner Jahrbuch für Bildende Kunst 6, 1911, 292 ff. — *L. Curtius*, Münchner Jahrbuch für Bildende Kunst 6, 1911, 173 ff. — *H. Diepolder*, Die attischen Grabreliefs des 5. und 4. Jahrhunderts v. Chr., 39, plate 34.

205

FEMALE HEAD. Found at Tegea in 1901. Parian marble. Height 11.4" (28.5 cm.). National Museum, Athens, No. 3602.

Among the sculptures from the sanctuary of Athene at Tegea that do not belong to the pediment carvings of Scopas, this head is pre-eminent for its beauty and great artistic merit. It seems to have come from a single figure that stood on a rectangular base in front of the Temple of Athene close to its south-east corner.

The long, narrow oval of the face leads straight up from the cheeks to the high back of the head, whose noble form is crowned by soft curls. The turn of the head on the slender neck, the expression of the face and the weight of the coiffure on the extended axis through chin and temple lend the work pride and grace in equal measure, a balance between outer mobility and a quietude that radiates from within. The head is turned slightly to one side (her right). The long, narrow eyes framed by broad, clearly defined lids look downwards. The nose leads from the lofty, upright forehead in an unbroken line to the small, slightly open mouth with the beautifully curved lips and the full, round chin. The hair is parted in the middle and brushed back over the ears. The thick hair at the back of the head is combed upwards and pinned in curls over the crown. A band that holds this hair in place at the back of the neck is also visible over the parting. The wavy hair at the sides is taken back diagonally from the temples over this band, combined with the combed-up curls and held in position by a second band or diadem.

The wealth of artistic means employed in the construction of individual forms such as the eyes or the mouth – here clearly defined, there more softly modelled – and the intricate arrangement of the hair combine in their effect to form a harmonious whole.

In the past the head was erroneously held to be the Atalanta from the east pediment of the Temple of Athene at Tegea, and then taken to be the remains of a statue of Hygieia by Scopas, which stood inside the temple beside the image of the goddess. A comparison with Scopas's heads from Tegea or the frieze on the Mausoleum at Halicarnassus (214, 215, top), however, shows the difference in the shape of the head, the eyes and the expression of the face. The ideal of beauty embodied in the noble and very feminine features tends rather to link the head with works from the middle period of Praxiteles (ca. 340 B.C.), such as the Cnidian Aphrodite or the Brauron Artemis, which have come down to us in Roman marble copies.

G. Mendel, Bulletin de Correspondance Hellénique 25, 1901, 260 f., plates 4—5.
— Ch. Dugas, J. Berchmanns et M. Clemmensen, Le Sanctuaire d'Aléa Athéna
à Tégée au IVe Siècle (Paris 1924), 117 ff., plates 113—115.

206

DEMETER. Parian marble. Height 32.2″ (80.5 cm.). Archae-ological Museum, Venice, No. 6 (Inv. No. 21). From the collection of Giovanni Grimani, Patriarch of Aquileia, which he gave to the Republic of Venice in 1586.

Like other female marble statuettes of the Classical period in Venice, this figure of Demeter is derived from a large-scale proto-type. Its severe pose is explained by the fact that the model was a cult statue, which, as such, was designed to be seen from the front. From the puffed-out drapery over the girdle downwards the long, heavy folds of the peplos with overfold conceal the lower part of the body on the side of the supporting leg. The toes of the free leg are set so far back that the thigh and knee appear beneath the taut drapery as though bare. The raised right hand held a sceptre. The left forearm was carved separately. In her left hand the goddess must have held ears of corn or a bowl. The head is turned very slightly to the right on the long, columnar neck. The parted hair provides a loose, abundant frame for the round face with the broad chin and full cheeks which, despite the very soft modelling of the surface, is austere in form and expression. Above the low *polos* the cloak is drawn round from behind like a veil to frame the head and neck with vertical folds, which only heightens the hieratic severity of the pose. It falls down the back as far as the left knee, covering both shoulders and hanging on the left side with one end under the arm, while the other end crosses the breast from the right shoulder in a wide arc and is laid across the left forearm.

Even though the statuette cannot be the equal of its prototype — which is lost to us — in inner grandeur and masterliness of execu-tion, it is none the less interesting and valuable for the freshness and vitality of its sculptural treatment and as a reflection of a Greek cult statue from the mid-4th century B.C.

In comparison with the figures of girls from the south hall of the Erechtheum, and also with the Eirene of Kephisodotus, the drapery has here acquired a more independent function in relation to the body. The body is carried just as much by the tubular folds in front of the supporting leg as by the visible free leg, and the folds of the veil hanging down from the *polos* form a support for the head and neck.

H. Dütschke, Antike Bildwerke in Oberitalien 5 (1882), No. 203. — A. Furt-wängler, Griechische Originalstatuen in Venedig, in: Abhandlungen der k. Baye-rischen Akademie der Wissenschaften, 1. Klasse 21, 2, 1898, 305 ff. (31 ff.), plate 5.
— E. Löwy, Antike Plastik. Festschrift zum 60. Geburtstag von W. Amelung (1928), 135.

207–209

THE 'WEEPING WOMEN SARCOPHAGUS'. Pentelic marble. Length of plinth 8′9″ (2.653 m.), width of plinth 5′7″ (1.383 m.), height of the whole sarcophagus to the tip of the central acroterium 5′9″ (1.797 m.). Istanbul, Archaeological Museum, Department of Classical Antiquities, No. 10 (368).

In 1887 an extensive cemetery was discovered at Sidon, on Phoenician soil, comprizing seven rectangular chambers that contained in all seventeen large marble sarcophagi, some of a roughly human shape, others shaped like houses or chests, dating from the 5th and 4th century B.C. It was evident from the scale of the cemetery, the only access to which was by a shaft over thirty feet deep leading to the centre, and by the imposing pro-portions and high artistic quality of some of the sarcophagi, that this must be the burial place of the Sidonian kings and their families. The contents of the sarcophagi had been plundered — perhaps back in antiquity. Almost all the sarcophagi had been more or less severely damaged in the process.

The 'Weeping Women Sarcophagus', as it has come to be called, stood in one of the chambers next to the entry shaft over a pit containing a mummy-shaped Egyptian sarcophagus dating from an earlier phase in the use of the cemetery. The 'Weeping Women Sarcophagus' was probably not designed to be placed in this parti-cular tomb chamber, for the relief-decorated balustrade that runs round the lid was originally crowned with a marble ornamentation in the form of vases, which had to be removed before the sarco-phagus could be introduced into this chamber.

Like the rest of the large relief-decorated sarcophagi from the Royal Cemetery at Sidon, the 'Weeping Women Sarcophagus' constitutes an elaborate whole worked out to the last detail, in the manner of 4th-century Greek art. The monumental chest with a roof-shaped lid stands on a base of rectangular profile encircled by a Lesbian cyma, above which runs a many-figured frieze showing hunting scenes. The walls of the chest dissolve to form a view into an open Ionic hall with slender columns, on which rest the architrave and dentil moulding, which in turn carry the gabled roof with the balustrade. Small lions' heads as gargoyles on the side cymas, seated sphinxes at the four corners of the roof and palmette acroteria over the ridge on both sides complete the over-all picture. Between the columns — replaced at the corners by pillars — and in front of a platform that extends all the way round, the artist has placed six female figures in long chitons and cloaks on each of the sides and three on each of the ends: striding, standing, leaning or half-sitting women who are mourning, lamenting and weeping — every figure different in attitude, posture and gesture. Some have their chiton drawn over their head like a veil, two of them are carrying cymbals, which form part of the music of the lamentation for the dead. The eighteen figures are combined in interconnected groups of varying sizes. Mourning women are also represented in the pediment triangles: a seated woman in the centre flanked by two recumbent ones. On the balustrades on either side of the roof we see the same solemn procession: single horses — evidently the favourite mounts of the dead prince — lead by their grooms, interspersed by quadrigas. One of the chariots bears a large vessel containing the mortal remains of the deceased. Over the triangles of the pediment we can distinguish mourning men in Asiatic costume.

All these scenes and figures combine to form a unified theme. They recount the life of the oriental prince here laid to rest, among whose special delights was the chase and who is mourned by his wives and hetaerae. Historical and art-historical evidence points to the sarcophagus being that of King Straton I (died c. 360 B.C.), of whom Theopompus relates in *Athenaeus XII*, 41, p. 531, among other things, that he led a licentious life and had many hetaerae sent to him from the Peloponnesus.

The paintwork on this sarcophagus is less well preserved than on other sarcophagi from the Royal Cemetery at Sidon, since a great deal of moisture entered the chamber in which it stood. Thus the blue has largely disappeared, whereas the red, brown and yellow colours on the garments have lasted better.

The affinity of the mourning women of the 'Weeping Women Sarcophagus' to similar female figures on Attic funerary reliefs, which can be dated on stylistic grounds from the middle of the 4th century B.C. (cf. H. Diepolder, *Die attischen Grabreliefs des 5. und 4. Jahrhunderts B.C.*, plates 41 ff.), gives us its probable dating. The artist of the 'Weeping Women Sarcophagus' — a sculptor from the Greek Orient — was firmly rooted in the Attic tradition; nevertheless, his figures lack the powerful expressiveness arising out of the spiritual concentration and profundity that characterizes the best Attic tomb reliefs of this period.

O. *Hamdi-Bey and Jb. Reinach*, Une Nécropole Royale à Sidon (Paris, 1892), 209 ff. and 238 ff., plates IV–XI. — *F. Winter*, Die Sarkophage von Sidon, in: Archäologischer Anzeiger 1894, 1 ff., and *do.* in: Antike Denkmäler III (1912), 12 f., plate 11. — *F. Studniczka*, Jahrbuch des Deutschen Archäologischen Instituts 9, 1894, 204 ff. — *G. Mendel*, Catalogue des Sculptures Grecques, Romaines et Byzantines dans les Musées Impériaux Ottomans I (1912), 48 ff., No 10 (368). — *L. Curtius*, Jahrbuch der preußischen Kunstsammlungen 61, 1940, 73 ff. — *J. Kleemann*, Der Satrapensarkophag von Sidon (Berlin, 1958), *passim*.

210

PORTRAIT OF AN AFRICAN. Found under a mosaic floor in the ruins of the Temple of Apollo at Cyrene, North Africa, in 1861. Bronze. Height 1' (30.5 cm.). British Museum, London. No. 268.

The physiognomy of this striking and important head, which is turned slightly to its right side on the powerful neck, has an un-Greek look. It is that of an African, an inhabitant of the region in which it was found. The face with the receding forehead, broad cheekbones, straight nose and very short chin is small. By contrast, the back of the head curves out in a wide arc. The hair of the head is rendered in sculptured curls, clearly separated from one another, full of movement but not restless, which cover the skull like thick fur. The beard, which is shaved into a regular curve, and the eyebrows, are chiselled to indicate the thin, soft down that is characteristic of the facial hair of dark-skinned peoples. The small eyes were inset in glass flux; their lower lids hang down in a slight arc towards the outer corners, the upper lids beneath the arched eyebrows are heavy with pads of fat. The full lips of the small mouth, which were inserted separately and overlaid with silver, form a clearly defined and beautifully mobile curve.

Opinions differ as to the exact age of the head, some writers ascribing it to various periods in the 4th century B.C. while others date it from the mid-3rd century. There are no other portraits directly comparable to the African. The closed outline and the relatively firm modelling make a date later than the middle of the 4th century B.C. unlikely. The structure of the head has affinities with such works as the so-called Lansdowne Hercules (Brunn-Bruckmann, *Denkmäler der griechischen und römischen Plastik*, Plate 691; now in the John Paul Getty Museum, Malibu, USA), which would suggest a date around 360 B.C.

Who was represented by the statue to which the head belonged we do not know. A king of Numidia or Mauretania has been suggested; but it might also portray a victorious athlete.

O. *Rayet*, Monuments de l'art antique (1880) 2, 195 ff., plate 57. — *H. Schrader*, Über den Marmorkopf eines Negers (60. Berliner Winckelmannsprogramm, 1900), 10 ff. — *A. Hekler*, Die Bildniskunst der Griechen und Römer, p. XV, plate 36. — *L. Laurenzi*, Ritratti Greci 98, No. 29, plate 10.

211–213

THE 'MAUSOLUS'. Marble. Height 3'4" (3 m.). British Museum, London, No. 1000.

The colossal statue was found during British excavations in 1857, accompanied by a female figure on the same scale and the remains of a marble chariot, on the north face of the Mausoleum at Halicarnassus. The two statues must have stood side by side to form a group. It was therefore natural to assume that the male figure, which bears clear marks of being a portrait, was Mausolus and the female figure his sister and wife Artemisia, and that they stood in the quadriga which crowned Mausolus's tomb. But this interpretation was later abandoned, because the figures were too small and because their posture and movements were not adapted for a chariot. Also their identity as Mausolus and Artemisia became dubious and it seemed possible that they were members of the family, perhaps the couple's parents. On the other hand, the original conjecture drew support from the fact that they were the only portrait statues on this scale, far above life-size, found at the Mausoleum, and as such would most likely be those of the occupant of the tomb and his wife. The position the statues occupied in or on the Mausoleum cannot be stated with certainty.

The male figure stands in the walking position, in an erect, self-confident posture appropriate to a ruler, the head turned slightly to his right, the eyes gazing into the distance. It is clad in a long robe held together on the shoulders, and over this a wide cloak one end of which hangs down over the left shoulder, while the rest is drawn to the left under the right arm with a broad over-fold, and wrapped round the lower body in sweeping folds. The left hand held a sheathed sword, remains of which have been found; the right hand probably rested on a sceptre.

The head is one of the most imposing portraits known from the mid-4th century B.C. The long hair is swept back from the low forehead and falls over the ears to the shoulders in long strands. The face is broad and rounded. A short, flocculent beard grows on the cheeks, the chin and the upper lip. The sharply drawn lips have a full and beautiful curve. The deep-set eyes with their heavy upper lids are placed wide apart and shadowed by large, powerful brows. Two folds run down from the wide nostrils to the corners of the mouth.

The figure immortalized by the sculptor in this work must have been a ruler from Asia Minor of eminent importance. Because of the finding-place and its connexion with the rest of the Mausoleum sculptures, whose approximate dates are known, this original statue is of particular importance for the history of the Greek portrait. It had already been associated earlier with the sculptor Bryaxis, who executed the reliefs that decorate the north side of the Mausoleum (cf. 216 above); more recently, indeed, actually attributed to him.

J. J. Bernoulli, Griechische Ikonographie, part 2 (1901), 41 ff. — *Fr. v. Lorentz*, „Maussolos" und die Quadriga auf dem Maussoleion. Dissertation, Leipzig 1931. — *E. Buschor*, Maussollos und Alexander (1950), 21 f. — *M. Bieber*, Who made the Statues of Maussolos and Artemisia?, in: Anthemon, Scritti di Archeologia e di Antichità Classiche in onore di Carlo Anti (1955), 67 ff. — B. *Ashmole*, Journal of Hellenic Studies 71, 1951, 20, note 40. — *E. Buschor*, Die Plastik der Griechen (1936 and 1958), 86.

214–217

RELIEF PANELS FROM THE MAUSOLEUM AT HALICARNASSUS. Coarse-grained, bluish marble from Asia Minor. Height 2'11" (0.89 m.). British Museum, London.

Mausolus (211–213) ruled in Caria as satrap of the Persian Kings Artaxerxes II and III from 377 to 353 B.C. In 359 he transferred

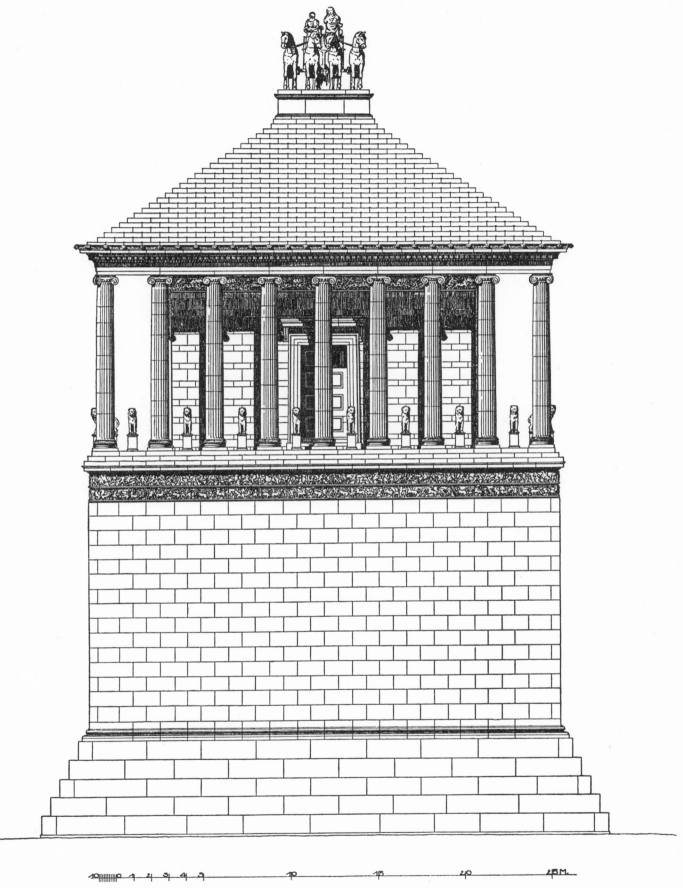

11 Mausoleum at Halicarnassus. Reconstruction of the front. After F. Krischen, *Der Entwurf des Maussolleions*

the residency of his father and predecessor Hecatomnus from Mylasa back to Halicarnassus on the coast of Asia Minor. In the centre of the replanned city stood his enormous tomb, which he began to build during his lifetime and which was numbered in antiquity among the Seven Wonders of the World. It was still referred to in the 12th century, and its ruins were later used by the Knights of St John in building fortifications. The remains were uncovered during British excavations under C. T. Newton from 1856 to 1858. Isolated frieze panels, which had been built into the walls of a citadel, had already found their way to London earlier.

We can form only a general idea of the colossal tomb, which combined ideas and architectural forms from Asia Minor, Egypt and Greece, from ancient descriptions and the surviving remains. It was over 150 feet (45 m.) high and divided into three tiers. On a rectangular foundation with a surface area of 95×117 feet (29×35.6 m.) rose an Ionic building supported by nine colums 40 ft. (12.30 m.) high at the ends and eleven at the sides, on top of which stood a stone stepped pyramid with twenty-four steps, each of them 1'5" (31 cm.) high. The whole structure was crowned by a quadriga.

All four sides were richly decorated with sculptural ornament, statues and continuous friezes. According to traditionary knowledge each face was decorated by a different sculptor: the front face in the east by Scopas of Paros; the south by Timotheus, the eldest, probably from Epidaurus; the north by Bryaxis, whose name is Carian, but who is described as an Athenian; the west by Leochares, an Attic master, the youngest of the four artists.

After Mausolus's death his sister and wife, Artemisia, had the work on the Mausoleum continued. At her death in 351 B.C. the building was not yet finished. According to Pliny in his *Naturalis Historia* (36, 31) the four sculptors did not stop work until the whole edifice was complete, for they regarded the Mausoleum as a memorial to their own fame and to that of art itself. Recent research, however, has led, on stylistic grounds, to the supposition that work on the building and its sculptural ornament was interrupted soon after Artemisia's death and only completed under Alexander the Great (c. 333).

Two relief friezes, one showing combats between Lapithae and Centaurs, the other showing combats between Greeks and Amazons, ran round the base. A third frieze depicting chariot-racing doubtless embellished the cella in the interior of the pillared court. We reproduce here various relief panels from the Amazons frieze, from which the styles of the four sculptors emerge with some clarity. These are as follows:

216, top. From the northern face. Bryaxis. Typical features are the diagonal movements that reach out sideways and run parallel with the background, the arrangement of the figures in several layers one behind the other, and the extension of the action of the combat from one figure to another (British Museum, No. 1019).

215, bottom; 216, bottom. From the southern face. Timotheus. The male bodies are clearly articulated in the manner of Polyclitus and his successors. The figures are built up with a similar lucidity into individual groups that do not extend beyond the edges of the panel. The Amazons' bodies and short garments form a single unit. The body carries the drapery, which follows its forms and movements (British Museum Nos. 1006 and 1022). Panel 1022, which reached London via Genova, was previously attributed incorrectly to Bryaxis.

214; 215, top. From the eastern face. Scopas. The powerfully built, passionately mobile figures race across the surface in a rhythmic rise and fall. They are linked less by their interlocking or closely planted feet than by their deep, significant glances. The broad diagonal lines and isolated small groups are characteristic of the composition (British Museum Nos. 1013, 1014, 1015).

217. From the western face. Leochares. The elongated figures, some of which are characterized by a spiral movement, as well as the continuous composition, possess a powerful dynamic quality. They thrust deep into space and are linked together by intersections (British Museum, No. 1020, 1021).

J. v. Breen, Het Reconstructieplan voor het Mausoleum te Halikarnassos, Amsterdam 1942. — *H. Drerup*, Pytheos und Satyros, in: Jahrbuch des Deutschen Archäologischen Instituts 69, 1954, 1 ff. — *P. Wolters* and *J. Sieveking*, Der Amazonenfries des Maussoleums, in: Jahrbuch des Deutschen Archäologischen Instituts 24, 1909, 171 ff. — *E. Buschor*, Maussollos und Alexander (1950). — *B. Ashmole*, Journal of Hellenic Studies 71, 1951, 15 ff. — *F. Krischen*, Der Entwurf des Maussolleions, in: Zeitschrift für Bauwesen, 1927, No. 10—12.

218–220

STATUE OF A YOUNG MAN. Bronze. Height 6'5" (1.94 m.). National Museum, Athens, No. 13396.

The bronze was found in 1900 in the sea off Anticythera, a small island in the south of the Peloponnesus, as part of a cargo of works of art that were being transported from Greece to Rome during the time of the Roman Empire. The statue has recently been pieced together anew from many small fragments. A few connecting parts have been restored. As was usual with large-scale bronzes in antiquity, the head, arms and legs were cast separately and then joined to the trunk.

To some, the posture of the figure has suggested a competitor who has thrown an object, probably a ball, at a target. Others have seen in it a representation of Paris, with the apple, which suggests the possibility that it may be no other than the famous Paris by Euphranor. The weight of the body rests on the left leg, which is placed to the front with the foot flat on the ground. The right leg with bent knee is set back and to the side, and all but the ball of the foot and the three inner toes are raised off the ground. The right arm is thrust diagonally forward and to the right; the hand, which is open in a semicircle, has just cast the object and is beginning to close again, as the arm starts to sink. The round head on the broad, powerful neck is turned half right and slightly bowed. The deep-set little eyes are gazing at the distant target. The left arm hangs straight down, splayed slightly out by the swing of the body. The natural position of the fingers suggests that the left hand might possibly, but not necessarily, have been holding something. The eyes are inlaid in a coloured material, the lashes cut out of bronze plate.

The Polyclitan tradition is evident in the powerfully built, muscular body of the athletically constructed figure. The individual parts are clearly marked off from one another. The broad head with the short, restlessly mobile hair above the round forehead and the mouth with its lowered corners is reminiscent of the intense and temperamental style of Scopas's sculptures (214; 215, top). The close affinity between the head of the Anticythera bronze and the youth on the Ilissus tombstone (226) places this figure in the period around 340 B.C. The connection of the statue with Euphranor's Paris must remain a matter for speculation so long as we have no clear picture of the activities and works of that artist.

In this context thanks are due to the Director of the National Museum, Athens, Dr. Chr. Karusos, for his permission to photograph this bronze statue for the first time after its reassembly – which was made possible by the munificence of J. Lagonikos – and to publish the photographs in this book.

J. N. Svoronos, Das Athener Nationalmuseum 1 (1908), 18 ff., No 1, plate 1 and 2. — H. Bulle, Der Schöne Mensch im Altertum, 2nd edition (1912), 115 ff., to plate 61.

221, 222, VII
STANDING YOUTH. Bronze. Height 4'3" (1.30 m.). National Museum, Athens, No. 15.118.

Like the youth and the head of the bearded philosopher which were found in the sea off Anticythera (218–220; 250, X), this bronze statue appears to have belonged to a consignment of works of art that suffered shipwreck in ancient times while on its way from Greece to Italy. It was found in 1925 off the coast near Marathon.

The under-life-size figure stands in a very natural position on the left leg, with the left hip curving outwards. The right foot is drawn back, so that only the ball and the toes – which were restored after rediscovery – touch the ground. The line of balance passes up from the supporting leg through the trunk to the comparatively small head, which is turned to the left and slightly bowed. The hair is short with a springy, curling growth. It is encircled by a narrow band, knotted at the back and with a forward-curving tongue at the top. This is the style worn by the competitors in the Palaestra and by Hermes, their god.

The young man's gaze is directed towards the object which he once held on the palm of his outstretched left hand, to which it was attached by means of a strong bronze pin. The right arm is raised at an upward and outward angle. The right hand is turned palm outwards, so that the thumb rests gently against the forefinger while the other three fingers curve free. As was customary, each arm was cast separately. Since their workmanship and rhythm do not tally with those of the rest of the body, it is assumed that they were added during restoration carried out in Roman times. Thus it is impossible to decide whether the figure, poised as if floating on air, was leaning on the raised right arm with the wrist against a tree or pillar.

A positive explanation for the subject has not yet been found. Among the theories put forward are that the youth held a bowl in his left hand into which he poured a curving stream of liquid from a slender, horn-shaped vessel held in his right; or that he was plucking fruit into a dish with his right hand. Others see him as the god Hermes himself, who – like the Olympian Hermes – bears on his left arm the little Dionysus, or possibly a tortoise – the prototype of the tortoise-lyre – at which he gazes thoughtfully. The balance of the body and the fluidity of the modelling have affinities with Praxitelian works of the third quarter of the 4th century B.C.; indeed, the youth has been attributed to Praxiteles himself, and executed before the Apollo killing a lizard (Sauroktonos) and the Hermes of Olympia (228–231). The head with its sharply defined eyes, whose lower lids curve deeply, and with its narrow-bridged nose, links it also with Lysippan heads. The eyeballs are of white stone, the iris of yellow glass-flux with a black rim; the pupils are missing. The nipples are inset copper.

K. A. Rhomaios, Deltion Archaiologikon 9, 1924—1925, 145 ff., plates 2—5 and the same, Antike Denkmäler 4, 1929, plates 30—37. — F. Studniczka, Der Bronze-

knabe von Marathon, Festgabe zur Winckelmannsfeier des Archäologischen Seminars der Universität Leipzig am 9. Dezember 1927. — W. H. Schuchhardt, Der Jüngling von Marathon, in: Die Antike 6, 1930, 332 ff., plate 28—32. — E. Buschor, Die Plastik der Griechen (1958), 91.

223
SCULPTURED BASE OF A COLUMN FROM THE LATER TEMPLE OF ARTEMIS AT EPHESUS. Marble. Height 5'11" (1.80 m.). British Museum, London, No. 1206.

The Archaic Temple of Artemis at Ephesus – dating from the 6th century B.C. – is said to have been burnt down during the night on which Alexander the Great was born (356 B.C.). The Ephesians immediately set about rebuilding it in all its original grandeur. In 334 B.C. it was not yet finished. For Alexander the Great had then said he would bear the rest of the cost of reconstruction if he himself was allowed to consecrate the temple of the goddess. His offer was refused by the Ephesians on the grounds that Alexander himself enjoyed divine honours and as a god could not consecrate a temple.

The Temple of Artemis, which, together with the Mausoleum at Halicarnassus and the Altar of Zeus at Pergamon, was counted among the Seven Wonders of the World, was surrounded by a double row of Ionic columns and was over a hundred yards long. Like its Archaic predecessor, a number of the new temple's columns stood on round bases decorated with reliefs. The artistic significance of these sculptured bases was no doubt primarily to mitigate or counteract the effect the excessively tall and slender fluted columns produced. One of the bases was the work of Scopas. The relatively best preserved of these column bases of the later Artemision shows on one face a standing female figure seen from in front holding one end of her cloak below her breast with her right hand and the other end over her shoulder with her left, so that the cloak falls in front of her body on her left side in heavy folds. She is standing between two young male figures: right (as one looks at it) Hermes, who pauses in the act of walking, looking up into the air, his left arm covered by a cloak resting on his hip, his round, shallow hat pushed back on to his shoulders. In his lowered right hand he carries his emblem – the *kerykeion*, the staff he bears as messenger of the gods and guide of the dead. On the other side is a winged youth with a long sword, perhaps Thanatos, Death. Behind Hermes come two figures that have been interpreted as Persephone (standing) and Hades (sitting); behind the winged youth stands a male figure thought to be Hercules. No satisfactory explanation of the whole relief has yet been found; in particular, the female figure between the winged youth and Hermes, recognition of which is rendered more difficult by the absence of the head, has not been identified.

The reliefs on the tambours are assumed to have been executed in situ, and not prior to the superimposed architecture, so that they should not be damaged during building. On grounds of style the base would appear to date from about 340 B.C. The splendid figure of Hermes pausing in his walk is modelled after a statue whose clearly constructed corporeality is reminiscent of works by the followers of Polyclitus. 'Persephone' and 'Thanatos' are based on works originating from Praxiteles's circle.

E. Curtius, Archäologische Zeitung 30, 1872, 72 ff., plates 65/66. — C. Friederichs-P. Wolters, Bausteine zur Geschichte der griechisch-römischen Plastik, No. 1242. — K. Süsserott, Griechische Plastik des 4. Jahrhunderts v. Chr., 174.

DEMETER. Found in the sanctuary of Demeter and Kore at Cnidus in 1812, excavated in 1858. Parian marble. The surface of the head, which is inset, is in a better state of preservation than that of most of the body. Height 5' (1.53 m.). British Museum, London, No. 1300.

The goddess is sitting on a throne with a high back-rest, narrow arm-rests and a cushion, her feet resting on a stool. The arms were made separately. The lowered right arm was no doubt supported by the arm-rest of the throne, the left fore-arm was raised and stretched out slightly to the left. The head is turned a little to the left, the vague – as though veiled – eyes are gazing into space.

Through the absence of the front legs of the throne and the arm-rests, and the fact that the two knees and the right shank have been damaged, the spectator's eye is now distracted by the slanting folds of the drapery between the right calf and the left knee. The feet of the enthroned goddess were not crossed; the legs stood side by side. The left foot is drawn back, remains of the toes are still visible on the foot-stool vertically below the left knee. The right foot is thrust out over the edge of the footstool and has pulled the border of the chiton out taut in the front. The shanks, which must therefore have been vertical, were framed by the perpendiculars of the legs of the throne, the horizontal thighs by the arm-rests. The splendid, richly folded drapery is stretched between these straight axes in long diagonal sweeps. The fine chiton is only visible at the throat and on the right arm, on the outside of the left elbow and over the feet. The great woollen cloak is wrapped tightly round the body and drawn back over the head to form a veil; one end hangs down in front under the left arm and over the leg of the throne. The other end is drawn under the right arm across the breast and thrown over the left shoulder. The double mass of cloth forms heavy folds whose ends spread out at the back on the seat of the throne.

Since the surface of the body had suffered a great deal more before excavation than the head, which was discovered somewhat later, the softly modelled neck and the regular oval of the face stand out in more gentle beauty from the now darker integument of the drapery. The wavy hair is parted in the middle and falls in long tresses behind the ears and forward on to the cloak.

The softly rounded shapes of the face with the deep-set, large eyes, the nose that runs straight down from the forehead, and the slightly open, full mouth, incorporate an ideal of beauty of the late Praxitelian period.

Detail in the statue's composition and execution indicate that it was not intended to be seen from an absolutely frontal view but slightly diagonally from its right side. Inscriptions and finds of statuettes in the sacred precincts of Demeter and Kore at Cnidus render it probable that the seated Demeter was accompanied by a standing figure, her daughter Kore, to form a cult group, which must have been produced in about 340/330 B.C.

B. Asbmole, Demeter of Cnidus, in: Journal of Hellenic Studies 71, 1951, 13 ff., plates 1—7.

226

ATTIC SEPULCHRAL MONUMENT OF A YOUTH. Pentelic marble. Height 5'6" (1.68 m.). Found in the bed of the Ilissus at Athens in 1874. National Museum, Athens, No. 869.

The great relief panel was surmounted, like the tombstone of Hegeso (187), by a pediment resting at either side upon antae, the ends of a projecting wall. This separately constructed architectural frame has now disappeared.

The composition has a unique grandeur. The deceased, shown as a young man in ideal nakedness, is half leaning, half sitting on a stele with a two-tiered base set at an angle, his left leg crossed over his right. His head with the short, curly hair is looking out from the picture plane, so that the full, round countenance with the deep-set eyes is seen full face. His eyes gaze away into the distance at no fixed point. His right arm had been across his chest. With his raised left hand the youth may well have been leaning on a long bronze spear standing on the ground between his left knee and the right ear of the dog, forming a stressed central vertical and separating the figure from its surroundings. A cloak falls over his left arm and forms a bundle on the stele for the figure to sit upon. On the youth's left arm there hangs a throwing club such as was used in hunting.

At the hunter's feet crouches a little naked servant, or the dead man's brother, helplessly sobbing. His arms lie with folded hands on his knees, his head has sunk on to his left arm. From behind the hunter his dog, a slender, finely-bred animal, emerges diagonally from the background snuffing the ground. To the right, facing the deceased youth, stands his father, in a long cloak and shoes. His left hand is supported by a stick, with his right he grasps his beard in agonized emotion. His gaze from his deeply shadowed eyes is directed upon his son, who is set apart from him by his posture, the turn of his head and his strangely unreal glance and here in the relief leads his own, remote existence.

The powerful modelling of the figures, the spatial quality of the composition and the independent relationship of the figures to the background stamp this tombstone as dating from the second half of the 4th century B.C. The hunter's head bears a close affinity to the sculptures in the Temple of Athene at Tegea and other works from the later period of Scopas. This would date the relief from 340 B.C. or soon after. It is the work of one of the leading Attic masters of this period, whose influence on Greek funerary sculpture can still be traced.

The two principal figures wore wreaths or fillets of metal, probably bronze, which were attached by small holes in the background beside the heads.

A. Conze, Die attischen Grabreliefs 2, No. 1055, plate 211. — H. Diepolder, Die attischen Grabreliefs des 5. und 4. Jahrhunderts v. Chr., 51, plate 48. — N. Himmelmann-Wildschütz, Studien zum Ilissosrelief, München 1956, 1 ff., see also H. Möbius, Gnomon 30, 1958, 48 ff.

227

ATTIC SEPULCHRAL RELIEF. Pentelic marble. Height 5'8" (1.75 m.). Found at Rhamnus (Attica) in 1879. National Museum, Athens, No. 833.

Like the Ilissus tombstone (226) this great relief panel was originally surrounded by an architectural framework at the top and sides, which held the figures together, made the work a closed whole and gave it artistic completeness.

The relief portrays a married couple, two tall, intimately linked figures. Turned towards one another, they clasped each other's hands; their eyes meet – and yet they belong to two different worlds, one of them to life, the other to the Beyond. On the left stands the man, in a cloak that leaves the upper half of his body uncovered. With his left leg crossed over his right, he was leaning on a staff under his left arm-pit. His feet are clad in high shoes. With his left hand he grasps his beard in pensive melancholy – the same gesture as that of the father on the Illissus relief – and gazes at the beautiful young woman whom death has taken away from him. While the weight of his body rests firmly on the right leg and is also supported by the staff, there is something unreal about the woman. She seems to be moving away from him, seems to be stepping into the background, into the realm of shades. The artist has depicted her – contrary to the husband – almost front face. Only the head with its earnest gaze is seen from the side, turned for the last time towards her husband. The loosely waved hair, swept back from a parting over the middle of the forehead, is taken up over a circlet at the back and sides. She is wearing a long sleeved-chiton, from beneath the hem of which the sandalled right foot peeps out, and a large cloak that firmly envelops the whole body. On the hip of the supporting leg and on the free leg it clings to the forms of the body, is thrown over the left shoulder and left upper arm with a diagonal bunch of folds across the breast and falls far down from the raised forearm on the side of the free leg in long vertical folds parallel with the frame of the relief.

Besides the beauty of the two figures and the unity of the composition, it is the depth of feeling and the ethos that informs the man and woman which give this relief its intrinsic greatness and significance. The slender proportions and small heads, the picturesque rendering of the hair and the extent to which the figures are isolated and released from the background indicate, in comparison with the Ilissus tombstone, a later stage in the development of 4th-century Attic relief sculpture. The Rhamnus sepulchral relief must date from the decade between 330 and 320 B.C., slightly later than the prototype of the statue of Sophocles in the Lateran, which Lycurgus had erected in the Theatre of Dionysus at Athens in about 330. (G. Helbig and W. Amelung, *Führer durch die Antiken Roms*, 3rd Ed. [1913] No. 1180. — Brunn-Bruckmann, *Denkmäler griechischer und römischer Skulptur*, (Plate 427). The head of the bearded man on this relief is closely allied to that of the Sophocles.

A. Conze, Die attischen Grabreliefs 2, No. 1084, plate 221. — *H. Diepolder*, Die attischen Grabreliefs des 5. und 4. Jahrhunderts v. Chr., 54 f., plate 54.

228–231

HERMES WITH THE CHILD DIONYSUS ON HIS ARM.
Parian marble. Height 7' (2.15 m.). Museum, Olympia.

The Greek travel writer Pausanias (5, 17, 3) mentions a Hermes carrying the Dionysus child in the Temple of Hera and says of the figure: 'the manner (τέχνη), however, is that of Praxiteles.' When the statue was found early in 1877, during German excavations at Olympia, in the cella of the Heraion, lying where it had fallen from its base, it was immediately connected with this statement of Pausanias's. The then director of excavations at Olympia, Gustav Hirschfeld, took the view – on the ground of the figure's stylistic and technical peculiarities and of Pausanias's statement – that the new find could not be Praxiteles's original, but only a copy. Soon, however, people were so impressed by the beauty of the statue and the skill of the marble work that they came to regard it as the original, which would place it among the most precious pieces of Greek carving from the chisel of one of antiquity's most celebrated

sculptors. This view is still the most widely held today, although it has been contradicted, especially recently, by various arguments that are not easily disposed of.

According to the legend, Hermes brought the little Dionysus to the nymphs of Nysa, who were to bring the boy up. The messenger of the gods is here depicted as a handsome young man resting while on his way to the nymphs. He has placed his left foot to the rear, free from weight. His right thigh curves outward, his right hip is drawn well in and the upper body tilted to his left. Hermes is supporting himself with his left arm, on which he carries the child, upon a tree trunk, over which his cloak of heavy cloth falls in abundant folds. The left hand held the herald's staff, which was of bronze. Dionysus has placed one of his little hands on his big brother's shoulder; the other is stretched demandingly towards a bunch of grapes that Hermes held out to him – the wine god – as though playfully, in his raised right hand. Hermes's well preserved head with the slightly open mouth, the dimple in the chin, the expanded nostrils and the forehead whose lower part arches forward has always been particularly admired for its delightful expression of serenity. The short, untidy hair is only partially carved. It was originally painted reddish brown and crowned with an ivy wreath of metal. The veiled glance goes right past the child.

The swinging rhythm of the figure, which draws the supporting tree trunk into the composition, the distribution of the whole work in space, the lively modelling of the naked body, the ideal beauty of the head and the conception of childhood revealed in the little Dionysus indicate that the Hermes was a late work of Praxiteles dating from the period 330/20 B.C. Not only the rendering of the tree trunk, the transverse stanchion that connects the latter with the figure, and the unfinished appearance of the back of the statue, but also the manner in which the marble has been treated on Hermes, Dionysus and the cloak seem to justify the assumption that this work is not the 4th-century original, but an interesting copy made by a Greek sculptor during the early period of the Roman Empire, designed for beauty of effect and intended to be placed between the columns in the cella of the temple.

The right shank apart from the foot, the whole of the left shank with the foot, and the lower part of the tree trunk have been restored in modern times. Traces of red-brown paint are visible on the thongs of the sandals and probably served as an undercoat for gilding, of which traces are also present.

G. Treu, Die Bildwerke von Olympia (= Olympia, Ergebnisse 3), 194 ff., plates 49—53. — *E. Buschor*, Erläuternde Texte zu Bruckmanns Wandbildern alter Plastik (1911), No. IV. — *C. Blümel*, Griechische Bildhauerarbeit (1927), 37 ff. with plate 43. — *C. Blümel*, Der Hermes eines Praxiteles (1948). — *R. Carpenter*, American Journal of Archaeology 58, 1954, 1 ff. — *J. Dobrn*, Attische Plastik vom Tode des Phidias bis zum Wirken der großen Meister des IV. Jahrhunderts v. Chr., 201 f.

232–237, VIII, IX

THE 'ALEXANDER SARCOPHAGUS'.
Pentelic marble. Length 10'6" (3.18 m.), width 5'6" (1.67 m.), height to the tip of the acroteria on the ridge 6'5" (1.95 m.). Istanbul, Archaeological Museum, Department of Classical Antiquities, No. 68 (370).

In the largest of the seven tomb-chambers in the Royal Cemetery at Sidon, which is also the most recent and the furthest from the entrance shaft, stood what has come to be known as the 'Alexander sarcophagus', accompanied by three small sarcophagi bearing only non-figurative decoration. This is the largest of all the sarcophagi found in the Sidonian cemetery and is noteworthy for its excellent state of preservation, which includes the plentiful paintwork. As with the 'Weeping women sarcophagus', if not to an even greater degree, the wealth of sculptural ornamentation on this one combines to form a unified whole in the manner of 4th-century Greek art.

It is made up of two separate parts: the rectangular chest and a heavy lid, which imitates the architecture of an Ionic temple. The high, stepped and profiled base and the upper edge of the chest are bordered by magnificent Ionic bands. Round the lower part of the lid, over two further, shallower bands, runs a vine trailer, surmounted by a dentil moulding and an egg-and-dart moulding. On the cyma as the places where in full-scale architecture lion's head gargoyles are to be found, there are three-horned heads of lion-griffins. The spaces between them, above the cyma, are occupied by female heads with a high leaf-shaped diadem between rosettes, instead of the frontal tiles. Similar heads recur along the sides of the ridge, alternating with eagles or sirens, of which only small remnants have been preserved. The four corner-acroteria consist of recumbent lions. Battle scenes are portrayed on the pediments. At the two ends, palmette acroteria flanked by horned lion-griffins project above the ridge.

The reliefs on the four sides of the sarcophagus chest are executed in deep, rectangular fields. Each of the long sides is coupled with a short side and the two pairs differ in theme and composition. The principal long side and its corresponding short side depict battles between Greeks and Persians. The figures are packed close and are occasionally ranged in two or three tiers one above the other. The second long side and its attached short side show hunting scenes. Here the arrangement of the figures and groups is more open. On both long sides the action is arranged in a freely symmetrical manner around a central group. In the battle scene we see, on the left, Alexander the Great on a rearing horse hurling his spear at a Persian, who is trying to defend himself with his weapon as he falls forward over the neck of his stumbling horse. Alexander is recognizable by the lion's skin, the attribute of Hercules, which he wears like a helmet. His is the only figure on the whole sarcophagus which can be named with complete certainty. To the right of this couple stands a group of three figures: a Greek and a Persian fighting on foot, and a Persian shooting an arrow at Alexander. On the right-hand extremity of the relief, corresponding to Alexander on the left, there is a second mounted Greek. He has raised his spear against a Persian who, wounded, is slipping from his horse and being caught by a comrade. To the left of this is a group showing an almost naked Greek seizing the reins of a galloping Persian, and in front of him a Persian archer who is aiming his arrow at the mounted Greek on the extreme right. In the centre of the relief a mounted Greek is stabbing a Persian who is begging for mercy. The bodies of dead Greeks and Persians lie on the ground.

The rider in the centre of the hunting scene on the other long side, whose horse is being torn to pieces by a lion, has – no doubt rightly – been identified as the prince who was interred in the sarcophagus. This is probably Abdalonymus, whom Alexander installed as King of Sidon after the battle of Issus (333). Correspondingly, the battle on the main side may well be Alexander's victory at Issus, as a result of which Sidon was freed from the Persians. The helmeted rider on the right-hand extremity of the main side has been interpreted as Antigonus, called 'the One-Eyed', Alexander's general and father of Demetrius Poliorcetes, who went to Asia Minor with the Macedonian king in 334 and was soon appointed by him satrap of Phrygia. The rider in the centre of the battle scene might be Hephaestion, Alexander's friend.

One of the short sides depicts a galloping Persian hurling his spear at a prostrate Greek and, to left and right of this, groups of warriors; the other short side shows four Persians slaying a panther they have encircled; to the left of this a young Persian is tyring to gain control of a runaway horse, and a hunting dog dashes towards the group surrounding the panther.

The colours employed by the artist on this sarcophagus, which have here been preserved as on no other piece of Greek sculpture and give each side the character of a painting or a sumptuously embroidered cloth, run through a wide scale from dark red, purple red and pink through a dark and a paler violet, dark brown, golden brown, pale brown and yellow to deep blue. Light and broken tones, in keeping with the style of the sculpture, predominate. The colours and tones are even less susceptible of verbal description here than in most cases. A reliable picture of the splendid colour-effect of the sarcophagus as a whole and in detail is afforded by Franz Winter's book of colour plates (1912).

The artist of the 'Alexander sarcophagus' must have been an Ionian Greek, who, in his own way, continued the tradition of the frieze on the Mausoleum at Halicarnassus. The style of the ornament and relief figures indicates that the sarcophagus was produced not long after the battle of Issus and probably during Alexander's lifetime.

O. Hamdi-Bey and Th. Reinach, Une Nécropole Royale à Sidon (Paris 1892), 64 ff.; 272 ff., plates XXIII—XXVII. — *F. Winter*, Die Sarkophage von Sidon, in: Archäologischer Anzeiger 1894, 1 ff. and do., Der Alexander-Sarkophag von Sidon (1912). — *F. Studniczka*, Jahrbuch des Deutschen Archäologischen Instituts 9, 1894, 204 ff. — *E. Buschor*, Erläuternde Texte zu Bruckmanns Wandbildern alter Plastik (1911), 8 ff. — *G. Mendel*, Catalogue des Sculptures Grecques, Romaines et Byzantines dans les Musées Impériaux Ottomans I (1912), 171 ff., No. 68 (370). — *G. Kleiner*, Alexanders Reichsmünzen, in: Abhandlungen der Deutschen Akademie der Wissenschaften zu Berlin, Philosoph.-histor. Klasse 1947 (1949), 5, 50, note 41 and do., Hellenistische Sarkophage in Kleinasien, in: Istanbuler Mitteilungen 7, 1956, 1. — *J. Charbonneaux*, Antigone et Démétrius sont-ils figurés sur le sarcophage d'Alexandre? in: La Revue des Arts 1952, 219 ff.

238, 239

HEAD OF A BOXER. Found at Olympia in 1880. Bronze, patinated dark green. Height 11.2" (28 cm.). National Museum, Athens, No. 6439.

The life-size head comes from the statue of a victor that stood in the sanctuary of Zeus at Olympia. The body has been lost and so it cannot now be said for certain whether the head belonged to a standing figure, or to a sitting figure in the style of the boxer in the Museo delle Terme (275–277). All that can be judged from the point of juncture with the neck is that it faced forward with a slight twist to his left. The stubborn, sombre-looking face with the small, half-closed eyes and the wide, firmly shut mouth is framed by the tangled, curly hair of head and beard. The lower lip protrudes, the nose hangs down flat and bulging, the under part of the low forehead curves outward. The ears are swollen from blows. Apart from the bare twigs, the ends of which are twined one under the other at the back, nothing is left of an olive wreath round the head but two small leaves. The eyes were inserted, the lips inlaid in bronze, the roof-shaped knitted eyebrows engraved in the form of two rows of parallel strokes.

In this very important portrait the artist has given a lifelike depiction of a particular boxer and over and above this a picture of a boxer as such, who is caught up in the toil and trouble of his harsh and unintellectual existence, but shows the pride of a victor in his mouth and eyes. Compared with the brutal verism of the Late Hellenistic bronze of Apollonios at Rome, with its ugly broken nose, grossly misshapen ears, the gashes in the flesh and the hair plastered with blood (275–277), this portrait is rather idealized in its artistic approach. The contours and forms are calmer and more unitary. The head derives from the still relatively more closed world of the outgoing Classical style of the late 4th century. It must date from the end of the Alexandrian period. Soon after its discovery it was ascribed to Lysippus. Later, however, it was taken with good reason to be the portrait of Satyros, a victorious boxer, which tradition states to have been made for Olympia by the metal-caster Silanion of Athens, the master of the Plato portrait.

A. Furtwängler, Die Bronzen von Olympia (Olympia, Ergebnisse Band IV), Text p. 10, 2.2a and plate 2. — *R. Kékulé von Stradonitz*, Über den Bronzekopf eines Siegers in Olympia (Sitzungsberichte der Kgl. Preußischen Akademie der Wissenschaften, Philos.-histor. Klasse 26, 1909, 694 ff. — *E. Schmidt*, Jahrbuch des Deutschen Archäologischen Instituts 49, 1934, 191 ff.

240, 241

FRAGMENT OF AN ATTIC FUNERARY RELIEF. Found in Attica. Pentelic marble. Height 5'3" (1.62 m.). National Museum, Athens, No. 2574.

This fragment must come from a tombstone similar to the Rhamnus relief (227). The bearded man in the cloak was balanced by another figure, to which he was linked in the act of parting. He was not reaching out his hand to this figure, however, but standing on his own like the old father on the Ilissus stele (226). If it is chiefly the fine spiritual and psychological relationship between the two tall, slender figures that gives the Rhamnus relief its importance, the effectiveness of this figure lies in its magnificently corporeal and statuesque appearance. The heavy, forward-leaning body was supported by a staff placed under the left arm-pit. The unclad upper body grows out of the folds of the thick robe, while in the lower part of the figure the sculptural unity of body and garment is more apparent. The left leg beneath the drapery is almost as much in evidence as the bare right arm.

The figure is more markedly free from the background than in either of the other two reliefs named above: it stands out from it almost like a piece of sculpture in the round. The autonomy of the figure is mirrored in the individual expression on the mourning man's fine face. The furrowed brow under the loose, untidy hair, the melancholy eyes above sunken cheeks and the mouth that seems to be opening as though in a cry make this likeness of an aging man resemble a portrait.

This fragment is the latest in our series of 5th- and 4th-century Attic sepulchral reliefs. It must date from about 320 B.C., only a few years before Attic funerary sculpture was brought to a sudden end by the laws against luxury promulgated by Demetrius of Phaleron.

S. Papaspiridi, Guide du Musée National d'Athènes, Marbres, Bronzes et Vases, 165, plate 11. — *H. Diepolder*, Die attischen Grabreliefs des 5. und 4. Jahrhunderts v. Chr., 54, plate 53.

242, 243

HEAD OF A GIRL. Parian marble. Height 14.4" (36 cm.). Museum of Fine Arts, Boston/Mass., No. 29 (Inv. 10.70). From the E. P. Warren Collection, 1910.

This extremely attractive head with neck to just above the shoulders was let into a clothed statue which is no longer in existence. Like the prototypes of the so-called 'women of Herculaneum', it was no doubt a funerary statue. Remains of drapery are visible over the left breast. The original edge has remained only at the back. On the right shoulder there is a rectangular hole for a peg which seems to be a relic of some ancient repair work. The head slopes away at the top from the parting towards the sides in large planes, rough on the right and smooth on the left for the application of hair – a technique occasionally employed when the marble block was not sufficiently large. The hair was covered by a cloak or veil that fell down to the shoulders. A hole bored in the front of the head near the parting indicates that it must have been so draped as to cast a slight shadow on the forehead and brows. This made the eyes appear more sharply modelled, deeper and more alert.

The head is turned to its right. Beneath the delicate lustre of the youthful face the structural forms are rendered clearly and in simple proportions. The hair is so arranged as to frame the forehead in a finely curving triangle. A gentle arch carries the latter over at the root of the nose to the straight, broad bridge. The eyebrows lead from the root of the nose to the temples in a long backward sweep in such a way that the inner corners of the deep-set eyes, half covered by the finely drawn lids, are in deeper shadow than the outer corners. In the well-proportioned oval of the lower part of the face the full lips of the small, closed mouth are softly embedded in the surrounding flesh. The top lip is drawn up at the corners as though in a slight smile. The wide nostrils and the lower eyelids grow out of the gently mobile cheeks without any marked transition.

All the shapes and contours of this glorious work appear as though seen through a gossamer veil and as though the surface were beginning to dissolve, a stylistic feature introduced during the late Praxitelian period which here – right at the end of the 4th century B.C. – reaches a high degree of effectiveness.

When the head was found on the island of Chios during the Crimean War (1854–1856) it was cleaned almost all over with acids, causing severe damage to the old patina.

John Marshall, Antike Denkmäler 2 (1908), plate 59. — *L. D. Caskey*, Catalogue of Greek and Roman Sculpture in the Museum of Fine Arts, Boston (1925), No. 29. — *R. Lullies*, Die kauernde Aphrodite, 69 f.

IV. HELLENISTIC EPOCH

From 300 B.C. to the Beginning of the Roman Empire

244

VOTIVE RELIEF FOR CYBELE AND ATTIS. Fine-grained grey marble. Length 32″ (80 cm.), height 23″ (57 cm.). Archaeological Museum, Venice, No. 17 (Inv. No. 118).

Cybele, the Great Mother, and Attis, her companion and beloved, were worshipped in orgiastic cults in Asia Minor, especially in Mysia, Lydia and Phrygia. This relatively small relief, dedicated to both deities, comes from Asia Minor, probably from Magnesia on the Sipylos or from Smyrna. It was originally framed by an architectural border at the top and sides. It was part of the collection which Giovanni Grimani, the Patriarch of Aquileia (died in 1593), gave to the Republic of Venice in 1586.

Two figures have entered the temple of the divine couple through a lofty door, one leaf of which is opened outwards. The foremost, a woman in a long chiton and cloak, which she has drawn over her head like a veil, is advancing towards the two great gods. In her left hand she holds a round box, the right is raised in the gesture of adoration. She is followed by a little serving-maid, a child still with a top-knot, likewise in chiton and cloak and carrying a salver in her hands. They are coming to Cybele and Attis, two tall, statuesque-looking figures standing in front of a wall in their sanctuary. On the left stands the goddess in a long, belted chiton and cloak, which is drawn up over the *polos*, the Greek crown of the gods, at the back, and holding a great round cymbal and a sceptre in her hands. At her feet sits a small lion, her sacred animal. She is turned towards Attis, who occupies the dominant centre of the relief. Dressed in the Oriental manner, he is wearing trousers, a belted chiton, a cloak and the Phrygian cap, from which dangle ribbons. With his left hand he is resting a thick knotted stick on a small rocky hummock.

Both the figures of the gods are based on 4th-century cult statues, which the Hellenistic artist has here translated into the style of his period. Thus there is something recalcitrant and cumbersome about the stance and movements of the figure of Attis, which distinguishes it from the clear, flowing rhythm of classical works. It is held together outwardly by the cloak that lies on the left shoulder, goes over the back, and then falls across the right forearm, held akimbo; the other part is wound round the left arm. Each figure stands separate and isolated against the background, to which the door gives the character of a solid wall. According to its composition, the style of the drapery and the relation of the figures to surrounding space, the relief must date from the mid-3rd century B.C.

M. *Collignon*, Monuments Grecs 10, 1881, 11, plate 2. — *H. Dütschke*, Antike Bildwerke in Oberitalien 5 (1882), 116 f., No. 297. — *W. H. Schuchhardt*, Die Antike 12, 1937, 103 ff., plate 7. — *H. Kähler*, Der große Fries von Pergamon, 75 f. and 173, note 70.

245

STATUE OF A PHILOSOPHER. From Delphi. Marble. Height with base 6′ 11″ (2.07 m.). Delphi, Museum.

The individual portraits of the great Greek philosophers from Socrates, Plato and Aristotle to the representatives of the Hellenistic schools of philosophy are comparatively well known. They have come down to us, above all, in the numerous copies made during the time of the Roman empire, chiefly in the shape of busts or herms, which represent only the subject's head and ignore the rest of his body. The Greek originals, from which these abbreviated copies were made, were bronze or marble statues showing the subject sometimes standing and sometimes sitting, but always entire. In Greek eyes, until into the 2nd century B.C., a man's portrait had to show the whole figure. Greek sculptors did not change over to the portrait bust or herm until the advent of late Hellenism, when the feeling for the organic connexion between all parts of the body had been lost and Greece had fallen increasingly under the influence of the Italo-Roman conquerors.

This over-life-size standing figure from the Delphic shrine is one of the few statues of Greek philosophers that have come down to us in their original form. The subject, whose name we do not know, must have been an important personage in his day to have had his statue placed in such an outstanding position. The sculptor has made him very much alive, as he stands — with his stick in his right hand — addressing an audience. Yet the statue does not give the impression of capturing a passing moment; on the contrary, this portrait of an individual has come to portray the philosopher of that day as such. The lover and teacher of wisdom is wearing a long cloak of thick cloth, which is wrapped over in front, cuts horizontally across the upper part of the body in a wide bundle of many folds and is thrown over the back and left shoulder, leaving the chest free. On his feet he has high, laced sandals. His beard is unkempt and bristling; his thin hair clings close to his head. His broad, domed skull has a high forehead; the small mouth is firmly closed; the gaze from the large eyes shaded by the bushy brows appears composed and withdrawn. The suggestion that this is the portrait of a Cynic is most probably correct.

The Delphic statue's individual quality and its place in the history of art become more evident if we place it between earlier portrait statues, such as the 'Mausolus' (211–213), and later ones like the 'Hippocrates' of Cos (266, 267). The positive, almost aggressive, rustic way in which the figure confronts the spectator is peculiar to the Delphic philosopher. The cloak envelops the body and enhances its statuesque effect by cutting it off from the outside world. The lower part of the body resembles an up-ended rectangle. At the same time, the figure seems as if built into the block. This effect is enhanced by such motifs as the heavy folds of the cloak falling vertically in front of the tree trunk on one side, and the manner in which it clings close to the right leg on the other; also by the horizontal bundle of drapery in front of the upper part of the body and the folds running diagonally up from the right shank and knee which form a shallow arc with the folds that pass over the shoulder. The 'Mausolus' possesses an integrated constructional dynamism in the classical sense. By contrast, the Delphic philosopher shows a firmness, a rigidity even, both of rhythm and of sculptural form. This hardening and tensing of the structural framework, however, also distinguishes it from the uncertain, rather dubious stance of the bearded figure from Cos, whose body structure appears to be, sculpturally, already in a state of general dissolution.

The statue of the Delphic philosopher must, therefore, date from roughly midway between the 'Mausolus' and the 'Hippocrates', that is to say around 250 B.C.

Fouilles de Delphes IV, plate 69 f. (as yet without detailed text). — *G. Kleiner*, Athenische Mitteilungen 65, 1940, 40 and *do.*, Tanagrafiguren 149. — *K. Schefold*, Die Bildnisse der antiken Dichter, Redner und Denker, 210. — *E. Buschor*, Das hellenistische Bildnis, 16 and *do.*, Die Plastik der Griechen² (1958), 103.

246

STATUE OF NIKOKLEIA, priestess of Demeter. Found in the sanctuary of Demeter and Kore at Cnidus in 1858. Marble. Height (without base) 5'2" (1.57 m.). British Museum, London, No. 1301.

The statue stands upon a high pedestal bearing the inscription:

Νικόκλεια Νικοχόρου
γυνὰ δέ ᾿Απολλοφάνευς
Δάματρι Καὶ Κούραι καὶ θεοῖς τοῖς
παρὰ Δάματρι εὐχάν

meaning: Nikokleia, daughter of Nikochoros, wife of Apollophanos, for Demeter and Kore and the gods with Demeter as a votive offering.

The head is inserted; the edge now visible round the neck was originally covered by drapery. The right hand under the cloak, the left forearm and a long strip on the left side of the figure were made separately. They are now lost.

The body beneath the drapery is as though enclosed in a block. The right leg is set a little to one side so that the bent knee pulls the cloak tightly forward. The raised right forearm and hand were covered by the drapery. The bent elbow draws the narrow cloak in the same direction as the right knee; the result is a marked division of the upper from the lower parts of the body by an overhanging fold which repeats the line of the lower border of the cloak in a shallow arc.

This movement of the body is counterbalanced by the mass of the cloth that drapes it. The vertical channels of the chiton of fine, crinkled fabric are brought to a stop by the ground, and together with the almost invisible legs beneath them seem like a supporting column, vaguely reminiscent of the Hera of Samos (32, 33) that is over 300 years older. In this case, however, the spare folds of the plain cloak above form a strong contrast to the richly folded lower garment. Lines of folds run diagonally across the body from the knee of the free leg and the right elbow, and point upwards to the head, slightly raised and turned to its left, the likeness of an elderly woman whose hair is covered at the back by a veil. The way in which the drapery is here employed to build up the figure, creating a delimiting outline for it, together with the contrasting relationship between body and drapery and between the different types of material, and the great use of intersecting lines in the composition, suggest a date soon after the mid-3rd century B.C. This estimate is borne out by the character of the inscription on the base.

A. H. Smith, A Catalogue of Sculpture in the British Museum, vol. 2 (1900), No. 1301. — *G. Kleiner*, Tanagrafiguren, 100; 165 ff., plate 52, a.

247

SACRIFICIAL SERVANT, THE 'ANTIUM GIRL'. Parian marble. Height 5'6.5" (1.70 m.). Museo delle Terme, Rome, No. 596.

This life-size statue was found in 1878 in the ruins of a Roman villa from the early Imperial period near Antium (Anzio) on the coast between Rome and Naples. It had stood in the villa on a brick

base in a niche in the rear wall of a large hall. The right arm, which was attached, and the left hand with half the round salver have so far not been traced. The head and neck, together with the right shoulder, are carved from a piece of marble of the same type as the rest of the body, but of finer quality. They were made separately and fixed on.

The powerfully built figure in intricately draped garments is holding a salver upon which her gaze is directed. The feet are sandalled. Pausing in her walk, the girl is standing firmly on her left leg; the right is placed well to the side with bent knee and raised heel. The difference between the free leg and the supporting leg is stressed, and the bust is tilted in the opposite direction to the pelvis. The shoulders and bowed head are turned to the left. The austere, maidenly profile is crowned by a double knot that joins the hair, which is parted at the back and twisted up from the ears over the forehead. The large cheeks are enlivened by fine curls in front of the ears. The eyes beneath the shallow arches of the brows look down at the salver.

The left elbow rests on the hip to take the weight of the salver. The right arm was reaching for the objects on the salver — a rolled-up strip of woollen cloth, a laurel twig and a vessel or implement, of whose three small feet in the shape of lion's claws only one is left. The girl must have been a sacrificial servant or a priestess portrayed in the performance of a religious rite.

The long chiton of ribbed linen has slipped off the girl's right shoulder. It is belted twice — below the breast and over the hips beneath the gathered bundle of the heavy woollen cloth, which is artistically draped like a cloak. One end has broken loose from this bundle in the front and is stretched in diagonal folds across the right thigh and carried round the back of the body in a series of wide arcs. The other end of the cloth is drawn upwards from the bundle at the back and falls down over the left shoulder, twisted inward. From the hips down, the chiton hangs in front of the body in vertical folds like a curtain, concealing the forms on the left side of the girl beneath it but leaving the foot and ankle bare. But on the right side it trails right down on to the foot, clinging closely to the free leg and forming a deep diagonal valley between the slanting ridges of the folds. Beside the foot and at the back the hem of the chiton lies firmly on the ground, thereby giving support to the figure.

The character of this work is determined by opposing and intractable movements, harsh intersections, irregular contours and seemingly disorderly and often ragged play of drapery. Equally characteristic of the essential nature of this statue, however, is the fact that the many divergent motifs are absorbed into other, superordinate motifs, which restore the figure's over-all unity. This proves the 'Antium girl' to be a typical example of the artistic tendencies of the mid-3rd century B.C. The manner in which the marble is worked seems to indicate that it is not a Hellenistic original, but more likely an excellent antique copy after a bronze dating from the early Roman Imperial period.

W. Amelung, Text zu Brunn-Bruckmann, Denkmäler griechischer und römischer Skulptur, plates 583/584. — *E. Buschor*, Erläuternde Texte zu Bruckmanns Wandbildern alter Plastik (1911) Nr. 15. Reprinted in *E. Buschor*, Von griechischer Kunst. Munich 1956, 166 ff. — *W. Helbig*, Führer durch die öffentlichen Sammlungen klassischer Altertümer in Rom (3rd edition, 1913), No. 1352. — *L. Curtius*, Interpretationen von sechs griechischen Bildwerken (Bern 1947), 106 ff.

248, 249

SLEEPING SATYR, the 'Barberini Faun'. Parian marble. Height 7' (2.15 m.). Glyptothek, Munich, No. 218.

The statue was found during the first half of the 17th century near the Castle of St Angelo, Emperor Hadrian's tomb, in Rome, and was first housed in the Palazzo Barberini. The right leg, the knee and foot of the left leg, the left forearm, the right elbow, the fingers of the right hand and the tip of the nose were missing. The restorations are the work of Bernini (1598–1680), who executed the lower parts of the rock with the plants and the tree trunk at the back, and the rectangular, shaped base, in marble, but made good the missing parts of the body in plaster. The latter were subsequently carried out in marble by the Italian sculptor and antiquary Pacetti, who acquired the statue in 1799, but had to return it to the house of Barberini in 1811 because it formed part of an entail. In 1813 it was bought by the Bavarian Crown Prince, later King Ludwig I. Since 1820 it has been at Munich.

The statue depicts a figure from the mythical retinue of Dionysus, a satyr, who, drunk with wine, has fallen asleep with slack limbs on a panther skin in a lonely mountain landscape. He wears a small horse's tail as an emblem of his half-animal nature. Only his buttocks, the lower part of his back and his left side rest on the rock. Apart from this the back and the whole of the right side of the body are free sculpture. The head has sunk heavily on to the left shoulder. One end of the panther-skin with the open mouth falls across the left upper arm, while the forearm hangs down from the rock. The right arm is raised up over the shoulders in an involuntary movement and rests against the head, a posture that reveals the relaxed state of the body and its deep breathing in sleep. Originally the right leg was not quite so much drawn up as it now appears in Bernini's reconstruction. The line of the thigh was more horizontal, the right foot, seeking a hold, was placed somewhat deeper and farther out on the rock in order to support the body. The whole figure was tilted correspondingly farther back and to its left, as is clear from the direction of the panther-skin in front, which runs in a vertical line from the arm to the top of the shin-bone. Since, in addition, the left forearm cannot have stood out from the body as much as it does now, the whole composition was formerly more compact and fitted into a large parallelogram.

The modelling of the mighty body's powerful, muscular forms is enlivened by light and shadow. In comparison with later figures, however, such as the Zeus from the Great Frieze at Pergamon, which conveys a sense of urgency (252), the figure of the satyr creates a more unitary and tranquil impression. The head of the Barberini Faun, with its broad cheek-bones and emaciated cheeks, its hollow, closed eyes below straight brows that almost join in the middle, its slightly open mouth and broad nostrils, has been particularly admired. The spectator can almost hear the heavy, regular breathing of the sleeper immersed in his dream-world. In the centre the hair grows straight up from the forehead in short, bristly tufts. At the sides thick, loosely dangling curls frame the face. The head is extended laterally by an ivy wreath with leaves and round berries, an emblem of the satyr's earthbound, Dionysiac sphere. The artist, one of the most important sculptors of the late 3rd century B.C., has created in this solitary sleeper a great and profound picture of nature that goes far beyond all naturalism.

In the rock under the head of the panther-skin there is a hole for a pipe, which was bored later when the satyr was used as a fountain figure.

A. Furtwängler and *P. Wolters*, Beschreibung der Glyptothek König Ludwigs I.

2nd edition (1910), p. 209 ff., No. 218. — *H. Bulle*, Der Barberinische Faun, in: Jahrbuch des Deutschen Archäologischen Instituts 16, 1901, 1 ff. — *H. Kähler*, Der große Fries von Pergamon, 171, note to II, 1, No. 34.

250, X

PORTRAIT OF A PHILOSOPHER. Bronze. Height 11.6" (29 cm.). National Museum, Athens, No. 13.400.

Like the large bronze Youth (218–220), this bearded head was part of the cargo that sank off Anticythera in the early days of the Roman Empire and was not recovered from the sea until 1900 and 1901. It comes from the life-size statue of a standing philosopher, of which the raised right arm, the sandalled feet with part of the shanks and the cloak, the left hand holding a stick, and further remains of the cloak from the upper body, were found at the same spot. Divers are said to have seen the missing trunk of the figure at the same time, but to have been unable to bring it to the surface.

This very important, curiously lifelike portrait depicts an elderly, bearded man with the earnest, introverted, intellectual features of a thinker. The hair is unkempt. It covers the head in long, loose strands; the restless tufts of the full beard are more finely chiselled. The forehead is furrowed by age and meditation. The eyebrows are drawn up at the sides above the small, worried-looking eyes. Two folds run diagonally downwards from the wings of the nose and, together with the slightly shrunken mouth, form a triangle into which the un-prominent nose seems to hang down. The effectiveness of the head lies in the synthesis between an extremely lifelike, and even realistic, portrait of an individual man and the portrayal of a standard type, the philosopher of the Hellenistic era. It goes far beyond the bronze head of a Boxer from Olympia (238, 239) in the apprehension and characterization of a unique personality. The calm objectivity of the expression and a certain austerity and calculation in the cast of the features suggest that it is related to,

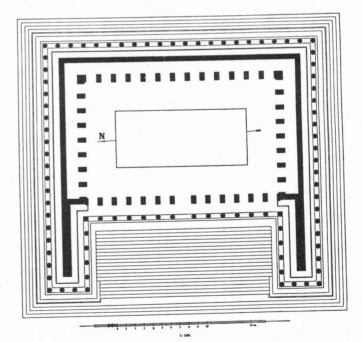

12   The Great Altar of Pergamon. Ground plan, reconstructed. After J. Schrammen, *Der große Altar*

but later than, the statue of a philosopher at Delphi (245), which would place it in the second half of the 3rd century B.C.

J. N. Svoronos, Das Athener Nationalmuseum (1908) 1, 29 ff., No. 2, plates 3/4. — L. Laurenzi, Ritratti Greci (1941), 124, No. 82, plate 32. — E. Buschor, Das hellenistische Bildnis (1949), 22 ff., fig. 18.

251–259

THE GREAT FRIEZE OF THE PERGAMON ALTAR. Marble from Asia Minor. Pergamon Museum, Berlin.

Eumenes II erected the great altar on the citadel mountain of Pergamon in about 180 B.C. as a memorial to the victories of his father and predecessor, Attalus I (241–197 B.C.). The huge building was dedicated to Zeus and Athene and stood on a large rectangular terrace overlooking the city's market-place. A 66-foot-wide (20 m.) monumental outside staircase of 28 steps cut into the almost square substructure, 120'3" × 112'10" (36.44 × 34.20 m.), from the west. It led through a double colonnade of Ionic columns into a rectangular court with the sacrificial altar in the centre. The inner face of the three walls of the court bore a relief frieze showing scenes from the legend of Telephus, the mythical founder of Pergamon and the first ancestor of the Pergamene royal house. Round the upper platform and the projecting flanks of the staircase ran Ionic columns that carried the roof.

Round the pedestal of the colossal monument, which itself stood on five steps, ran a frieze 7'6" (2.30 m.) in height and almost 400 feet (120 m.) long; this was not a decorative addition but an essential element in the construction of the altar. In extent it is, next to the Parthenon frieze, the largest work of relief in antique, indeed in the whole of western art. In the Greek fashion, it projects the historical events, the victories of the Pergamenes, into the mythological world. Its theme is the war of the gods with the giants, the triumph of order and light over chaos and darkness. The giants, sons of the earth, rose against the Olympian gods. According to an oracle the latter could only vanquish the giants if a mortal fought on their side. The gods gained the support of Hercules, who decided the battle in their favour with his arrows. Because of the length of the frieze, other mythological figures, associated with the gods, were included in the composition fighting alongside them. The names of some figures are inscribed on the fillet above the denticulation. Some of the giants are portrayed in human shape, others have serpent legs or wings on their backs, while a few have animals' heads.

This frieze, generally called the 'Great Frieze' to distinguish it from the Telephus frieze in the altar court, comprised more than a hundred individual panels varying in width between 1'11" (0.60 m.) and 3'7" (1.10 m.). More than a dozen sculptors engaged on the frieze have chiselled their names on the foot-fillet. The over-all design of the frieze, however, is the work of a single brilliant master.

Anyone entering the altar terrace from the market-place below through a door was confronted by the eastern face. It is the longest side of the altar, set against the outside staircase, and the main face of the frieze. Here Zeus and Athene (252, 253), fighting, occupy a significant position. In the central axis to the entrance stood the towering figure of Zeus, brandishing the aegis in his left hand and hurling a thunderbolt at two giants with his right. The supreme god with his mighty lunging body and trailing cloak is seen from the front view; facing him on his left – seen in a magnificent rear view – is serpent-footed Porphyrion, one of the strongest of the giants,

who has fallen to his knees. His eyes were inlaid in brightly coloured stones. His left arm is wrapped in a lion's skin. Between his head and arm rises one of his serpents, upon which an eagle of Zeus's swoops down from above. Another thunderbolt beneath Zeus's raised fist has struck a fallen giant in the thigh and caused him to go up in flames. Hercules was depicted on Zeus's left and on his other side Athene being garlanded by a hovering Nike. Athene has seized the winged Alcyoneus by the hair. Gaia, the mother of the giants, rises before her to beg mercy for her sons. Alcyoneus is touching his mother's breast with his outstretched left foot: according to the legend he was unconquerable as long as he was in contact with the Earth that had borne him. Athene is shown striving to pull him off the ground. The main group, Zeus between Hercules and Athene, was further framed by two chariots and their teams. On the left the winged steeds of Hera reared up towards the centre; on the right the horses of Ares.

In the left half of the eastern face, at its southern extremity, the three-bodied Hecate (254) is striking with torch, spear and sword at a bearded, serpent-legged foe; to her right the huntress Artemis (255) rushes over a dead giant lying on the ground at helmeted Otos. Mesmerized by the goddess's beauty he has lowered his sword. Both goddesses are accompanied by their dogs, which have attacked the despairing giants. Further towards the centre Leto and Apollo are shown in battle.

On the southern face the gods of light are fighting: In the centre Helios with his chariot and team, Eos and Selene on horseback, then the luminous star-gods and Rhea-Cybele on her lion.

On the northern face the central figure was Nyx, the goddess of night, who crashes a vessel encircled by serpents down upon a giant (257), the Moirae (258), the splendid figure of a lion-goddess (259) and in the corners Poseidon and Aphrodite with Eros. On the left flank of the stairs were the sea gods, on the front face Triton and Amphitrite (251), on the side facing the steps Nereus, Doris and Oceanus (?); the less well preserved right flank of the stairs was occupied by Dionysus with his retinue.

The Great Frieze is the supreme achievement of Pergamene art. Drawing upon an inexhaustible fund of invention, the immense drama passes before the eyes of the spectator like a cosmic event. The passions unleashed in the cruel struggle are mirrored in the bold, far-flung movements, the strength and weight of the figures with their swelling muscles, and the loud rustle of the drapery. The garments cling to the bodies in great sweeping curves and arcs, in rugged ridges or deep valleys, or seem to have broken free of them and to be living a life of their own. The background of the relief, artistically speaking, is the actual solid wall of the pedestal, before which the figures move in sculptural monumentality, in powerful contrast to the architectural function of the pedestal. The extent to which the ideal sphere of the relief reaches out into the structure of the altar is most strikingly shown on the inner face of the northern flank of the staircase, where the serpent leg of one giant winds its way up the stairs and another giant supports himself in falling with his knee and his hand upon the steps. The fact that the composition of the main group on the eastern face, showing Zeus and Athene framed by the two chariots and teams, is based on that of the west pediment of the Parthenon, where Athene and Poseidon are straining away from one another framed by their chariots, has often been noted. Features derived from the Classical relief style of the 5th century may also be observed in the way in which the individual figures are expanded in the plane, the avoidance of an effect of a multiplicity of planes and of depth in the relief by keeping the figures and groups apart, and the manner in which the whole of the background is covered with figures.

Altertümer von Pergamon, III, 1 = J. Schrammen, Der große Altar. Der obere Markt (Berlin 1906); III, 2 = H. Winnefeld, Die Friese des großen Altares (Berlin 1910). — A. v. Salis. Der Altar von Pergamon (1912). — W. H. Schuchhardt, Die Meister des großen Frieses von Pergamon (Berlin 1925). — H. Kähler, Der große Fries von Pergamon. Untersuchungen zur Kunstgeschichte und Geschichte Pergamons (Berlin 1948). — D. Thimme, The Masters of the Pergamon Gigantomachy, in: American Journal of Archaeology 50, 1946, 345 ff. — G. Kleiner, Zur Rangstellung der pergamenischen Kunst, in: Neue Jahrbücher für Antike und Jugendbildung 1938, 254 ff.

260, 261

HEAD OF ALEXANDER THE GREAT. White, fine-grained marble. Height 16.4" (41 cm.). Found at Pergamon, Autumn 1900. Istanbul, Archaeological Museum, Department of Classical Antiquities, No. 538 (1138).

A number of portraits of Alexander the Great in sculpture and painting, produced during his lifetime, are known to us indirectly through ancient literature and from copies made during the period of the Roman Empire. Of the original portraits, the statues by Leochares and Lysippus, Alexander's court sculptor, seem to have exercised the greatest influence on representations of Alexander produced at a later date. From the information available concerning Lysippus's likeness of Alexander, it seems reasonable to assume that this enormous head, the remains of an over-life-size standing figure of the Macedonian king, was also modelled on one of Lysippus's portraits of Alexander.

The head, set upon the thick neck, was turned a little to the left and slightly upwards. The full, curved lips are parted. Cut into the middle of the not very high forehead are two horizontal furrows, the upper one deeply incised; above these the forehead slopes back more markedly than in the outcurving part underneath. The intense and at the same time visionary gaze from comparatively small, deepset eyes shadowed by bushy eyebrows is directed upon some distant goal. Seen in profile, the nose continues the slope of the forehead. By comparison with the broad, full cheeks, the chin is rather small and round. The dishevelled hair lies loosely on the head, the individual, curved strands spreading from the crown. It covers the upper parts of the ears and falls loosely over the nape. It rises vertically above the centre of the forehead, quickly parting to right and left in great waves, in the *anastolé*, Alexander's traditional and characteristic hair-style. Seen from in front, the restless fullness of the hair, in conjunction with the cheeks and the chin, forms an impressive oval frame for the bold face with its composed countenance.

Soon after its discovery, this head was linked with the art of the Great Frieze on the altar of Zeus at Pergamon. The modelling — like that in the frieze of the giants — is filled with movement and effects of light and shade, but these effects are individually finer and more differentiated. Everything in this portrait bespeaks youthful fire, a passionate will and the genius of a world-conqueror. Out of a lofty view of the great historical personality, the deified founder of the Hellenistic empire, one of the most important of the Pergamene artists has here refashioned the portrait of Alexander with the aid of the stylistic devices of the high Hellenistic period. With good reason, the head has been declared the work of the leading master engaged on the Great Frieze, the same

sculptor who was responsible for the centre groups on the east side of the altar of Zeus (252, 253).

Altertümer von Pergamon VII, 1 = F. Winter, Die Skulpturen mit Ausnahme der Altarreliefs I, No. 131, plate 33. — Antike Denkmäler II (1899/1901), plate 48 (A. Conze). — G. Mendel, Catalogue des Sculptures Grecques, Romaines et Byzantines dans les Musées Ottomans II (1914), No. 538 (1138). — E. Buschor, Das hellenistische Bildnis, 27, 29, 31 ff. — G. Kleiner, Das Bildnis Alexanders des Großen, in: Jahrbuch des Deutschen Archäologischen Instituts 65/66, 1950/51, 208 f. and do., Zur Rangstellung der pergamenischen Kunst, in: Neue Jahrbücher für Antike und deutsche Bildung 1938, 263 and in: Charites, Studien zur Altertumswissenschaft (1957), Festschrift für E. Langlotz, p. 102.

262

NIKE. Found on Samothrace in 1863. Parian marble. Height 8' (2.45 m.). Louvre, Paris, No. 2369.

The Rhodians erected this vastly over-life-size image of the winged goddess of victory near the sanctuary of the Cabiri on Samothrace, in c. 190 B.C., in gratitude for their victories over Antiochus III of Syria (222–187 B.C.). The figure stood on the prow of a victorious ship in front of a wall overlooking a deep gorge, facing northward out to sea – a monument visible from a great distance.

The tall figure is shown at the instant of alighting on the prow of the ship. Her long, abundantly plumed wings are still open behind her. With all her gathered strength she is breasting the wind that comes surging towards her. Her feet on straddled legs are firmly planted on the solid surface. Her broad, out-turned left hip and the forward-thrusting torso turned in the opposite direction show that the weight of the body, with the contrasting movements of its various parts, rests equally on both feet. The right leg stands upright beneath the intricate concealing drapery; the left leg, which emerges clearly from beneath the robe, is set back and leads the eye in steep S-curves via the bunched up chiton across to the right shoulder and the raised right arm.

The goddess of victory is wearing a long chiton of thin fabric, girded close under the breast, with a broad overfold. The wind has pressed her garment so close to her body that the parts round the breasts, the stomach and the left leg stand out as though bare. A cloak has slipped from her shoulders and been caught up on the forward-thrust right leg, so that one end is blown round the right side of the figure and out at the back. In the front it is bunched up between the legs in great sweeping folds that follow the movement of the rear leg – forming sharp ridges and broad, deep valleys – and pile up on the ground in front of the left foot. The impetus of the drapery corresponds to the refractory movements of the body and heightens the figure's restlessness. Set free from the body, the drapery enjoys a largely independent existence full of surging movement, like the breakers of a sea whipped up by the storm.

The head was turned to its left. The right arm was raised, the left lowered.

The stump of the right hand and the upper part of the right ring-finger came to light during fresh excavations on Samothrace in 1950. By a fortunate coincidence, a thumb and the lower part of a ring finger, both of which fitted exactly on to the right hand, were discovered in the storehouse of the Museum of Art History at Vienna the same year. Marks on the hand and the two extended fingers suggest that the index finger was bent towards the thumb and that the goddess held in her right hand a victor's fillet of metal.

These finds and the fact that study of the attachment surface of the neck has revealed that the Nike's head was turned to the left and not, as was formerly thought, to the right have proved the inaccuracy of earlier reconstructions according to which the Victory of Samothrace was blowing a trumpet held in her right hand. This reconstruction was based on the image of a Nike, preserved on coins, set up by Demetrius Poliorcetes in 306 B.C. to celebrate his victory over Ptolemy I at Salamis on Cyprus. This late 4th-century statue was still constructed according to the Classical principles of composition: a difference was made between the free and the supporting leg, the forward-thrust right leg and outstretched arm demanding that the head should be turned to the right in a sequence of flowing movements on the part of the speeding goddess. The early 2nd-century artist gave his figure another kind of solidity, making the axes irregular, balancing forward movement of the body by a backward swing of the drapery and turning the Nike's head away from the raised right arm towards the left shoulder, in conformity with the system of contrasts employed in the construction of the figure. He placed it in front of a wall in the sanctuary in such a way that it was looked at mainly aslant towards its left side. Seen from this broad diagonal view the Victory of Samothrace, one of the most magnificent statues of the early 2nd century B.C., displays all its wealth of artistry.

A. Conze, A. Hauser and O. Benndorf, Neue Untersuchungen auf Samothrake (1880) II, 55 ff. — H. Thiersch, Die Nike von Samothrake, ein rhodisches Werk und Anathem, in: Nachrichten der Gesellschaft der Wissenschaften zu Göttingen, Philosoph.-Histor. Klasse 1931, No. 3, 337 ff. — H. Kähler, Der Große Fries von Pergamon, 76 ff. and 173 ff., note 75. — J. Charbonneaux, La Main Droite de la Victoire de Samothrace; in: Hesperia 21, 1952, 44 ff., plates 12/13.

263

HEAD OF HELIOS. Parian (?) marble. Height 22" (55 cm.). Museum, Rhodes.

This greatly over-life-size head was found during digging operations in 1938 in a medieval wall in the upper part of the Knights' Way on Rhodes, in a spot close to what is thought to have been the site of the sanctuary of Helios, the chief god of Rhodes.

The head is twisted vehemently round to its right. The eyes look upwards. The lips are parted, the chin and cheeks full and round. The face is framed by the great oval of a restless abundance of hair, which grows up from the forehead in long, tongue-like locks separated from one another by deep grooves cut with the running drill. The mass of the hair is separated from the temples, cheeks and neck by deep, shadowy interstices.

The gaps now present in the hair were originally filled in with stucco. The whole of the back of the head and part of the back of the neck were also of stucco. The combination of stucco and stone was a technique frequently employed – especially in Hellenistic times – in places where good marble was lacking. It seems to have been particularly usual in Alexandria. The differences of material were rendered invisible by painting.

In the hind part of the hair, running round the head in a three-quarter circle, are fifteen small holes slanting towards the centre. They held long metal rods which formed the sun god's halo of rays. A large hole in the rear of the head, tapering inwards, contained an iron peg or dowel. The size of this hole suggests that it was intended not only to hold together the stucco and the marble, but also to fix the head more firmly to the body or to balance the weight.

The neck is broken right round at the base. The pronounced tension of the neck muscles indicates that the right shoulder was thrust

considerably farther forward than the left, and that the rest of the body showed a tilt and twist from right to left. It must have been a mighty figure full of contrasting movements. Whether the god was naked or clothed, alone or set on a chariot driving his quadriga can for the present no longer be determined with certainty; on the other hand, it has been authoritatively suggested that the statue to which the head belonged was a freely treated copy of the famous Colossus of Rhodes. The vigorous twist of the head, the emphatic gaze, the turbulent rendering of the hair and the magnificent mobility of the sculptural forms place this head in direct succession to the Great Frieze of Pergamon, close to the so-called Attalus I from Pergamon at Berlin (Altertümer von Pergamon VII, 1, 144 ff., No. 130, Plates 31/32) and the heads of Alexander from Pergamon and Cos at Istanbul (E. Buschor, Das hellenistische Bildnis, Figs. 27/28. – Here: 260, 261). This would give it a date in the second quarter of the 2nd century B.C.

L. Laurenzi, Un' Immagine del Dio Sole Rinvenuta a Rodi, in: Memorie Pubblicati a Cura dell' Istituto Storico-Archeologico di Rodi 3, 1938, 21 ff., plates 23—25. — G. Kleiner, Helios und Sol, in: Charites, Studien zur Altertumswissenschaft. Festschrift für E. Langlotz (Bonn 1957), 101 ff. with Pl. XIII, 1—2.

264, 265

PORTRAIT STATUE OF A RULER. Bronze. Height to the tip of the left index finger 7'9" (2.37 m.). The staff has been restored. Found in Rome in 1884. Museo delle Terme, Rome, No. 544 (Inv. 1049).

The over-life-size, imposing figure of a man in ideal nakedness stands with the left foot set far back. The upstretched left hand held a spear, the right rests, palm outwards, against the back.

The massive, muscular body bears a relatively small head which is turned to the right. The eyes gaze into the distance. The face is framed by short, tangled curls of hair and the engraved down of a thin beard. The eyes are deep-set between the projecting cheekbones and the low, beetling brow, close together and slightly narrowed. They were originally inset in coloured material. The small mouth with the thick lips is open, the nose short and fleshy, the ears curiously misshapen.

In type and pose the bronze recalls a statue of Alexander the Great by Lysippus, which must have served the artist as a model. Compared with late Classical works, however, the rhythm of this figure appears irregular and inhibited. The forms have become restless, losing their firmness and as if they were swelling up from within, so that light and shade create a pictorial effect on the surface of the sculpture. The expression of the face is nervous and as if tormented by doubt.

The statue has been taken to represent various historical personages, most recently and with great probability Demetrius I Soter of Syria, who came to Rome as a hostage in 175 B.C. while still a boy, fled from Rome to his homeland at the age of twenty-four and was recognized by the Roman Senate as King of Syria (162–150 B.C.). Judging by the style, and especially by the subject of the portrait, the bronze must date from about the middle of the 2nd century B.C.

W. Helbig, Antike Denkmäler 1 (1886), plate 5. — W. Helbig, Führer durch die öffentlichen Sammlungen klassischer Altertümer in Rom (3rd edition, 1913), vol. 2, No. 1347. — Ph. L. Williams, American Journal of Archaeology 49, 1945, 330 ff. — G. Kleiner, Münchner Jahrbuch für Bildende Kunst 1, 1950, 19 ff. — E. Buschor, Das hellenistische Bildnis, 31 f.

266, 267

MALE PORTRAIT STATUE. Found near the Odeion on Cos. Marble from Cos. Museum, Cos.

The over-life-size portrait statue depicts a handsome, bearded man in a long cloak. The right foot bears no weight and is set far back. The missing right arm, which was originally pieced on, was raised and probably supported on a tall staff. The robe is wound round the body with an overfold, crosses the chest horizontally, goes round the back and over the left shoulder, covers the left arm and falls straight down in front of the figure and on its left side. The left hand grasps the robe, so that it forms a long, straight edge which intersects the body. The unbroken head is slightly lowered and turned to the left. The face with the evenly shaped nose is framed by short, thick hair and a flocculent beard. The somewhat small, tired eyes, overshadowed by heavy brows and set between broad lids, gaze into the distance.

The rear of the figure is strikingly flat and has been neglected by the sculptor. There is a large, rectangular hole in the back for a peg, by means of which the statue was fixed to a wall.

In type this portrait is based on works from the 4th century B.C. such as we see in Attic sepulchral reliefs or portraits like that of Sophocles in the Lateran. It cannot be a 4th-century original, however. The pose lacks the inner firmness, and the composition the compactness, of Classical statues. The way in which the vertical edge of the robe that falls down the front from the left shoulder, and the deep fold running down between the legs, divide the body in two halves is typical of Late Hellenistic sculpture. Correspondingly, the whole of the left side of the figure is intentionally extended in a lateral direction so as to appear to the best effect from the front view and against a background. The outward brio and feeling with which the robe as a whole and the individual folds are arranged, and the ideal of beauty expressed in the head, which recalls the Aphrodite of Melos (270, 271), also indicate that the statue was carved during the second half of the 2nd century B.C., which was a golden age for the island of Cos.

Soon after its discovery it was – not unnaturally – interpreted as a likeness of the celebrated physician Hippocrates, who was born on Cos in about 460 B.C. This designation might well have been correct; but the statue from Cos bears no individual resemblance to a bearded portrait bust from Ostia which is now thought, from an inscription on a nearby pillar, to represent Hippocrates. At one time it was believed to depict Periander, the Tyrant of Corinth, since the head bears a certain, though not irrefutable, resemblance to a portrait of Periander which is unmistakably identified by an inscription, while in type the figure from Cos is comparable to one in the mosaic with the Seven Wise Men from Torre Annunziata at Naples. It is most likely that the statue portrays an unknown citizen of Cos, to whose lasting memory his countrymen erected this monument in Late Hellenistic times.

£. *Laurenzi*, Clara Rhodos V, 2 (1932), 71 ff., plates 1—3. — *V. H. Poulsen*, Acta Archaeologica 14, 1943, 72 ff. — *G. Becatti*, Il Ritratto di Ippocrate, in: Atti della Pontificia Accademia Romana di Archeologia (Series III), Rendiconti 21, 1945—46, 123 ff.

268

VOTIVE RELIEF. SACRIFICE IN A RURAL SANCTUARY. Pentelic marble. Height 24.4" (61 cm.), width 31.6" (79 cm.). From Greece, exact site of find unknown. Munich, Glyptothek, No. 206. Acquired from dealer, 1882.

The scene, which is contained within an architectural framework, shows a sacrifice in which gods and men are brought together. On the left we see a huge old plane, a sacred tree, whose thick, wrinkled trunk is adorned with a broad sacrificial band. On a tall pillar close to the tree stand the small figures of Apollo and Artemis, represented in an old-fashioned style. A curtain, which also serves as a background for the two deities to whom the relief was dedicated, stretches in a wide arc from the lowest of the tree's gnarled branches to the right-hand edge of the relief. The deities appear as in their cult images: on the right a dignified, bearded god in a cloak on a chair of state, the arm of which is supported by a lion-griffin, and his goddess – smaller in stature and seen in front view – in a chiton and belted peplos, leaning against a pillar. Each holds a long sceptre in the right hand. The two gods cannot be identified with certainty, since further attributes or inscriptions are lacking; but the suggestions that they are Asklepios and Hygieia or Serapis and Isis may well be correct.

In front of the gods stands their altar, which a line of worshippers is approaching from the left. These are members of a family. Behind the altar, turned towards the deities and taller than the rest of the family, stands the father, in profile. His hair is short and curly; he holds his cloak with his left hand as he inserts his right into a sacrificial basket held out to him by his eldest son. Next comes his wife; like the son, she is shown in front view; she has drawn her cloak over her head like a veil and her right hand is raised in prayer. In front of her a small girl is walking towards the altar with a covered basket on her head. Beside the girl stand two small children, facing outwards: one boy is holding a cock and a bucket, the other, shorter one, is tightly wrapped in his cloak. Two bigger girls in long mantles bring up the rear; like their mother, each has drawn her mantle over her head and raised her right hand in the gesture of adoration. The girl on the left – who is seen in profile and thus terminates the composition on this side by balancing the figure of the god on the right – is wearing a mushroom-shaped hat with a high point on top.

The style and dating of this charming relief of unusual character have been variously interpreted by scholars. Some have ascribed it to the end of the 3rd century B.C. But opinion is veering more and more towards the view that it can only be the product of late Hellenistic times. This late dating is supported not only by the style of the individual figures – such as the complex and mobile image of the goddess with its mutually displaced axes, or the head of the sacrificing father, reminiscent of late Hellenistic portraits – but also by the elements suggestive of a landscape and above all by the absence of tension between the figures and the ground of the relief.

A. Furtwängler and *P. Wolters*, Beschreibung der Glyptothek König Ludwigs I (2nd ed. 1910), 183 ff., No. 206. — *E. Buschor*, Die Plastik der Griechen (1936), 98. — *L. Laurenzi*, Römische Mitteilungen 54, 1939, 42 ff., plate 11. — *G. Kleiner*, Tanagrafiguren, 266. — *H. G. Beyen*, Bulletin van de Vereeniging tot Bevordering der Kennis van de Antieke Beschaving 27, 1953, 1 ff. — *E. Thiemann*, Hellenistische Vatergottheiten, 93 ff., plates 1—3. — *K. Schefold*, Griechische Kunst als religiöses Phänomen, 127.

269

STATUETTE OF POSEIDON. Bronze with dark green and brownish-red patina. Height 11.8" (29.5 cm.). Munich, Museum Antiker Kleinkunst. From the J. Loeb Collection (No. 15).

The figure is poised in the act of taking a step, the unweighted left leg set far back. Construction and rhythm are governed by the figure's purposeful movements. In his raised left hand Poseidon holds the trident (the one seen here has been restored). With his slightly open right hand stretched forward and outward, he seems to be taming the waves of the sea. The supposition that he formerly held a dolphin in his right hand is certainly incorrect. The relatively small head with the untidy beard and long, dishevelled hair, which was adorned with a crown of reeds, is turned in the direction indicated by the supporting leg, following the pull of the right arm. The eyes are gazing into space. The relaxed posture and the baroque swing of the arms are echoed in the portrayal of the powerful, muscular body with its athletically fashioned forms and splendidly mobile modelling.

Compared with the bronze portrait of a ruler in the Museo delle Terme (264, 265), this statuette appears more generous and unified in its movements and shapes. The modelling is more powerful and firmer, in the manner of the Classical statues of athletes; the figure fits into this tradition and is a significant and important follow-up of the great figures of the gods produced in the late Hellenistic period. There is not much doubt that it dates from the end of the 2nd century B.C.

The right foot and leg from the middle of the shinbone downwards, and the left foot below the ankle, have been restored in modern times.

J. Sieveking, Die Bronzen der Sammlung Loeb, 41 ff., text figure and plates 17 f. — G. Krahmer, Römische Mitteilungen 38/39, 1923/24, 150. — W. H. Schuchhardt, Die Kunst der Griechen, 420 ff., fig. 390 f. — E. Thiemann, Hellenistische Vatergottheiten, 82 ff.

270, 271

APHRODITE. Found on the island of Melos in 1820. Parian marble. Height 6'8" (2.04 m.). Louvre, Paris, No. 399/400.

This much admired image of the goddess of love has become for generations, under the title of the 'Venus de Milo', the incarnation of feminine beauty, ever since 1821 when the statue came to occupy an effective position in the Louvre.

The tall body with the broad hips and high waist, the full, diverging breasts, narrow shoulders and relatively small head represents an ideal of feminine beauty of the Late Hellenistic period. The weight of the figure rests on the right leg. The left foot is placed on a small eminence, thus taking the weight off the leg, the knee of which is bent inwards – towards the goddess's right side. The upper part of the trunk is twisted to the left, in the opposite direction to the slanting thigh. The head on the extended neck is looking towards the left. The face is seen to best advantage in three-quarter view, when it lies in the same plane as the upper part of the body. The hair is parted in the centre and held together with a band. It is taken back from the temples in long waves and tied above the band in a knot from which a curl has escaped and is hanging down the back of the neck. The arms reached outwards, the right across the body, the left upwards.

A wide cloak has slipped down over the hips. It lays bare the upper part of the torso with all its charms and thus effectively emphasizes the contrast between the naked and the clothed areas of the body. The drapery is arranged in a spirited pattern of steep ridges and deep valleys in which the shadows gather. Here, too, the dominant impression is one of contrasts: the supporting leg is hidden beneath folds while the material clings so smoothly to the free leg that it discloses rather than conceals its forms.

To judge by the wealth of contrast in the structure of the figure, the spiral movements and the modelling, the Melos Aphrodite was carved during the last quarter of the 2nd century B.C. It is not an independent creation of this period, but derived from a type of Aphrodite dating from the second half of the 4th century, the best preserved example of which is a statue from Capua at Naples, a marble copy after a bronze (Brunn-Bruckmann, Denkmäler griechischer und römischer Skulptur, Plate 297. – H. Bulle, Der Schöne Mensch, Fig. 169). In the original the left foot rested on the helmet of Ares, while the goddess held his shield in her hands and gazed at her reflexion in it. In the Aphrodite of Melos the still comparatively lucid construction of this tall, majestic figure of the Alexandrian period is broken up, the simpler axial framework complicated and transformed into a multiplicity of conflicting axes. The heroic character of the model is heightened to an intense emotionalism. The artist has remodelled the long oval of the face with the triangular forehead, the small, far-gazing eyes and the softly curved lips to achieve a more conscious, august and at the same time cooler charm and beauty than were given to it during the 4th century.

The statue in the Louvre is made up of two blocks that meet just above the drapery. The left arm was made out of a separate piece and attached. The tip of the nose has been restored. The goddess wore metal jewellery on her ears.

W. Fröbner, Notice de la Sculpture Antique du Musée Impérial du Louvre (1869), No. 136. — A. Furtwängler, Meisterwerke, 601 ff. — R. Horn, Römische Mitteilungen 53, 1938, 83. — J. Charbonneaux, La Vénus de Milo, = Die Venus von Milo, Opus Nobile, Chefs d'Oeuvre de l'Art Antique; No. 6 (1958) [French]; No. 6/1 (1959) [German].

272

APHRODITE. Terra-cotta. Red-brown clay, traces of white and bright red paint. Height 15" (37.8 cm.). State Museum, Berlin, Department of Classical Antiquities Inv. 31272. Acquired from the Baron Heyl Collection in 1930.

The goddess is shown poised in the middle of a movement with her left leg raised, her arms lifted to the left. Her shoulders and beautiful, expressive head are turned to the right. The long, close-drawn garment has slipped from her shoulders and is held in front of the breast by the right arm; one end lies on her raised leg as a bundle of folds. Her hands were close together and held some object whose nature can no longer be determined. Her pensive, smiling eyes are looking downwards, perhaps at an Eros that may have stood beside her. Her hair is parted over the centre of her forehead and taken back in soft waves. It is adorned with a broad diadem.

The tall, slender body is activated from the centre outwards in a variety of divergent axes, twists and intersections. In spite, however, of the finely rounded limbs and the long, sweeping folds of the drapery round the lower part of the body and legs, the figure is intentionally flat and designed to be seen from one angle only. There is something statuesque about it and the effect it creates is that of a piece of monumental sculpture. It has behind it an important prototype from the second half of the 4th century B.C., to which the artist from the end of the 2nd century has given an entirely fresh shape in line with the style of his own period. The broken, mutually conflicting rhythms of movement, the treatment of the drapery, aimed at a sensuous effect, which in places clings so closely to the body as to create an impression of nakedness, and the restless play of the folds are combined with the classicizing ideal of beauty of the Late Hellenistic period to form a new unity. This extremely fine terra-cotta comes from one of those workshops in Asia Minor – Myrina or Pergamon – that took the first place in the manufacture of Greek terra-cottas after production ceased at Tanagra in the 2nd century B.C.

P. Arndt and *W. Amelung*, Photographische Einzelaufnahmen antiker Skulpturen (Series 5, Munich 1902) No. 1451, Text by *H. Bulle*. — Die Kunstsammlungen Baron Heyl/Darmstadt. part 2. Auktionskatalog Helbing, 30. Oktober 1930, No. 72, plate 19, Text by *E. Langlotz*. — *G. Kleiner*, Tanagrafiguren, 149 ff., plate 48 a.

273

CROUCHING APHRODITE. Found on Rhodes in 1923. Parian marble. Height 19.6″ (49 cm.) (without base). Museum, Rhodes.

Doidalses of Bithynia, an artist from Asia Minor of the 3rd century B.C., was the first to sculpt a statue of naked Aphrodite in a crouching position. The original, a life-size bronze, is lost. Its fame and popularity is attested by numerous antique copies and the widespread influence it exercised on the art of later generations.

The goddess was represented almost kneeling. The left foot was placed flat on the ground with the shank almost vertical, while the right thigh and shank were parallel with the base and only the toes of the right foot rested on the ground. The left hand covered the pubic area, the right reached over to the left side of the head to capture a loose curl or smooth back the hair. The head was turned far round to the right and looked down over the right shoulder. The goddess's body was portrayed in full, luxuriant forms with long, deep folds cutting into the opulent flesh. As was customary during the mid-3rd century B.C., the individual limbs were contrasted with one another in opposing movements, the whole figure being firmly self-enclosed by its gathered-in pose; the position of the arms, the turn of the head and the direction of the gaze all cut it off from the outside.

This 3rd-century work was translated by a Rhodian sculptor at the turn of the 2nd to the 1st century B.C. into the idiom of his own time in the shape of the statuette here reproduced. Instead of bronze, with all the characteristic qualities of the metal, he has selected a white, fine-crystalled marble resembling alabaster in its transparency. He has reduced the life-size scale of Doidalses's statue, which must have been a cult statue or a votive offering, by more than half. Above all, however, he has radically altered the proportions, pose and composition of his model. The body is slenderer, but less supple. The right leg is tilted downwards at a greater angle, so that the right knee is closer to the ground. It rests upon a round box such as women used for their toilet. The torso is erect with the arms and head turned into a frontal position and thus spread out in a single plane. Both hands are grasping the loose hair that is held round the head by a broad band and falls down on either side of the parting – an arrangement which the Late Hellenistic sculptor has borrowed from another type of Aphrodite, the goddess emerging from the sea.

The complicated movements of the older model have been simplified in the statuette. The 3rd-century composition, closed on all sides, has been opened up and arranged to be viewed from one particular angle. The sculptural form is looser, the modelling soft and the coordination indistinct. The symmetrical oval of the face represents a new, late ideal of beauty in Greek art.

A. Maiuri, Bollettino d'Arte (series 3) 3, 1923/24, 385 ff. — *S. Reinach*, Fondation Eugène Piot. Monuments et Mémoires 27, 1924, 119 ff., plate 12. — *A. Adriani*, L'Afrodite al Bagno di Rodi e l'Afrodite di Doidalses, in: Annales du Service des Antiquités de l'Egypte 44, 1945, 37 ff. — *R. Lullies*, Die kauernde Aphrodite (1954), 84, fig. 51.

274, XI

MALE PORTRAIT HEAD. Found in the old Palaestra on Delos in 1912. Bronze with a dark green patina. Height (with the neck) 13″ (32.5 cm.). National Museum, Athens, Inv. 14.612.

The expressive and eloquent head was cast together with the neck and set in a clothed statue. Set on a thick, fleshy neck, it is turned emphatically to its left and upwards. The full, indecisive mouth is slightly open, the despondent glance from the inlaid, coloured eyes, which were originally fringed by bronze lashes, is directed upwards. The difference in the set of the eyes adds to the look of instability about the expression. The brows have the appearance of wings and are so drawn together as to form two folds above the straight nose, which becomes fuller towards the tip. The modelling of the undeveloped, dimpled chin accords with that of the pendulous cheeks. The forehead is furrowed in the centre by two long, vertical folds. The short hair lies flat on the head in untidy, restless tufts divided by single, slanting engraved lines and smallish strands.

The subject of this portrait must have been a nervous man, shaken and tormented by anxious doubts, typical of a late period. The dissolving sculptural form, the surface of which is enlivened by the play of light and shade, goes far beyond the level of the Ruler in the Museo delle Terme (264, 265), without yet attaining the classicizing hardness of modelling which we see in the Boxer (275–277). The bronze head from Delos must date from the early 1st century B.C. It has been associated in style and date with the so-called 'Borghese warrior' in the Louvre – according to the inscription, the work of Agasias, son of Dositheos of Ephesus – and even attributed to the same artist.

Exploration Archéologique de Délos, 13 = C. *Michalowski*, Les Portraits Hellénistiques et Romains (1932), 1 ff., plates 1—6. — *G. Kleiner*, Der Bronzekopf von Delos, Grieche oder Römer?, in: Münchner Jahrbuch der Bildenden Kunst 1, 1950, 9 ff. — *G. Hafner*, Späthellenistische Bildnisplastik (1954), 30, M K 2 and plate 10.

275–277

BOXER. Found at Rome in 1884. Bronze. Height 4'2″ (1.28 m.). Museo delle Terme, Rome, 545 (Inv. 1055).

The athlete sits with legs apart and torso bent forward, the front part of his coarse, broad feet lifted slightly off the ground by the twist of his raised head. His arms lie stiffly on his thighs, made clumsy by the thongs and bandages with which the knuckledusters for his hands are fastened to his forearms. The unintelligent, small face that seems to be raised ill-humouredly towards someone who has disturbed the exhausted boxer during the rest between rounds is in keeping with the heavy, compact body, the powerful chest, the burly bull-neck and the short, thick throat.

Long gashes on the right shoulder and right elbow are due to an opponent's blows. The coarse, short nose is flattened, the upper front teeth seem to have been knocked out. The mouth is open as though the nose were blocked with congealed blood. The ears are swollen from blows and covered with fresh wounds out of which drops of blood are oozing. The eyes were inset in coloured material. Their empty cavities now intensify the disconsolate expression.

An inscription on the thongs of the left hand describes the statue as the work of Apollonios, son of Nestoros, of Athens. The famous Belvedere torso in the Vatican bears the signature of the same sculptor. Both figures are characterized by the same strongly contrasting movements and disjointed rhythm. There is something harsh and discordant about the artist's handling of forms. Thus the rough, battered face is in striking contrast to the treatment of the hair, which is based on Classical models and which, despite its general disorder, exhibits areas where individual tufts of hair are arranged symmetrically or fashioned into rigid ornamental shapes. The bronze dates from the mid-1st century B.C. It may represent a mythological boxer and have been combined with a second figure to form a group. As model or inspiration the Late Hellenistic artist may have used a seated Hercules by Lysippus, a bronze colossus which once stood upon the acropolis of Taranto and which was brought to Rome by the Roman general Q. Fabius Maximus Varrucosus after the town was conquered anew by the Romans in 209 B.C.

The rock on which the figure is seated has been restored.

W. Helbig, Antike Denkmäler 1 (1886), plate 4. — W. Helbig, Führer durch die öffentlichen Sammlungen klassischer Altertümer in Rom (3rd edition 1913), vol. 2, No. 1350. — Ph. L. Williams, American Journal of Archaeology 49, 1945, 332 ff. — On artist's mark: R. Carpenter, Memoirs of the American Academy at Rome 6, 1927, 133 ff. — On the Hercules of Lysippus: J. Dörig, Jahrbuch des Deutschen Archäologischen Instituts 72, 1957, 19 ff.

278, 279

DEATH OF LAOCOÖN AND HIS TWO SONS. White, fine-crystalled marble. Height 8' (2.42 m.). Vatican Collections, Belvedere, Rome, No. 74.

According to Greek legend, Laocoön, a Trojan and a priest of Apollo, married against the god's prohibition and begot two sons. As a punishment he and his sons were killed by two serpents. In the magnificent section of the second book of the *Aeneid* Virgil has clad the Greek material in Roman garb, by giving the Laocoön episode the character of a prodigy, a grandiose augury foreshadowing the downfall of Troy: the terrible fate that overtook these individuals – Laocoön and his sons – would later befall all Trojans.

The Vatican group was found in 1506 in the spacious palace of Nero on the Esquiline. It did not stand there by chance: the incident from the Trojan legend was linked with the city of Rome and the Julio-Claudian imperial house through Aeneas, who came to Latium after the destruction of Troy and became the ancestor of the Romans and the Julian family.

In the group the ghastly occurrence is taking place in front of an altar approached by two steps. The elder of the two sons is still unhurt and striving to free himself from the serpent's coils. The eyes of the younger boy, into whose right side the same beast is plunging its fangs, are already glazed. Laocoön is being bitten in the flank by the other serpent, which he is trying to pull away with his left hand. Racked with pain, his abdomen drawn in, his chest mightily raised, his head thrown convulsively back, he opens his mouth in a groan of agony. This group has been much admired for the vividness with which it captures in stone, at the

'psychological moment', suffering humanity fighting in vain against disaster ordained from above.

According to ancient tradition, the Laocoön group was the work of three Rhodian sculptors, Agesandrus, Athanodorus and Polydorus. It is a perfect example of the Late Hellenistic group spread out in one plane like a relief and intended to be looked at from one side only, indeed from a single point. In the inward dissolution of its sculptural form, the extensions of the bodies and the virtuosity with which it reproduces intense emotion the group represents a late phase of Hellenistic sculpture. Some scholars ascribe it to the mid-1st century B.C., while others place it in the early Augustan period (c. 30 B.C.).

Laocoön's raised right arm with the serpent has been restored. It was originally bent more acutely at the elbow and touched the back of the head, which materially alters the outline of the whole group. In addition to numerous other details, the right arm of the younger son and the right hand of the elder have also been restored.

W. Amelung, Katalog der Skulpturen des Vatikanischen Museums 2 (1908), 181 ff., No. 74, plate 20. — G. Krahmer, Die einansichtige Gruppe und die spät-hellenistische Kunst, in: Nachrichten der Gesellschaft der Wissenschaften zu Göttingen 1929, No. 1, 1 ff. — H. Kleinknecht, Laokoon, in: Hermes, Zeitschrift für klassische Philologie 79, 1944, 66 ff. — M. Bieber, Laocoon. The Influence of the Group since the Discovery (New York 1942). — H. Sichtermann, Laokoon. Opus Nobile, Meisterwerke der antiken Kunst, No. 3 (1957).

280, 281

BOY IN A CLOAK. Parian marble. From Tralles (Aidin, Caria). Height with plinth 4'10" (1.475 m.). Istanbul, Archaeological Museum, Department of Classical Antiquities, No. 542 (1191).

This statue represents a palaestrite in boyhood; tired, his head thoughtfully bent, he is leaning against one of the quadrangular pillars that mark the starting- turning- or finishing-point for runners or chariot races in the stadium. The weight of the body, in so far as it is not taken by the pillar, rests upon the right leg. The left shank is crossed over the right leg and probably only the tip of the left foot was touching the ground. The feet as far as the heel were carved out of a separate piece of marble and attached. They are now missing.

The boy, whose ears are swollen from fighting in the palaestra, is wearing high leather shoes tied with thongs. He is dressed in a brief, possibly belted undergarment with short sleeves, and a cloak of thick cloth that is gathered on the right shoulder and encircles the neck like a wide collar. The left arm rests on the chest beneath the cloak. One end of the cloak is wrapped round the boy's lowered right arm, which thus pulls the rear part of the cloak forward. The hair is depicted in many separate tousled tresses and parted above the forehead.

At first glance the palaestrite may recall similar draped marble statues from the second half of the 4th century B.C., such as Daoches I from the Delphic votive offering (*Fouilles de Delphes IV*, plate LXVI right). In that the treatment of the hair appeared to have parallels in even earlier Greek heads, the statue was previously thought to date from Classical times. Later it was ascribed to the 3rd century B.C., because the figure lacked the rhythm of Classical works and was sharply cut off from surrounding space. Both datings seem unlikely. Although the sculptor of the Tralles boy took works like the aforementioned Delphic statue as a model, the way in which one leg is here crossed over the other, the way in which the body is divided in front by the long diagonal fold of the cloak and the figure in combination with the pillar is composed to be looked at from one view only, coupled with the schematic parallelism between the vertical and the horizontal axes, the tired expression on the face and the portrayal of the hair with a parting over the forehead – which is more reminiscent of Augustan portraits than of 5th-century heads, – all combine to suggest that it can only be a classicizing re-creation in the manner of the early period of the Roman empire.

M. Collignon, Monuments Piot 10, 1903, 29 ff., plates 4, 5. — G. Mendel, Catalogue des Sculptures Grecques, Romaines et Byzantines II (1914), No. 542 (1191). — M. Schede, Meisterwerke der türkischen Museen zu Konstantinopel I, p. 10, plate 15. — G. Krahmer, Römische Mitteilungen 38/39, 1923/24, 158 f. — G. Becatti, Rivista del R. Istituto d'Archeologia e Storia d'Arte 7, 1940, 75 f. — W. H. Schuchhardt, Die Epochen der griechischen Plastik, 116 ff.

282

FEMALE HEAD. Found at Satala, near Erivan, Armenia. Bronze. Height 15.2" (38 cm.). The height of the whole figure was about 7' (2.10 m.). British Museum, London, No. 266. Purchased from the Castellani Collection in 1873.

Apart from the head, all that remains of the over-life-size statue is the left hand that held a garment. The back of the head is missing. The eyes were inlaid in coloured material. There are two rectangular holes and cavities in the circlet that runs round the head, on both sides of the parting, which served for the attachment of a diadem.

The head is slightly tilted towards the left shoulder. The face is modelled in a triangle but creates an impression of roundness because of the small, soft chin and the symmetrical waves of the hair. Fine curls emerge in front of the ears and lie close to the cheeks, longer curls hang down behind the ears and form in falling a curved ornament resembling the meander. Two thin strands have been combed down over the forehead on either side of the parting in the shape of a pair of open tongs. The emphatically severe, straight nose and the shallow curve of the finely drawn eyebrows above the close-set eyes constitute a formal framework whose severity is mitigated by the mouth and eyes. The heavy upper lids give the eyes a thoughtful expression; the small, full-lipped mouth with the sharply defined Cupid's bow of the upper lip is slightly open.

This decorative head had as a model an Aphrodite-type of the 4th century B.C. A late Greek artist has transformed it, with the aid of a carefully thought-out composition and a cool rendering of forms, which may already be called Classicizing, into the ideal of beauty held by his own age. It is hard to imagine that the statue to which the London head belonged was cast before the Augustan epoch.

R. Engelmannn, Ein Bronzekopf des Britischen Museums, in: Archäologische Zeitung 36, 1878, 150 ff., plate 20. — H. B. Walters, Catalogue of the Bronzes in the British Museum No. 266 and the same, Select Bronzes (1915), plate 13.

CHRONOLOGICAL TABLE

B.C.

776	Beginning of time-reckoning by Olympiads. Coroebus victor at Olympia.
750—650	Homer's great epic poems collected to form the *Iliad* and *Odyssey*.
c. 750	First Greek colonies established in southern Italy and Sicily (Cumae 754; Syracuse 735; Taranto 708; Gela 690; Selinus 628).
after 750	Bronze statuette of a horse. State Museum, Berlin, Department of Classical Antiquities (Plate 1).
c. 700	Warrior from the Acropolis. National Museum, Athens (Plate 2).
c. 660	The oldest monumental stone carvings in Greece.
c. 640	The 'Auxerre Statuette'. Louvre, Paris (Plate 6).
before 600	Attic statue of a youth in the Metropolitan Museum, New York (Plates 11–13).
c. 600	Statues of Cleobis and Biton. Delphi, Museum (Plates 14, 15).
594	Solon is Archon at Athens.
c. 590	West pediment of the Temple of Artemis, Corfu (Plates 16–19).
c. 570	Calf-bearer from the Acropolis. Acropolis Museum, Athens (Plates 24, 25).
560—527	Peisistratus, Tyrant of Athens. Succeeded by his sons Hippias and Hipparchus.
c. 550	Funerary statue from Tenea. Glyptothek, Munich (Plates 36–38).
534	First tragedy performed at Athens (Thespis).
c. 530	Statue of a girl in chiton and peplos from the Acropolis. Acropolis Museum, Athens (Plates 43–45). – Head of a youth in Copenhagen (Plates 46, 47).
before 525	Siphnian treasury at Delphi (Plates 48–55).
c. 520	Funerary statue of Kroisos from Anavyssos. National Museum, Athens (Plates 57–61).
514/10	End of the tyranny at Athens. The Athenians erect a bronze group of the tyrannicides Harmodius and Aristogeiton by Antenor in their market-place in memory of the murder of Hipparchus (514) and the expulsion of Hippias (510), and as a monument to the new democracy.
c. 510	Funerary stele of Aristion. National Museum, Athens (Plate 71). – West pediment of the 'Temple of Aphaia', Aegina (Plates 72–77). – Metopes of the Athenian treasury in Delphi (Plate 79).
509	Kleisthenes promulgates his laws, which are a democratic extension of the Solonic constitution. The proscription of luxury by Kleisthenes brought Attic funerary sculpture to an end until the Parthenon period.
c. 500	Phidias and Sophocles († 406/05) born.
500—449	Persian Wars (revolt of the Ionian Greeks 500; Battle of Marathon 490; Salamis 480; Plataea 479).
494	Miletus destroyed by the Persians.
before 480	East pediment of the 'Temple of Aphaia', Aegina (Plates 82–87). – Standing boy from the Acropolis. Acropolis Museum, Athens (Plates 89–91).
480	Destruction of the Athenian Acropolis by the Persians. Carthaginians attack Greek towns in Sicily. Carthaginians defeated at Himera.
477	A new bronze group of the tyrannicides by Kritios and Nesiotes erected in the Athenian market-place to replace the original group by Antenor, which was removed by the Persians.
c. 470	Charioteer at Delphi (Plates 102–104, IV). – Terracotta group of Zeus and Ganymede at Olympia (Plates 105, V).
472	Performance of *The Persians* of Aeschylus.
469	Socrates born.
c. 460	Bronze statue of Poseidon from Cape Artemision. National Museum, Athens (Plates 130–132, VI). – The 'Ludovisi Throne'. Museo delle Terme, Rome (Plates 134–137).
458	*Oresteia* of Aeschylus.
456	Temple of Zeus at Olympia completed (Plates 107–125). –Aeschylus dies at Gela in Sicily.
448—432	Beginning and completion of the Parthenon (Plates 142–171). – In 438 the image of Athene (in gold and ivory around a wooden core) made by Phidias was consecrated.
444	The 'sophist' Protagoras of Abdera in Athens for the first time ('Man is the measure of all things').
440	*Antigone* of Sophocles.
c. 440	Statue of a spear-bearer by Polyclitus. — Dying Niobid. Museo delle Terme, Rome (Plates 174–177).
431—404	Peloponnesian War which ended, after changing fortunes, in the defeat of Athens.
c. 430	The great Eleusinian votive relief. National Museum, Athens (Plates 172, 173).
429	Death of Pericles.
c. 420	Equestrian relief in the Villa Albani (Plates 179–181).
410/400	Sepulchral relief of Hegeso. National Museum, Athens, (Plate 187). – Reliefs of the Nike balustrade. Acropolis Museum, Athens (Plates 189–191).
406/05	Death of Sophocles and Euripides (born c. 480).
399	Socrates, aged seventy, forced to drink the cup of hemlock.
394	Tombstone of Dexileos. Ceramicus Museum, Athens (Plate 192).

387	Plato (429–347) founds the Academy at Athens.
c. 370	Funerary *lekythos* with leave-taking couple. Glyptothek, Munich (Plate 204). – Early works of Lysippus.
c. 360	Early works of Scopas and Praxiteles. – 'Weeping Women sarcophagus' from Sidon, Turkish Museums, Istanbul (Plates 207–209).
353	Death of Mausolus, viceroy of the Persian kings in Caria. During his lifetime he had his colossal tomb erected at Halicarnassus; after the death of his sister and wife Artemisia (351) the tomb was richly decorated by the sculptors Scopas, Timotheus, Bryaxis and Leochares (Plates 211–217).
c. 340	Funerary relief from the Ilissus. National Museum, Athens (Plate 226). – Bases of the columns from the later Temple of Artemis at Ephesus. British Museum, London (Plate 223).
338	Philip of Macedon, the father of Alexander the Great, defeats the allied Greeks at the Battle of Chaeronea.
330	Lycurgus has the statues of the three great tragic poets set up in the newly erected Theatre of Dionysus at Athens.
330/20	Funerary relief of Rhamnus. National Museum, Athens (Plate 227). – Hermes of Praxiteles. Museum, Olympia (Plates 228–231). – 'Alexander sarcophagus' from Sidon, Archaeological Museum, Istanbul (Plates 232–237, VIII, IX).
336–323	Alexander the Great. After his death his successors (the Diadochi) struggle for predominance. Five monarchies develop out of Alexander's empire: Macedonia under the Antigonids, Egypt under the Ptolemies (capital Alexandria), Syria under the Seleucids, Bithynia (capital Nicomedeia), and Pergamon under the Attalids.
322	Death of Aristotle (born 384), the teacher of Alexander the Great.
c. 310	The end of Attic funerary reliefs as the result of a law forbidding luxuries issued by Demetrius of Phaleron. – Girl's head from Chios. Museum of Fine Arts, Boston (Plates 242, 243).
280	Athenians vote to erect a statue of Demosthenes (384–322) by Polyeuktos in the market-place at Athens.
272	Taranto occupied by the Romans.
270	Death of Epicurus (born 341).
264	Death of Zeno (born 336), founder of the Stoic philosophy.
264—146	Rome's wars with the Carthaginians (Punic Wars), which ended after varying fortunes in the reconquest of Sicily (Syracuse 212) and southern Italy (Taranto 209) and the destruction of Carthage (146) by the Romans.
241—197	Attalus I, King of Pergamon.
c. 240	Sacrificial servant, the 'Antium girl'. Museo delle Terme, Rome (Plate 247). – Statue of Nikokleia from Cnidus. British Museum, London (Plate 246). – Bearded bronze head from Anticythera. National Museum, Athens (Plates 250, X).
c. 210	Sleeping satyr, the 'Barberini Faun', Glyptothek, Munich (Plates 248, 249).
209	Taranto is finally won back by the Romans, after it had been occupied by Hannibal in 212.
c. 190	Nike of Samothrace. Louvre, Paris (Plate 262).
c. 180	Eumenes II (197–159) erects the great altar at Pergamon as a monument to the victory of the Pergamenes over the Gauls (Galatians) (Plates 251–259). – Portrait head of Alexander the Great from Pergamon (Plates 260, 261).
168	Victory of the Romans over Perseus of Macedonia at Pydna. L. Aemilius Paullus brings vast quantities of Greek sculptures in triumph back to Rome.
c. 160	Bronze statue of a Hellenistic ruler. Museo delle Terme, Rome (Plates 264, 265).
156	Delegation of Greek philosophers at Rome (Diogenes, Critolaus, Carneades).
146	The Romans destroy Corinth. Mummius brings countless art treasures from Greece in triumph to Rome. — The kingdoms of the Diadochi fall to the Romans, some by conquest, some by legal testament: Macedonia 148; Pergamon 133; Bithynia 74; Syria 63; Egypt 30.
c. 120	Statue of Aphrodite of Melos. Louvre, Paris (Plates 270, 271).
c. 90	Bronze head from Delos. National Museum, Athens (Plate 274, XI).
86	Sulla conquers Athens. The fortifications in the Piraeus are dismantled.
c. 40	The Laocoön group. Vatican Collections, Rome, Belvedere (Plates 278, 279).
31	Octavian defeats Antony at Actium and becomes emperor – Caesar Octavianus Augustus († A.D. 14).

A. D.

117—138	Emperor Hadrian. Makes repeated visits to Greece, whose art he admires and fosters. 124/25 he receives the great sacraments at Eleusis.
c. 160	The Greek travel-writer Pausanias in Greece.
267	Heruli and Goths conquer Athens and plunder shrines throughout Greece.
323—337	Constantine the Great. Christianity is made state religion in the Roman Empire.
393	Last Olympic Games under Theodosius.
410	Rome plundered by Alaric.
476	Romulus Augustulus, last West Roman Emperor.
529	The Academy at Athens closed by an edict of Emperor Justinian.

1204—1456	Greece under the Franks and Venetians.
1456—1821	After the conquest of Constantinople by the Turks (1453), Greece falls into their hands. The Venetians retain fortified trading bases.
1506	The Laocoön group found in Rome (Plate 278, 279).
1764	J. J. Winckelmann's *History of the Art of Antiquity* published.
1766	Lessing's essay *Laocoön, or concerning the Limits of Painting and Poetry, Part I* published.

110

1786—88	Goethe in Italy.
1802	The Parthenon sculptures brought to London by Lord Elgin.
1811	The pediment sculptures of the 'Temple of Aphaia' on Aegina found [now in the Glyptothek, Munich] (Plates 72–77 and 82–87).
1812	The metopes and frieze of the Temple of Apollo at Phigalia found (now in the British Museum, London).
1821—33	Greek wars of liberation against the Turks. They evacuate the Athenian Acropolis in 1833 on the insistence of the Great Powers, after Prince Otto of Bavaria was proclaimed King of Greece in 1832.
1857—58	British excavations at Halicarnassus, Cnidus and Miletus (C. T. Newton).
1870—74	Terra-cottas found at Tanagra (Boeotia).
1871—90	Heinrich Schliemann's excavations at Troy, Mycenae, Orchomenus and Tiryns.
1875—81	First German excavations at Olympia. They have been continued since 1936.

since 1876/80	French excavations on Delos and at Delphi.
1878—86	First German excavations at Pergamon, resumed after 1900.
1885—91	Rediscovery of Archaic sculpture on the Athenian Acropolis through systematic Greek excavations under P. Kavvadias and G. Kawerau begun in 1882.
1893	*Masterpieces of Greek Sculpture* by Adolf Furtwängler.
since 1896	American excavations at Corinth.
since 1900	British and Italian excavations on Crete (Sir Arthur Evans and others).
1903/08	R. M. Rilke's sonnets to Apollo in his *Neue Gedichte* ('Early Apollo' and 'Archaic Torso of Apollo').
1908/13	Crete, which had for so long been under the sovereignty of Turkey, is united with Greece.
since 1910	German excavations in the Heraion, Samos.
since 1914	German excavations in the Ceramicus, Athens.
since 1930	American excavations on the Agora, Athens.

LIST OF PUBLISHED WORKS ON GREEK SCULPTURE

SELECTED FOR THEIR BEARING ON THE WORKS OF ART REPRODUCED IN THIS BOOK

GENERAL WORKS. ARRANGED CHRONOLOGICALLY

H. Brunn: Geschichte der griechischen Künstler. Vol. 1: Die Bildhauer. 2nd edition, Stuttgart 1889.

A. Furtwängler: Meisterwerke griechischer Plastik. Leipzig-Berlin 1893.

G. Lippold: Kopien und Umbildungen griechischer Statuen. Munich 1923.

G. M. A. Richter: The Sculptures and Sculptors of the Greeks. 1st edition, New Haven 1929; 3rd edition 1951.

W. Lamb: Greek and Roman Bronzes. London 1929.

G. M. A. Richter: Animals in Greek Sculpture. London 1930.

J. D. Beazley and B. Ashmole: Greek Sculpture and Painting to the End of the Hellenistic Period. Cambridge 1932.

A. J. B. Wace: An Approach to Greek Sculpture. Cambridge 1935.

Ch. Picard: Manuel d'Archéologie Grecque. La sculpture. I–IV. Paris 1935–59.

E. Buschor: Die Plastik der Griechen. Berlin 1936. Revised new edition, Munich 1958.

F. Gerke: Griechische Plastik in archaischer und klassischer Zeit. Zürich-Berlin 1938.

G. Rodenwaldt: Die Kunst der Antike (Propyläen-Kunstgeschichte, Vol. 3, 3rd edition, Berlin 1938; 4th edition 1944).

L. Curtius: Die antike Kunst II, 1. Die klassische Kunst Griechenlands (Handbuch der Kunstwissenschaft). Potsdam 1938.

W. Zschietzschmann: Die antike Kunst II, 2. Die hellenistische und römische Kunst (Handbuch der Kunstwissensch.). Potsdam 1939.

W. H. Schuchhardt: Die Kunst der Griechen. Berlin 1940.

E. Buschor: Vom Sinn der griechischen Standbilder. Berlin 1942.

G. Lippold: Die griechische Plastik (Handbuch der Archäologie, 5th instalment). Munich 1950.

R. Bianchi Bandinelli: Storicità dell'Arte Classica. Florence 1950.

G. M. A. Richter: Three Critical Periods in Greek Sculpture. Oxford 1951.

R. Hamann: Geschichte der Kunst von der Vorgeschichte bis zur Spätantike. Munich 1952 (pp. 408–778 on Greek art).

L. Alscher: Griechische Plastik I–VI. Berlin 1954–1957.

G. M. A. Richter: A. Handbook of Greek Art. London 1959. In particular: Werke der großen Plastik und der Kleinplastik, pp. 45 ff.

W. H. Schuchhardt, Die Epochen der Griechischen Plastik. Baden-Baden 1959.

ON ARCHAIC SCULPTURE

F. Matz: Geschichte der griechischen Kunst I. Die geometrische und früharchaische Form. Frankfurt a. M. 1949.

G. M. A. Richter: Archaic Greek Art. New York 1949.

E. Homann-Wedeking: Die Anfänge der griechischen Großplastik. Berlin 1950.

G. Karo: Greek Personality in Archaic Sculpture. Cambridge/Mass. 1948.

E. Langlotz: Frühgriechische Bildhauerschulen. Nürnberg 1927.

— Zur Zeitbestimmung der streng rotfigurigen Vasenmalerei und der gleichzeitigen Plastik. Leipzig 1920.

G. M. A. Richter: Kouroi. A Study of the Development of the Greek Kouros from the Late Seventh to the Early Fifth Century B.C. New York 1942.

E. Buschor: Frühgriechische Jünglinge. Munich 1950.

— Altsamische Standbilder. Berlin 1934–35.

R. J. H. Jenkins: Dedalica. A Study of Dorian Plastic in the Seventh Century B.C. Cambridge 1936.

F. R. Grace: Archaic Sculpture in Boeotia. Cambridge/Mass. 1939.

H. Payne and G. M. Young: Archaic Marble Sculpture from the Acropolis. A Photographic Catalogue. London. 1st edition 1936, 2nd edition 1950.

H. Schrader, E. Langlotz und W. H. Schuchhardt: Die archaischen Marmorbildwerke der Akropolis. Frankfurt a. M. 1939.

E. Langlotz und W. H. Schuchhardt: Archaische Plastik auf der Akropolis. Frankfurt a. M. 1940.

K. Schefold: Griechische Plastik I. Die großen Bildhauer des archaischen Athen. Basel 1949.

G. M. A. Richter: Archaic Attic Gravestones. Cambridge/Mass. 1944.

ON SCULPTURE OF THE 5th AND 4th CENTURIES B.C.

V. H. Poulsen: Der strenge Stil. Studien zur Geschichte der griechischen Plastik 480–450 (Acta Archaeologica 8, 1937, 1 ff.).

E. Buschor und R. Hamann: Die Skulpturen des Zeustempels zu Olympia. Text and Plates. Marburg/Lahn 1924. The text is reprinted, somewhat abbreviated and without the notes, in: E. Buschor, Von griechischer Kunst. Munich 1956, pp. 65 ff.

A. W. Lawrence: Classical Sculpture. London 1929.

G. von Lücken: Die Entwicklung der Parthenonskulpturen. Augsburg-Cologne-Vienna 1930.

B. Schweitzer: Prolegomena zur Kunst des Parthenonmeisters I. – Zur Kunst des Parthenon-Meisters II. – Pheidias, der Parthenonmeister (Jahrbuch des Deutschen Archäologischen Instituts 53, 1938, 1 ff.; 54, 1939, 1 ff.; 55, 1940, 170 ff.).

E. Langlotz: Phidiasprobleme. Frankfurt a. M. 1947.

E. Buschor: Phidias, der Mensch. Munich 1948.

G. Becatti: Problemi Fidiaci. Milan-Florence 1951.

T. Dohrn: Attische Plastik vom Tode des Phidias bis zum Wirken der großen Meister des IV. Jahrhunderts v. Chr. Krefeld 1957.

K. Süsserott: Griechische Plastik des vierten Jahrhunderts v. Chr. Untersuchungen zur Zeitbestimmung. Frankfurt a. M. 1938.

E. Buschor: Maussollos und Alexander. Munich 1950.

H. Diepolder: Die attischen Grabreliefs des 5. und 4. Jahrhunderts v. Chr. Berlin 1931.

K. F. Johansen: The Attic Grave-Reliefs of the Classical Period. Copenhagen 1951.

HELLENISTIC SCULPTURE

G. Dickins: Hellenistic Sculpture. Oxford 1920.

A. W. Lawrence: Later Greek Sculpture and its Influence on East and West. London 1927.

M. Bieber: The Sculpture of the Hellenistic Age. New York 1955.

G. Krahmer: Stilphasen der hellenistischen Plastik (Römische Mitteilungen 38/39, 1923/24, 138 ff.).

— Nachahmungen des 5. Jahrhunderts in Pergamenischen Statuen (ibid. 40, 1925, 67 ff.).

G. Krahmer: Die einansichtige Gruppe und die späthellenistische Kunst (Nachrichten der Gesellschaft der Wissenschaften in Göttingen 1927, 1 ff.).
— Hellenistische Köpfe (ibid. 1936, 217 ff.).
R. Horn: Stehende weibliche Gewandstatuen in der hellenistischen Plastik. Römische Mitteilungen, Suppl. vol. 2. Munich 1931.
G. Kleiner: Tanagrafiguren. Untersuchungen zur hellenistischen Kunst und Geschichte. 15. Suppl. vol. of Jahrbuch des Deutschen Archäologischen Instituts, 1942.
H. Kähler: Der große Fries von Pergamon. Untersuchungen zur Kunstgeschichte und Geschichte Pergamons. Berlin 1948.

K. Schefold: Die Bildnisse der antiken Dichter, Redner und Denker. Basel 1943.
G. Lippold: Griechische Porträtstatuen. Munich 1912.
E. Buschor: Bildnisstufen. Munich 1947, pp. 168 ff.
— Das hellenistische Bildnis. Munich 1949.
G. Hafner: Späthellenistische Bildnisplastik. Berlin 1954.
E. Pfuhl: Die Anfänge der griechischen Bildniskunst. Munich 1927.
B. Schweitzer: Studien zur Entstehung des Porträts bei den Griechen. Berichte über die Verhandlungen der Sächsischen Akademie der Wissenschaften zu Leipzig, Philolog.-histor. Klasse 91, 1939, vol. 4 (1940).

RELIEFS, METOPES, FRIEZES AND PEDIMENTS

G. Rodenwaldt: Das Relief bei den Griechen. Berlin 1923.
R. Binnebössel: Studien zu den attischen Urkundenreliefs. Leipzig 1932.
H. Kähler: Das griechische Metopenbild. Munich 1949.
R. Demangel: La Frise jonique. Paris 1933.
E. Lapalus: Le Fronton sculpté en Grèce dès origines à la fin du IVe siècle. Paris 1947.
Th. Wiegand: Die archaische Porosarchitektur der Akropolis zu Athen. Kassel-Leipzig 1904.
E. Buschor: Größenverhältnisse attischer Porosgiebel. Athens 1924.
W. H. Schuchhardt: Archaische Giebelkompositionen. Freiburg/Br. 1949.

ON PORTRAIT SCULPTURE

R. Delbrück: Antike Porträts. Bonn 1912.
A. Hekler: Die Bildniskunst der Griechen und Römer. Stuttgart 1912.
L. Laurenzi: Ritratti Greci. Florence 1941.

ON TECHNIQUE

C. Blümel: Griechische Bildhauerarbeit. 11th Suppl. vol. of Jahrbuch des Deutschen Archäologischen Instituts, Berlin 1927..
— Griechische Bildhauer an der Arbeit. 4th edition, Berlin 1953. Transl. into English under the title: Greek Sculptors at Work. London 1955.
St Casson: The Technique of the Early Greek Sculpture. Oxford 1933.
K. Kluge: Die Gestaltung des Erzes in der archaisch-griechischen Kunst. Jahrbuch des Deutschen Archäologischen Instituts 44, 1929, 1–30.
— Die antike Erzgestaltung und ihre technischen Grundlagen. Berlin and Leipzig 1927.
G. M. A. Richter: Polychromy in Greek Sculpture (American Journal of Archaeology 48, 1944, 321 ff.).
J. Winter: Der Alexander-Sarkophag aus Sidon. Straßburg 1912 (for the colour-painting of Greek marble sculpture).
H. Koch: Studien zum Theseustempel in Athen. Abhandlungen der Sächs. Akademie der Wiss. zu Leipzig, Philol.-histor. Klasse 47,2 (1955), 82 ff. (for polychromy in Greek architecture).

The photographs newly taken for this work were supplemented by pictures from the undermentioned archives:
Berlin, State Museums, Department of Classical Antiquities: 1, 20–23, 42, 97–101, 140, 141, 251–259, 272 – German Archaelogical Institute, Athens: 2, 4, 5, 8, 9, 16–19 – Boston/Mass., Museum of Fine Arts: 3, 242, 243 – New York, Metropolitan Museum: 11–13 – Prof. Friedrich Krauss, Munich: 78 – Archaeological Seminary of Munich University: 126, 127 – Prof. Ernst Langlotz, Bonn: 128, 129 – German Archaeological Institute, Rome: 179–181.

ALPHABETICAL LIST OF PRESENT LOCATIONS OF WORKS ILLUSTRATED